# Human Rights in the Global Information Society

**The Information Revolution and Global Politics**
William J. Drake and Ernest J. Wilson III, editors

*The Information Revolution and Developing Countries*
Ernest Wilson, 2004

*Human Rights in the Global Information Society*
edited by Rikke Frank Jørgensen, 2006

# Human Rights in the Global Information Society

edited by Rikke Frank Jørgensen

The MIT Press
Cambridge, Massachusetts
London, England

MIT Press books may be purchased at special quantity discounts for business or sales promotional use. For information, please email special_sales@mitpress.mit.edu or write to Special Sales Department, The MIT Press, 55 Hayward Street, Cambridge, MA 02142.

This book was set in Stone Sans and Stone Serif by SNP Best-set Typesetter Ltd., Hong Kong and was printed and bound in the United States of America.

Library of Congress Cataloging-in-Publication Data

Human rights in the global information society / [edited by] Rikke Frank Jørgensen.
   p. cm.—(The information revolution & global politics)
Papers originally presented at the World Summit on the Information Society, November 2005. Includes bibliographical references and index.
ISBN 0-262-10115-7—ISBN 978-0-262-10115-8 (alk. paper)
ISBN 0-262-60067-6—ISBN 978-0-262-60067-5 (pbk. : alk. paper)
1. Human rights—Congresses. 2. Information society—Congresses. I. Jørgensen, Rikke Frank. II. World Summit on the Information Society (2005 : Tunis, Tunisia) III. Series.

JC571.H76954   2006
323—dc22

                                                                2005058046

10  9  8  7  6  5  4  3  2  1

# Contents

# Foreword

Adama Samassékou

## The Promise of Information and Communication Societies

The year is 2006. The first World Summit on the Information Society was held in December 2003, with a follow-up in November 2005. Governments of the world have adopted the first political Constitution of Cyberspace, thereby formally acknowledging the potential benefits stemming from the use of information and communication technologies, and have agreed to help narrow the digital gap between the developed and the developing countries: a gap that is unacceptable for all humanity and that represents both a cause and a consequence of the unequal distribution of wealth in the world and within countries.

Formally recognized by all is the premise that the development of the information society must be based on the framework of human rights, and should respect and uphold the standards laid down in the United Nations Charter and the Universal Declaration of Human Rights. Human rights are universal, indivisible, interrelated, and interdependent, as reaffirmed at the 1993 Vienna World Conference on Human Rights. Hence, a crucial premise for realizing the vision of the information society is a commitment to effectively implement and enforce all human rights: civil and political as well as economic, social, and cultural.

Furthermore, there is a general recognition that information and communication technologies should be used to advance and implement the U.N. Millennium Development Goals, the indicators to end human poverty by 2015.

The human rights standards require governments to ensure that the information society does not result in discrimination or in deprivation of existing rights. On the contrary, information and communication technologies should be used to advance the effective implementation of human rights at the local level. The principle of nondiscrimination mandates universal access to information and communication as an overall goal. All individuals, communities, and countries should be empowered to take part in the information society, using their own languages to create, disseminate, and share information and knowledge. Ensuring information and education for all is essential if information and communication technologies are to play a vital role in helping to reach the U.N. millennium goal of eradicating poverty, hunger, and diseases, particularly in the developing world, where nearly half of the population is living below the poverty line. But it is also important in the developed world, where the regulatory framework for information access, ownership, and privacy is being developed and debated.

The information society has communication as its nerve center. It provides new and easy access to information and to communication, to find like-minded persons, and to build bridges that cross traditional geographical and cultural borders. Information can be power; communication is empowering. As societies transform into information societies, the ability to communicate and learn becomes the most important societal skill. Seizing this opportunity requires openness and the ability to embrace and reflect on a number of different perspectives and realities. If we are willing to meet this challenge, the information society can provide an enormous learning opportunity for all of us.

And this is why I wish to stress that we are indeed entering a new global society: that of information, human communication, and shared knowledge.

## The Challenge for Human Rights

At the core of human rights are the dignity, integrity, and vulnerability of the individual. Human rights are about people on the ground and their rights. The right to a decent standard of living and to a life lived in freedom, without hunger, violence, and suffering. The right to participate in society, to voice opinions, and to be free from arbitrary intrusions or restrictions by the state. As expressed by Eleanor Roosevelt, who chaired the U.N. Human Rights Commission in its first years:

Where, after all, do universal human rights begin? In small places, close to home—
so close and so small that they cannot be seen on any maps of the world. Yet they
are the world of the individual person; the neighborhood he lives in; the school or
college he attends; the factory, farm or office where he works. Such are the places
where every man, woman and child seeks equal justice, equal opportunity, equal
dignity without discrimination. Unless these rights have meaning there, they have
little meaning anywhere. Without concerned citizen action to uphold them close
to home, we shall look in vain for progress in the larger world. (Eleanor Roosevelt
at the presentation of *"In Your Hands: A Guide for Community Action for the Tenth
Anniversary of the Universal Declaration of Human Rights,"* March 27, 1958, United
Nations, New York)

Access to information is essential for self-determination, for social and
political participation, and for development. However, at present only one
third of the world population has access to information and communication technologies; the great majority is excluded from them. The poor
remain poor and the rich remain rich. The great challenge facing the world
is how to expand the reach of information to all human beings, no matter
their social, economic, cultural, and geographical position. A region such
as Africa has wealth and cultural diversity, but also represents a tremen-
dous challenge in empowering illiterate people and ensuring that ordinary
citizens, who speak only local languages, are included in the information
society.

Human rights, democracy, and development are intertwined. Unless
human rights are respected, international peace and security and the promotion of economic and social development cannot be achieved. Often
the political debate leaves one with the impression that conflicts and terror
require us to diminish human rights and freedoms. This rhetoric has put
human rights on the defensive. It is important to insist that effective implementation of human rights is actually the best way to prevent conflict and
terror, the best way to end suffering and inequality. All actions to secure
international peace and security must be firmly based on the human rights
framework, and respect and uphold the standards—not least in times of
fear and heated public emotions.

When the Universal Declaration of Human Rights was adopted in 1948,
it was one of the first major achievements of the United Nations. After
more than fifty years it remains an instrument that has a significant effect
on people's lives all over the world. Its adoption was the first time in

history that human rights and fundamental freedoms were formulated in such detail. At this point in history, and within an information society perspective, human rights face not only great potentials but also strong pressure—not least in regard to new technological developments. As democratic societies we need to constantly reflect on how we respond to the challenges presented by new technologies and new political developments.

Rapid advances in surveillance and security measures, especially in the post–9/11 environment, can have a chilling effect on privacy and on freedom of expression and freedom of association, and new technologies can be used to restrict access to information. The deployment of communication infrastructures, combined with central data storage, biometrics, and pervasive computing, threatens the right to privacy in new and intrusive ways. The growing commodification of information and knowledge contradicts some of the basic potentials of enhanced access to, and sharing of, information, and thus the development of a rich public domain. Information and communication technologies can be used to promote diversity and respect for cultures, but also to spread racial hatred, and hence restrict or suppress diversity. The digital divide represents an unequal access to information and to the means of communication, and therefore requires special measures to improve the situation of those who are vulnerable, exposed, or excluded. Applications need to be developed and used to advance the realization of economic, social, and cultural rights and to support human rights to education and learning, in order to build, all around the world, a real democratic culture. As Nelson Mandela said, we need to create a new political culture based on human rights. Indeed, the so-called digital divide represents a knowledge divide, a social and economic divide, that we must address with the participation of all stakeholders.

I welcome this book as an attempt to explore these many difficult questions, and I hope it will fuel ideas and knowledge on how the agenda of information, human communication, and shared knowledge societies can be used to advance the protection of human rights.

# Human Rights in the Global Information Society

# Introduction

William J. Drake and Rikke Frank Jørgensen

Since the mid-1990s, the term "global information society" (GIS) has gained currency in the lexicon of information and communication technology (ICT) policy discussions. The GIS has been invoked in analyses, policy statements, and initiatives undertaken by national governments, businesses, civil society organizations (CSOs), and academics. Similarly, it has been the subject of declarations and work programs in such international organizations and collaborations as the European Commission (EC), the Organization for Economic Cooperation and Development (OECD), the International Telecommunication Union (ITU), and the Group of Eight (G-8) industrialized countries. And most recently, the term has received even wider play as a result of the United Nations' 2002–2005 World Summit on the Information Society (WSIS) process.

There is no precise and widely accepted definition of the GIS. Even so, when employing the term in global policy discussions, participants appear to believe that they all mean essentially the same thing. The most common usage seems to be as a loose umbrella rubric for the wide array of national and global effects and policy issues resulting from the information revolution. Many people additionally embrace variants of the analytical propositions that the technologically enabled creation, distribution, and manipulation or application of information is becoming a key driving force and defining feature of social change worldwide, and that the resulting GIS is some respects qualitatively different from antecedent forms of social organization.

In principle, these constructions of the concept are essentially neutral with respect to policy prescriptions, in that one can embrace them without advocating any particular type of programmatic response. But in practice, critics on the political left maintain that they are ideological and prescriptive, in that asymmetries in wealth and power mean that the information society is not really global, and because the term GIS is often invoked to argue that the combination of market liberalization and private control is the only logical and natural way to govern ICT. In addition, some of these critics disagree with the analytical propositions. They variously argue that the causal role of information pales in significance when compared with state and corporate control of material resources; or that information is indeed a driving force of social change, but it is overwhelmingly controlled by these power centers and manipulated to promote patterns of social order favorable to their interests.

Wherever one comes down on these and related questions, clearly the GIS term has caught on in global ICT discourse. Moreover, the vast range of policy issues the GIS is thought to entail—telecommunications and media regulation, digital convergence, radio frequency spectrum management, technical standardization, Internet governance, trade in networked goods and services, competition policy, intellectual property, privacy and consumer protection, freedom of speech and censorship, network security and cybercrime, cultural and linguistic integrity, development and the global digital divide, e-commerce, e-government, e-education, e-everything—are all pressing and moving up the global agenda. They also are increasingly interrelated, often intrinsically so; it is impossible to effectively address security without considering privacy, intellectual property without considering freedom of speech, trade without considering consumer protection, and so on across the board. There is thus a growing tendency to view these issues in a more holistic manner—as elements of a single overarching policy space rather than as a random assortment of disconnected topics that are somehow related to ICT. And regardless of whether or not one views the term GIS as misleading or ideological, it increasingly is being employed by governments and other stakeholders to refer to that space. Accordingly, while recognizing at the outset that the term is contested, in this volume we will use it to refer to the policy space described above.

Today, much of the GIS policy arena is in flux. Leading governments and transnational corporations are pushing for often sweeping changes in national, regional, and global policies. In general, the overarching objectives of these efforts are to increase private-sector control over the economic sphere and, particularly in the post-9/11 context, state control over security-related matters. While some elements of this agenda have met with resistance from various quarters, overall the drive to transform ICT governance along these lines is moving ahead.[1] In the process, other perspectives and priorities generally are being pushed to the side, at best acknowledged but not really accommodated. One such perspective positions development promotion as the baseline for evaluating policy options and calls for the special and differential treatment of developing countries in ICT global governance arrangements. Another semimarginalized perspective, which has been advanced by progressive CSOs in particular, sets public-interest criteria as the evaluative baseline and calls, inter alia, for more democratic participation in policymaking, better oversight of state and corporate power, and a better balance between commercial and noncommercial objectives.

Even more marginalized in GIS debates has been the international human rights perspective. GIS policy discussions generally have not internalized as key criteria for evaluation the various human rights that have been recognized and institutionalized in treaties and related instruments since the late 1940s. Indeed, to the extent that analytical and programmatic links have been drawn between human rights and the issues arising from the information revolution, the focus typically has been on just two issues.

The first issue concerns the use of ICT to increase global awareness of human rights violations—pertaining in particular to civil and political rights—in authoritarian and semiauthoritarian countries. For example, the 1980s saw the burgeoning use of video cameras and satellite television links to reveal the violent suppression of political dissent within the Soviet bloc and various developing countries. In the 1990s, the focus of attention shifted to the Internet, which, insofar as some governments find it difficult to monitor and censor transmissions, provides a vital means for international and local actors to get out the word about human rights abuses.[2] The second and related issue concerns the efforts by governments, especially but not only in nondemocratic societies, to impose laws and regulations restricting privacy and free speech on the Internet. Despite all the talk about the Internet's ability to "route around" censorship, many governments have proven increasingly adept at extending state control into cyberspace. Accordingly, both traditional human rights and civil liberties groups and organizations specializing in the cyberspace environment have been cataloging and publicizing the growing number of governmental restrictions being imposed around the world in the name of public morality, cultural integrity, and political control.[3] Some of these watchdog organizations draw explicit linkages between such actions and the internationally agreed human rights they violate, but others are less attentive to the human rights framing.

While these two issues are critically important, they are just the tip of the iceberg. International law and policy have enshrined a broad range of human rights pertaining to multiple dimensions and contexts of social life. These rights go well beyond the rights to freedom of expression and physical security involved in the above examples, to cover such matters as access to information, privacy, nondiscrimination, access to public services, freedom of assembly and political participation, due process, mobility, education, working conditions, women's rights, development, peace, and much more. The protection and promotion of these rights are often affected in a direct and negative manner by the ways in which ICT is used and governed by both public- and private-sector actors. Conversely, beginning assessments of ICT usage and governance from the baseline of human rights standards will often point toward policies and practices that are at variance, sometimes sharply, with the approaches currently being pursued.

Given the rapid pace and direction of change in GIS policy, there is an increasingly pressing need to put human rights considerations firmly on the global agenda. Whether the issue at hand is trade, intellectual property, Internet governance, "information security," or something else, compliance with the full range of internationally agreed human rights standards should be a key criterion for the development and evaluation of policy frameworks. Unfortunately, the communities of expertise and practice involved in human rights and ICT policy have not undertaken the sort of reciprocal and sustained dialogue required to move in this direction.

To the contrary, there has been a significant disconnect between the two fields. On the one hand, members of the ICT policy communities typically are not trained in the intricacies of human rights, are unsure how human rights standards might apply to issues such as Internet governance or intellectual property, are unclear on the potential practical implications of such an effort, and have not been under what they would consider to be salient political pressures to figure these things out. On the other hand, most traditional human rights groups have largely eschewed delving into the full complexities of the GIS arena. Those which have launched programs on ICT issues usually focus on challenging governmental restrictions on freedom of expression rather than protecting and promoting the broader array of political, economic, and social rights in light of the information revolution. In parallel, the specialized CSOs launched in the 1990s to defend cyber civil liberties have usually stuck to their original mandates, such as freedom of expression and privacy protection, instead of expanding their focus to the broader human rights agenda. Moreover, their initiatives often concentrate on opposing specific new laws, policies, and programs rather on framing the issues in terms of long-standing and internationally agreed human rights. And, for their part, intergovernmental organizations concerned with human rights have only occasionally devoted any attention to the matter, and generally have done so in a loose, schematic, and aspirational manner.[4] In short, integrating human rights criteria into the assessment and development of GIS policies will require, as a first step, that members of both communities overcome these and other barriers and enter into sustained dialogue.

Over the past few years, elements of the human rights community at least have begun to take steps in this direction. The major impetus for this movement was the United Nations' World Summit on the Information Society (WSIS). As is discussed in more detail below, the WSIS comprised a pair of global summits held in Geneva in December 2003 and Tunis in November 2005, as well as an elaborate preparatory process involving a series of large regional conferences and meetings held between May 2002 and the Tunis summit. Broadly stated, the overarching objectives of WSIS were to foster a global dialogue about the GIS; adopt shared principles and a plan of action to help guide the international community's GIS initiatives; and define an approach to follow-up and implementation of efforts related to the action plan.

As part of a larger civil society coalition that came together around the WSIS, a group of concerned CSOs launched the Human Rights Caucus at the first preparatory conference (hereafter PrepCom) in July 2002. Comprising (at the time of writing) over sixty national and transnational organizations—including traditional human rights organizations, cyber-liberties organizations, trade unions, and more—from all continents, the Caucus pressed governments to make internationally agreed human rights principles an overarching consideration of the WSIS framework.[5] In the

end, the Caucus's efforts yielded decidedly mixed results: while the negotiated texts acknowledged the importance of some international human
rights agreements and principles, particularly with respect to freedom of
expression, others of direct relevance were overlooked. Moreover, there was
little real engagement on how the broader corpus of human rights might
apply to diverse GIS policy issues such as telecommunications regulation,
network security, intellectual property, the global digital divide, or Internet governance. Human rights considerations simply did not figure much
in the governments' negotiations on these topics, and many in their delegations would have been hard pressed to see the connections. As such,
the WSIS experience demonstrated that there is a pressing need to flesh
out the linkages between human rights and information society issues, and
to translate these into concrete policy recommendations.

With these considerations in mind, the purpose of this volume is to
provide an initial assessment of the relevance of internationally agreed
human rights to the GIS. The cases examined herein by no means constitute an exhaustive listing of the human rights that are impacted by, and
should inform, ICT policies and practices. Rather, they are particularly
important and illustrative examples of a broader range of rights and related
issues that merit sustained consideration and dialogue over time. They are
also in some senses among the more controversial rights when considered
in relation to the ICT environment.

The human rights considered herein include freedom of expression and
access to information, the right to privacy, the right to development, the
prohibition against discrimination, gender equality, freedom of association
and assembly, procedural rights, the right to participate in public affairs,
and the right to enjoy one's own culture. These rights are enshrined in
the Charter of the United Nations and the International Bill of Human
Rights—which, in consequence, are the principal starting points for the
chapters' analyses—as well as in other multilateral instruments. In each
case, activists, academics in different scholarly disciplines, and policy practitioners specializing in different fields or subfields may have varying
perspectives on the interpretation and implementation of these rights. As
such, it is hoped that the essays in this volume may contribute to some
conceptual and programmatic bridge-building among these diverse analysts and stakeholders.

The chapter authors are activists and scholars who have been involved
in the Human Rights Caucus or related advocacy work in the WSIS and

other ICT policy debates. At the time of writing, the volume's editor, Rikke Frank Jørgensen, and Meryem Marzouki, the author of chapter 8, served as the co-coordinators of the Caucus. Hence, while the authors come from different disciplinary backgrounds, they all share a firm commitment to promoting human rights standards as an essential baseline for the assessment and governance of the GIS.

To contextualize the chapters that follow, the remainder of this Introduction proceeds in three steps. First, it briefly surveys the international human rights arrangements that serve as points of departure in the subsequent chapters. Second, it summarizes the dynamics and outcomes of the WSIS process with respect to human rights. The WSIS is important here not only because it catalyzed the development of the civil society Human Rights Caucus, but also and more importantly, because it constituted the first serious encounter between human rights advocacy and policy debates on the GIS as a whole. Not surprisingly, then, if one enters the key words "human rights" and "global information society" into a Internet search engine such as Google, a majority of the top-ranked Web sites listed pertain to the WSIS. Third and finally, the Introduction provides an overview of the chapters that follow.

## The International Human Rights Regime

The institutionalization of international human rights standards has constituted one of the most important normative shifts in world politics since World War II. Viewed in a broad historical perspective, the notion that human beings hold inalienable and universal rights simply by virtue of their personhood that should trump state prerogatives is fairly radical. Indeed, as one scholar has argued, "Virtually everything encompassed by the notion of 'human rights' is the subject of controversy . . . the idea that individuals have, or should have, 'rights' is itself contentious, and the idea that rights could be attached to individuals by virtue solely of their common humanity is particularly subject to penetrating criticism."[6]

Nevertheless, and despite the complaints from some governments that human rights are a matter of cultural relativism or are contrary to so-called Asian values, the core concept has been enshrined in international law and policy, and is now effectively uncontested. All but the more egregious vi olators have abandoned challenges to the concept of inherent, universally applicable, and multidimensional human rights, such as the once persistent assertions that rights apply only to collectivities rather than individuals, or that a state's treatment of its citizens is a purely domestic matter. Nowadays they typically settle for denying charges that their actions violate international norms and/or seek positions on monitoring bodies such as the U.N. Commission on Human Rights so that they can influence the agenda and water down resolutions regarding their performance.

Of course, none of this is to suggest that human rights are not consistently violated all around the world, often on a massive scale. Compliance with human rights obligations is highly variable, and so are the incentives for noncompliance. There are the usual suspects of states with bad human rights records, but there are also states which will not subject themselves to standards beyond the nation-state or which trump civil liberties for state concerns in relation to national security and/or the "war on terror." Nevertheless, the existence of a global framework for human rights provides mechanisms through which political and legal pressure can be continually applied to inch states toward greater conformity. This is true not only for well established and obvious violations such as torture, human trafficking, or the violent suppression of expression, assembly, and political participation, but also for newly recognized problems, such as those covered in this volume. It should be noted that human rights traditionally concern the relationship between state and individual, but that "horizontal effect" is part of this relationship, implying that state obligations include a positive obligation to protect a private party against another private party, by legislation and/or preventive measures or by investigating violations.

The establishment of this global framework was a long time in coming. The idea that citizens should enjoy certain freedoms and protections from the arbitrary exercise of government authority took hold early in the development of some nation-states. The origins of guarantees provided by law to individuals against the arbitrary use of the state power can be traced back to the Magna Carta (or Great Charter) promulgated in 1215. Notions of humans holding innate and inalienable rights were subsequently elaborated by Enlightenment philosophers and incorporated into such constitutional texts as the Virginia Declaration of Rights and the American Declaration of Independence of 1776, as well as the French Déclaration des Droits de l'Homme et du Citoyen of 1789, but their rules were applicable only within the lands of the respective sovereign states. Early international mechanisms—such as the Conference of Vienna's Declaration on the Abolition of the Slave Trade in 1815, the League of Nations' "minority treaties," and the Constitution of the International Labour Organisation—established multilateral mechanisms regarding slavery, minorities within states defeated in World War I, and workers, respectively—but these specialized agreements fell short of the contemporary conception of universal and multidimensional human rights.[7]

It was only in the context of World War II and its aftermath that this conception would be elaborated and enshrined in broad and binding international agreements. Revulsion against fascist atrocities played a catalytic role in expanding the scope and domain of human rights concepts. Let us note just a few of the key steps along the way. In a January 1941 speech to the U.S. Congress, President Franklin D. Roosevelt declared that freedom means the supremacy of human rights everywhere, and spoke of the centrality of four essential freedoms in particular—freedom of speech, expression, and religion, and freedom from fear. Eight months later, the U.S.–U.K. Atlantic Charter stated a desire to construct a postwar world in which "men [sic] in all the lands may live out their lives in freedom from fear and want"; while these words were probably not written with people living under colonial subjugation in mind, they did point toward the future universalization of human rights.[8]

In 1944, the American Jewish Committee supported the publication in New York of British legal scholar Hersch Lauterpacht's book *The International Bill of the Rights of Man,* and also issued a call for an International Bill of Rights that was signed by 1,300 prominent Americans. In 1945, the Committee met with President Roosevelt and Secretary of State Edward Stettinius to press for the inclusion of human rights protections in the pending Charter of the United Nations. As one of the most detailed accounts of these developments concludes, the Charter's "human rights provisions were products of [nongovernmental organizations'] determination and persistent lobbying in which the American Jewish Committee played the leading role."[9] In addition, a group of Latin American countries pushed for the listing and guaranteeing in the Charter of a complete set of human rights, perhaps in an effort to lock in protections against potential future nondemocratic governments.[10]

The United States and the other great powers were not willing to accept legally binding commitments on a detailed list of human rights. Nor did the Charter offer a clear definition of human rights. Nevertheless, it did include seven important references to them. The Charter's Preamble positions the international community's "faith in fundamental human rights, in the dignity and worth of the human person, [and] in the equal rights of men and women and of nations large and small" as an overarching principle of the United Nations. Similarly, Article 1 states that the United Nations' mission is, inter alia, to "achieve international co-operation . . . in promoting and encouraging respect for human rights and for fundamental freedoms for all without distinction as to race, sex, language, or religion." To this end, subsequent articles establish that the General Assembly is to initiate studies and make recommendations to assist in the realization of human rights and fundamental freedoms; the United Nations and its then relevant trusteeship system are to promote universal respect for, and observance of, human rights and fundamental freedoms; all member states are to take joint and separate action in cooperation with the United Nations to achieve these purposes; the Economic and Social Council (ECOSOC) may make recommendations to the same ends, and may call international conferences and prepare draft conventions for submission to the General Assembly on matters falling within its competence; and ECOSOC is to set up a commission for the promotion of human rights.[11]

Collectively and read in context, these seven references underscored human rights' multidimensional and universal character. In addition, they linked the promotion of human rights both to the progressive development of international law and institutions, and to the realization of objectives such as international peace and stability and economic and social progress. Going forward, such issue linkages to other valued objectives would prove to be tactically important in persuading states to accept the imposition of rules that could be seen as unilaterally imposing burdens without benefits.

In accordance with the Charter's mandate, the U.N. Commission on Human Rights (CHR) was established in 1946. Under the leadership of Eleanor Roosevelt, the CHR began deliberations in January 1947 on the development of an International Bill of Human Rights that would build out and translate into operational commitments the relevant principles contained in the Charter. The new body decided on a two-part structure comprising a nonbinding declaration by the General Assembly that could be taken up immediately, and a binding covenant that would require more extensive negotiations. This decision contained the kernel of an approach that would be elaborated and generalized in the years to follow: "International human rights law now usually progresses through similar stages: issue identification, debate, adoption of nonbonding declarations, negotiation of binding agreements (treaties), establishment of supervisory institutions and procedures, and further elaboration of the rights through decisions and judgments of supervisory institutions."[12]

In December 1948, the U.N. General Assembly approved the resulting Universal Declaration of Human Rights (UDHR) by a vote of 48 to 0, with 8 abstentions. Later referred to by U.N. Secretary-General U Thant as the "Magna Carta of Mankind," the UDHR comprised thirty articles dealing with two broad categories of human rights: civil and political rights; and economic, social, and cultural rights. The General Assembly subsequently decided that the two categories would be detailed in separate treaty instruments—the International Covenant on Civil and Political Rights (CCPR) and the International Covenant on Economic, Social and Cultural Rights (CESCR), both agreed upon by the General Assembly in December 1966. Together, the UDHR, CCPR, and CESCR constitute the International Bill of Human Rights, which is the overarching framework for global human rights today.

The UDHR's Preamble states that the Declaration is meant to serve as a common standard of achievement for the international community, and that every individual and every organ of society is to strive, by teaching and education, to promote respect for human rights, and to secure their universal and effective recognition and observance by progressive measures, national and international. Article 2 elaborates on the U.N. Charter's nondiscrimination principle by holding, inter alia, that "Everyone is entitled to all the rights and freedoms set forth in this Declaration, without distinction of any kind, such as race, colour, sex, language, religion, political or other opinion, national or social origin, property, birth or other status." Articles 3 to 21 then deal with fundamental civil and political rights, such as the right to life, liberty, and security of person; the prohibition of slavery, torture, and arbitrary arrest, detention, or exile; the rights to recognition as a person before the law, to the presumption of innocence until proven guilty, and to equal protection, effective remedies, and fair and public hearings by competent national tribunals; the rights to a nationality, to freedom of movement and residence within the borders of each state, to leave any country to return to one's country, and to seek and to enjoy in other countries asylum from persecution; and the rights to marry, create a family, and own property.

As we will see in subsequent chapters of this volume, in addition to Article 2 on nondiscrimination, and the procedural rights laid down in Articles 7, 8, 10, and 11, particularly important civil and political rights in the GIS context are the following UDHR provisions:

Art. 12: No one shall be subjected to arbitrary interference with his privacy, family, home or correspondence, nor to attacks upon his honour and reputation. Everyone has the right to the protection of the law against such interference or attacks.

Art. 19: Everyone has the right to freedom of opinion and expression; this right includes freedom to hold opinions without interference and to seek, receive, and impart information and ideas through any media and regardless of frontiers.

Art. 20: Everyone has the right to freedom of peaceful assembly and association. . . .

Art. 21: (1) Everyone has the right to take part in the government of his country, directly or through freely chosen representatives. (2) Everyone has the right to equal access to public service in his country. . . .

UDHR Articles 22 to 27 deal with economic, social, and cultural rights. Under their provisions, everyone has the right to social security and is entitled to realization of the economic, social, and cultural rights indispensable for his or her dignity and personality development. Further, everyone has the rights to work, to choose their employment, to just and favorable conditions of work, to equal pay for equal work, to protection against unemployment, to form and to join trade unions, and to rest and leisure, including reasonable limitation of working hours and periodic holidays with pay. In parallel, everyone has the right to a standard of living adequate for their health and well-being, including food, clothing, housing, and medical care and necessary social services, and the right to security in the event of unemployment, sickness, disability, widowhood, old age, or other causes of lack of livelihood in circumstances beyond their control. Mothers and children are entitled to special care and assistance, and all children, whether born in or out of wedlock, are to enjoy the same social protection. Everyone has the right to education, which is to be free, at least in the elementary and fundamental stages. Finally, and of particular relevance in the GIS context, the UDHR in Article 27 embraces both cultural participation and authors' right to protection. Hence, it states that everyone has the right to participate freely in the cultural life of the community, to enjoy the arts and to share in scientific advancement and its benefits; as well as the right to the protection of the moral and material interests resulting from any scientific, literary, or artistic production of which he or she is the author.

The UDHR concludes with three provisions on the application of the abovementioned rights. Article 28 lays down the ambitious requirement that everyone is entitled to a social and international order in which the rights and freedoms set forth in the Declaration can be fully realized. In deference to the collectivist rather than individualist vision favored by the Soviet Union and like-minded states, Article 29 says that everyone has duties to the community in which alone the free and full development of his or her personality is possible. It further holds that in the exercise of these rights and freedoms, everyone shall be subject only to such limitations as are determined by law solely for the purpose of securing due recognition and respect for the rights and freedoms of others and of meeting the just requirements of morality, public order, and the general welfare in a democratic society; and that these rights and freedoms may in no case be exercised contrary to the purposes and principles of the United Nations. Finally, Article 30 specifies that nothing in the Declaration may be interpreted as implying for any state, group, or person any right to engage in any activity or to perform any act aimed at the destruction of any of the rights and freedoms set forth therein.[13]

A political instrument, the UDHR was drafted and approved in the remarkably short period of just two years. In contrast, negotiations over the two legal instruments dragged on for over a decade before concluding in 1966, and the process of national ratification, thus getting binding commitment from a large number of states, has taken much longer and is still incomplete. The treaties build directly on the UDHR, reinforcing through repetition and codification the strength of its injunctions. At the same time, some of the UDHR's principles are specified in more detail, and some new principles are added into the mix. To avoid repetition in this brief summary, and because those most directly related to this volume's concerns are cited in the chapters to follow, the principles contained in the two covenants will not be listed here.

The CCPR and the CESCR have elements in common, and the U.N. General Assembly and other relevant international bodies repeatedly have affirmed that the rights they contain are all intrinsically interrelated and of equal status. Nevertheless, there are important differences between the two, some of which are particularly worth noting here. First, since the rights they cover have different historical origins, many observers distinguish between first and second "generations" of rights. Civil and political rights are referred to as first-generation rights because they were recognized at the national level in a number of eighteenth- and nineteenth-century constitutions, whereas economic, social, and cultural rights were generally developed in national constitutions and international instruments in the post–World War II era. As such, the former are more deeply embedded in multiple legal systems and traditions, and are usually what the layperson thinks of as human rights. Moreover, political and civil rights have often been described as "negative" rights, in that they proscribe state interference with individual freedoms, whereas economic, social, and cultural rights have been described as "positive" rights that require states to create the conditions in which individuals and collectivities can enjoy a certain quality of life, or to provide certain goods or services to that end. In operational terms, though, the distinction is not so clear-cut, as we shall see below.

Second, the CCPR calls for the strict and immediate application of human rights protections to individuals, whereas the CESCR calls for progressive realization subject to state resources. Many experts argue that while the CESCR also is a legally binding treaty, it is more aspirational and progressive in nature, and the realization or violations of the rights it entails are open to greater latitude in interpretation.[14] As one proponent of this view has suggested:

> Whereas the CCPR requires strict compliance with its stipulations, essentially its sister instrument boils down to a promotional obligation which, furthermore, is not owed to the individuals concerned. In fact, a close reading of the "rights" listed in the CESCR reveals that it deliberately refrains from establishing true individual rights. . . . Economic and social rights are to a large degree context-dependent, more than civil liberties. They have as their backdrop a concept of the state as a potent provider, but with the proviso that the duties owned to citizens can never be set out in absolute terms, but must take into account the scarcity of resources which any human community has to reckon with.[15]

In recent years, the "positive/negative" dichotomy stemming from the traditional distinction between economic, social, and cultural rights and civil and political rights has been replaced by the tripartite typology *to respect, protect, and fulfill,* which has been adopted in a variety of contexts, thus adding more nuances to the types of state obligations entailed in the two set of rights.[16] The obligation to respect requires states to refrain from interfering with the enjoyment of human rights. The obligation to protect requires states to prevent violations of such rights by third parties, and the obligation to fulfill requires states to take appropriate legislative, budgetary, judicial, and other measures toward the full realization of such rights. Accordingly, the human rights obligations of the state should be examined at three levels, going from the predominantly cost-free and passive obligation to respect, to the gradually more active and costly obligations to protect and to fulfill. The Committee on Economic, Social and Cultural Rights has also chosen to incorporate this tripartite typology in its work.[17] As one scholar argued:

The tripartite terminology bridges the two sets of rights by illustrating that compliance with each and every human right—economic, social, cultural, civil and political—may require various measures from (passive) non-interference to (active) ensuring of the satisfaction of individual needs, all depending on the concrete circumstances. A social right like the right to housing can be complied with by the State at the first or secondary level by abstaining from eviction or by preventing third parties from doing that, and the tertiary level is primarily activated if there is no home to *respect* or *protect.* Likewise, the civil right to freedom of expression may require that the State abstains from interfering with the enjoyment of the right or prevent third parties from doing so, and the tertiary level only becomes relevant if other obstacles stand in the way of individuals expressing themselves, such as lack of access to the media or—more seriously—lack of ability to express themselves due to illiteracy or disabilities.[18]

Third, the political configurations underlying the negotiation of the two sets of rights were different. At the risk of drawing an overly bald generalization, whereas the Western democracies attached particular importance to the civil and political rights of individuals, in keeping with their own constitutional traditions and limitations on state power, the Soviet Union and like-minded states were more favorably inclined toward economic, social, and cultural rights. To Western governments, economic, social, and cultural objectives were better realized via normal legislative means than by enshrining them as "constitutional" rights, but the aspirational character of the CESCR and the overall negotiated package made it acceptable. Even so, exactly how economic, social, and cultural rights are to be interpreted and enforced remains a subject of some ambiguity and controversy.

Fourth, the two covenants take tellingly different approaches to monitoring compliance. The CCPR established a Human Rights Committee comprising a group of independent experts to review and comment on periodic reports that the treaty parties are obliged to submit, and provides for an optional interstate complaint mechanism. Moreover, the First Optional Protocol to the CCPR allows individual victims of violations to file complaints against state parties. In contrast, compliance with the CESCR thus far has been assessed only via periodic state reports, and there are no procedures for handling individual complaints, although an optional protocol is currently being considered.[19] In short, while both instruments are binding, it is reasonable to suggest that the CCPR is more demanding with respect to monitoring and compliance.

While the International Bill of Human Rights provides the overarching foundation, the global human rights system also entails a range of other universal instruments. For example, five additional core treaties, with their dates of conclusion, are the Convention on the Elimination of All Forms of Racial Discrimination (1965); the Convention on the Elimination of All Forms of Discrimination Against Women (1979); the Convention Against Torture and Other Cruel, Inhuman or Degrading Treatment or Punishment (1984); the Convention on the Rights of the Child (1989); and the International Convention on the Protection of the Rights of All Migrant Workers and Members of Their Families (1990). Many of the core treaties are supplemented by optional protocols imposing additional obligations on the states that have chosen to be parties to them.

In addition, there are many other universal instruments dealing with the interpretation and application of rights in particular issue areas or contexts. These take a variety of legal forms, ranging from "hard law" covenants and conventions to "soft law" declarations, guidelines, and recommendations. A nonexhaustive listing by subject area from the Web site of the Office of the U.N. High Commissioner on Human Rights (the lead U.N. official responsible for human rights, a post created in 1993) includes the instruments shown in the box below. Additional related instruments, which are not in the list below, include a number of conventions from the International Labour Organisation (ILO), specifically on the rights of

## THE INTERNATIONAL BILL OF HUMAN RIGHTS

- Universal Declaration of Human Rights (1948)
- International Covenant on Civil and Political Rights (1966)
- International Covenant on Economic, Social, and Cultural Rights (1966)

## UNIVERSAL HUMAN RIGHTS INSTRUMENTS

### World Conferences on Human Rights and the Millennium Assembly
- Vienna Declaration and Programme of Action
- United Nations Millennium Declaration

### The Right to Self-Determination
- United Nations Declaration on the Granting of Independence to Colonial Countries and Peoples
- General Assembly resolution 1803 (XVII) of December 14, 1962, "Permanent Sovereignty over Natural Resources"
- International Convention Against the Recruitment, Use, Financing and Training of Mercenaries

### Rights of Indigenous Peoples and Minorities
- Indigenous and Tribal Peoples Convention, 1989 (no. 169)
- Declaration on the Rights of Persons Belonging to National or Ethnic, Religious, and Linguistic Minorities

### Prevention of Discrimination
- Equal Remuneration Convention, 1951 (no. 100)
- Discrimination (Employment and Occupation) Convention, 1958 (no. 111)
- International Convention on the Elimination of All Forms of Racial Discrimination
- Declaration on Race and Racial Prejudice
- Convention Against Discrimination in Education
- Protocol Instituting a Conciliation and Good Offices Commission to Be Responsible for Sseeking a Settlement of Any Disputes Which May Arise Between States Parties to the Convention Against Discrimination in Education
- Declaration on the Elimination of All Forms of Intolerance and of Discrimination Based on Religion or Belief
- World Conference Against Racism, 2001 (Durban Declaration and Programme of Action)

**Rights of Women**
- Convention on the Elimination of All Forms of Discrimination Against Women
- Optional Protocol to the Convention on the Elimination of All Forms of Discrimination Against Women
- Declaration on the Protection of Women and Children in Emergency and Armed Conflict
- Declaration on the Elimination of Violence Against Women

**Rights of the Child**
- Convention on the Rights of the Child
- Optional Protocol to the Convention on the Rights of the Child on the Sale of Children, Child Prostitution and Child Pornography
- Optional Protocol to the Convention on the Rights of the Child on the Involvement of Children in Armed Conflict
- Minimum Age Convention, 1973 (no. 138)
- Worst Forms of Child Labour Convention, 1999 (no. 182)

**Rights of Older Persons**
- United Nations Principles for Older Persons

**Rights of Persons with Disabilities[20]**
- Declaration on the Rights of Mentally Retarded Persons
- Declaration on the Rights of Disabled Persons
- Principles for the Protection of Persons with Mental Illness and the Improvement of Mental Health Care
- Standard Rules on the Equalization of Opportunities for Persons with Disabilities

**Human Rights in the Administration of Justice: Protection of Persons Subjected to Detention or Imprisonment**
- Standard Minimum Rules for the Treatment of Prisoners
- Basic Principles for the Treatment of Prisoners
- Body of Principles for the Protection of All Persons Under Any Form of Detention or Imprisonment
- United Nations Rules for the Protection of Juveniles Deprived of Their Liberty
- Declaration on the Protection of All Persons from Being Subjected to Torture and Other Cruel, Inhuman or Degrading Treatment or Punishment
- Convention Against Torture and Other Cruel, Inhuman or Degrading Treatment or Punishment

- Optional Protocol to the Convention Against Torture and Other Cruel, Inhuman or Degrading Treatment or Punishment (not yet in force)
- Principles of Medical Ethics Relevant to the Role of Health Personnel, Particularly Physicians, in the Protection of Prisoners and Detainees Against Torture and Other Cruel, Inhuman or Degrading Treatment or Punishment
- Principles on the Effective Investigation and Documentation of Torture and Other Cruel, Inhuman or Degrading Treatment or Punishment
- Safeguards Guaranteeing Protection of the Rights of Those Facing the Death Penalty
- Code of Conduct for Law Enforcement Officials
- Basic Principles on the Use of Force and Firearms by Law Enforcement Officials
- United Nations Standard Minimum Rules for Noncustodial Measures (Tokyo Rules)
- United Nations Standard Minimum Rules for the Administration of Juvenile Justice (Beijing Rules)
- Guidelines for Action on Children in the Criminal Justice System
- United Nations Guidelines for the Prevention of Juvenile Delinquency (Riyadh Guidelines)
- Declaration of Basic Principles of Justice for Victims of Crime and Abuse of Power
- Basic Principles on the Independence of the Judiciary
- Basic Principles on the Role of Lawyers
- Guidelines on the Role of Prosecutors
- Principles on the Effective Prevention and Investigation of Extralegal, Arbitrary and Summary Executions
- Declaration on the Protection of All Persons from Enforced Disappearance

**Social Welfare, Progress, and Development**
- Declaration on Social Progress and Development
- Universal Declaration on the Eradication of Hunger and Malnutrition
- Declaration on the Use of Scientific and Technological Progress in the Interests of Peace and for the Benefit of Mankind
- Declaration on the Right of Peoples to Peace
- Declaration on the Right to Development
- Universal Declaration on the Human Genome and Human Rights
- Universal Declaration on Cultural Diversity

**Promotion and Protection of Human Rights**
- Principles Relating to the Status of National Institutions (Paris Principles)
- Declaration on the Right and Responsibility of Individuals, Groups and Organs of Society to Promote and Protect Universally Recognized Human Rights and Fundamental Freedoms

**Marriage**
- Convention on Consent to Marriage, Minimum Age for Marriage, and Registration of Marriages
- Recommendation on Consent to Marriage, Minimum Age for Marriage, and Registration of Marriages

**Right to Health**
- Declaration of Commitment on HIV/AIDS

**Right to Work and to Fair Conditions of Employment**
- Employment Policy Convention, 1964 (no. 122)

**Freedom of Association**
- Freedom of Association and Protection of the Right to Organise Convention, 1948 (no. 87)
- Right to Organise and Collective Bargaining Convention, 1949 (no. 98)

**Slavery, Slavery-like Practices, and Forced Labor**
- Slavery Convention
- Protocol Amending the Slavery Convention Signed at Geneva on September 25, 1926
- Supplementary Convention on the Abolition of Slavery, the Slave Trade, and Institutions and Practices Similar to Slavery
- Forced Labor Convention, 1930 (no. 29)
- Abolition of Forced Labour Convention, 1957 (no. 105)
- Convention for the Suppression of the Traffic in Persons and of the Exploitation of the Prostitution of Others
- Protocol to Prevent, Suppress and Punish Trafficking in Persons, Especially Women and Children, Supplementing the United Nations Convention Against Transnational Organized Crime

**Rights of Migrants**
- International Convention on the Protection of the Rights of All Migrant Workers and Members of Their Families (ICPMW)
- Protocol Against the Smuggling of Migrants by Land, Sea and Air, Supplementing the United Nations Convention Against Transnational Organized Crime

**Nationality, Statelessness, Asylum, and Refugees**
- Convention on the Reduction of Statelessness
- Convention Relating to the Status of Stateless Persons
- Convention Relating to the Status of Refugees

- Protocol Relating to the Status of Refugees
- Declaration on the Human Rights of Individuals Who Are Not Nationals of the Country in Which They Live

### War Crimes and Crimes Against Humanity, Including Genocide
- Convention on the Prevention and Punishment of the Crime of Genocide
- Convention on the Nonapplicability of Statutory Limitations to War Crimes and Crimes Against Humanity
- Principles of International Co-operation in the Detection, Arrest, Extradition, and Punishment of Persons Guilty of War Crimes and Crimes Against Humanity
- Statute of the International Tribunal for the Former Yugoslavia
- Statute of the International Tribunal for Rwanda
- Rome Statute of the International Criminal Court

### Humanitarian Law
- Geneva Convention Relative to the Treatment of Prisoners of War
- Geneva Convention Relative to the Protection of Civilian Persons in Time of War
- Protocol Additional to the Geneva Conventions of August 12, 1949, and Relating to the Protection of Victims of International Armed Conflicts (Protocol I)
- Protocol Additional to the Geneva Conventions of August 12, 1949, and Relating to the Protection of Victims of Noninternational Armed Conflicts (Protocol II)

Source: Office of the U.N. High Commissioner on Human Rights, www.ohchr.org/english/about/hc/index.htm

indigenous people, discrimination in employment and occupation, and workers' rights more generally.

While the above list is not exhaustive, its breadth and diversity are sufficient to underscore two points of direct relevance to the analyses in this volume. First, while many of these instruments amplify rights previously established in the International Bill of Human Rights, there are also additions. These rights are often described as "third-generation" human rights. Leading examples include the rights invoked in the U.N. General Assembly's 1984 Declaration on the Right of Peoples to Peace and its 1986 Declaration on the Right to Development. The aspirational principles of these declarations have been affirmed in subsequent political statements or soft law, but they have not been embodied in binding treaties. Moreover, the rights established would seem to be very multidimensional, contextual, and based on progressive realization, and their full enjoyment would require not only agreement on what constitutes peace or development, but probably also large-scale social, political, and economic changes at both the national and international levels. Not surprisingly, there has been a good deal of controversy about their proper interpretation and application, and efforts to develop the concepts and work through the programmatic implications for human rights advocates, governments, and international organizations are ongoing.[21] The right to development is of particular concern with respect to the GIS, and as such is discussed in chapter 12.

Second, the global governance of human rights is substantively and architecturally very complex. As the list indicates, it includes a wide array of principles and instruments of varying degrees of precision, scope, strength, and so on. Human rights is a deeply institutionalized field involving, at the global level, the U.N. Human Rights Commission, a multitude of monitoring mechanisms, interpretation guides (general comments on specific rights), special rapporteurs, and so on—working in a dense policy space to elaborate and interpret internationally agreed rights, build capacity, and promote compliance.

Despite this complexity, there is also an overarching unity and coherence between the core universal instruments—the U.N. Charter, the International Bill of Human Rights—and the other conventions, declarations, protocols, and related instruments. As such, these collectively may be said to constitute an international human rights regime. International regimes are conventionally defined as "principles, norms, rules, and decision-making procedures around which actor expectations converge in a given issue-area" of international affairs.[22] A number of international relations scholars have analyzed the human rights regime, using the same explanatory theories and conceptual vocabulary that have been employed to assess the formation, evolution, and transformation of international regimes in a wide variety of other global issue areas, from monetary and trade policy to arms control, the environment, and beyond.[23] While the participants in the present volume do not attempt to enter into the theoretical debates among political scientists about how best to explain the human rights regime's development, operation, and impact, we do take its key principles, norms, rules, and procedures as embodied in the abovementioned universal instruments as a starting point for the analysis of GIS issues.

The universal, U.N.-based human rights regime is not, however, our only baseline. There are also regional human rights regimes, and these, too, are at times directly relevant to the analyses. Not surprisingly, the regional regimes vary widely in constitution and effectiveness. Nevertheless, at least one—the European regime—is more "legalized," and hence stronger, than the international regime, and as such provides an impressively robust model when considering options for future progress.[24]

The European regime is based on the European Convention on Human Rights (ECHR), which was agreed upon by the Council of Europe in 1950 and in the years to follow took on a series of additional protocols. Developed in the shadow of World War II and in the gap between the completion of the UDHR and of the CCPR and CESCR—during which time it became clear that global compliance mechanisms would not be strong— the ECHR laid the foundation for the strongest and most institutionally developed human rights framework anywhere, and took the first steps toward making the International Bill of Human Rights' requirements truly operational. It established a European Court of Human Rights, to which unresolved cases could be presented for binding rulings. Governments are obliged to report on their compliance with these rulings, and routinely adjust their national laws and policies to achieve conformity. Reform of the Court is an ongoing topic of discussion, since it is overloaded with cases and judgments may take seven to eight years. The Council of Europe also has adopted a series additional human rights instruments. And in parallel, within the European Union (EU), the European Court of Justice and other EU institutions have been progressively expanding the scope and strength of human rights protections and have reinforced the ECHR's influence. The most recent example is the Charter of Fundamental Rights of the European Union, which is included in the proposed Constitutional Treaty for Europe.

The inter-American regime also is institutionally well developed, and shares broad commonalities with the European system. The Charter of the Organization of American States (OAS), signed in 1948, lists human rights as one of the organization's guiding principles. In 1959, the OAS created an expert Inter-American Commission on Human Rights, which later acquired the ability to receive complaints from individuals. The American Convention on Human Rights, which was agreed upon in 1969 and came into force in 1978, created an Inter-American Court of Human Rights that can issue nominally binding rulings. But notwithstanding these institutional arrangements and the substantial improvements that have accompanied the spread of electoral democracy since the 1980s, the overall track record of compliance and enforcement falls rather short of the European model.

Regional regimes elsewhere are less developed and operate under far more difficult and constraining conditions. The African Charter of Human Rights and Peoples' Rights, adopted in 1981, is supposed to extend protections not only to individuals but to collectivities as well. It also contains an expansive menu of third-generation rights, including the rights to a healthy environment, development, and peace, and has bolder provisions on economic, social, and cultural rights than its counterparts in Europe and the Americas. The Charter also created an African Commission on Human and Peoples' Rights. Similarly, the League of Arab States adopted an Arab Charter on Human Rights in 1994, and there is an Arab League Human Rights Committee. In contrast, Asia lacks even an ineffective human rights regime.

Finally, complementing the international and regional regimes and associated organizations are a variety of national mechanisms. These include national human rights institutions (NHRIs), which increasingly interact and cooperate on promoting human rights compliance and national capacity-building. The NHRIs operate under a mandate established by the U.N. Paris Principles that were adopted by the U.N. General Assembly in 1993.[25]

In sum, as this overview indicates, the international community has made very significant progress in establishing human rights standards and mechanisms for the ongoing monitoring of progress toward their realization. Moreover, none of the rights listed in the core instruments has ever been withdrawn or formally curtailed by subsequent decisions; to the contrary, they have been progressively reinforced through reiteration and incorporation into successive intergovernmental agreements and court rulings. These successes can be attributed to a variety of factors, including the moral character of human rights claims and the desire of many states to avoid being publicly "named and shamed"; powerful democratic countries' interest in using human rights as a foreign policy tool against certain authoritarian regimes, and small and medium-sized democracies' interest in consolidating their own open societies; the substantial catalytic influence of CSOs at every stage and level of the process; the attendant development of a transnational "epistemic community" comprising committed experts in government, civil society, international organization secretariats, and, at times, the private sector and global media; and the attendant institutionalization of organizational programs mandated to carry the agenda forward through mechanisms of monitoring, assessment, and codification.[26]

Despite these gains, two major challenges remain. The first, of course, is promoting state compliance. Sanctions and other "hard" measures, such as the withholding of development assistance or curtailing of diplomatic and economic relations, have been employed in some extreme cases, but the realities of international power relations and larger foreign policy objectives generally limit the resort to such techniques. The newly established International Criminal Court could prove to be an important tool to dissuade dictators from undertaking particularly egregious violations of human rights, but it remains to be seen how thoroughly the United States will undercut its authority. In the meanwhile, normative pressure remains the principal means of promoting compliance with the international human rights regime, a circumstance that invites depressing gamesmanship around the composition of the U.N. Commission, the drafting of reports and resolutions, and so on. In the current context of globalization, the desires to attract foreign investment, development assistance, and political support have sometimes provided previously intransigent states with additional incentives to comply, although the strategic partnerships being formed in the "global war on terror" have provided new cover for others. Conversely, some of the regional systems, most notably the European regime, provide more effective methods for redressing individual grievances and bringing national policies into alignment with human rights standards.

The second challenge is to give greater detail to the internationally agreed rights, and to clarify their meaning and applicability under diverse conditions. In particular, as new types of behavior and policy emerge that were not envisioned when they were established, it is essential to consider how human rights can be not only respected but also advanced in the resulting environments. On the one hand, this means ensuring that states refrain from establishing national or international laws, policies, and practices that erode the agreed principles and their application. On the other hand, it means proactively taking steps to create conditions in which they can be realized more fully and effectively. Increasingly important in the latter connection is the growing need to establish national and international public policy frameworks that discourage practices by private actors, most notably the business sector, that could undercut the strength of human rights protections.[27]

The present volume was organized with this latter challenge in mind. As we have indicated, there has been no sustained and probing discussion either within the human rights epistemic community or among governments and other actors about how the protections established by the international human rights regime and related instruments should be protected and promoted with respect to the GIS. To the contrary, with few exceptions, national, regional, and global ICT policies are routinely being formulated without giving any real attention to the relevance of or impact on internationally agreed human rights standards. Hence, as the following chapters demonstrate, governments are actively pursuing initiatives that may work against guarantees concerning freedom of expression, the right to seek information, privacy protection, the right to enjoy one's culture, the right to freely assemble and associate or participate in political processes, procedural protections, freedom from discrimination, the rights of women, minorities' rights, and the right to development. At a minimum, then, there is a pressing need to think through how these rights apply in a globally networked and information-intensive world, identify specific policies and practices that could be contrary to their preservation and promotion, and suggest specific reforms that would rectify such problems.

Collective analysis and dialogue along these lines will not be easy. Three examples illustrate the kinds of problems that must be confronted. First, in some cases, the relevant rights and violations thereof can be specified and observed with great precision. For example, nobody could plausibly argue that the increasingly common arrest and imprisonment without due process of Internet users who have simply expressed their political views on e-mail listservs, Web pages, or blogs does not constitute a significant violation of human rights. But in many other cases, particularly involving so-called second- and third-generation rights, there may be greater ambiguity and less consensus. Does the right to express oneself, seek out information, or participate in political dialogue, culture, and development mean that governments are obliged to provide the technological means to these ends? Is the failure to provide affordable access to telecommunications or the Internet inconsistent with human rights obligations? Some analysts and advocates would argue that it is, but others would undoubtedly view this as an overly expansive claim that risks diluting the moral force and legal coherence of rights guarantees.

Second, the transnational character of cyberspace forces a direct collision between diverse national legal cultures and ways of balancing competing human rights standards. The celebrated French court case concerning Yahoo! and the distribution of Nazi memorabilia was just the tip of the iceberg with respect to the interplay of freedom of expression, on the one hand, and nondiscrimination, on the other. In such cases, there may be no consensus even within the epistemic community, much less in the larger global polity, in part because many advocates concentrate on defending the particular human rights they specialize in at the expense of a more holistic perspective.

And third, there are difficult questions concerning the role of private actors in the GIS. An obvious example here is the growing propensity of technology companies to provide authoritarian regimes with the technical tools to violate the personal privacy and suppress the speech of Internet users. Are governments of the countries in which these companies are incorporated obliged to adopt policies barring such complicity in authoritarian practices abroad? What about the lack of privacy protections, outside the European Union, for World Wide Web domain name owners, who are listed in the privately controlled and publicly accessible WHOIS data base?

Until recently, there was no organized setting in which the human rights and GIS policy communities could come together to begin working through such issues. The 2002–2005 WSIS provided the first serious opportunity to launch the collective analysis and dialogue that are required. Alas, on the whole, this opportunity was not taken, and we are still at the starting gate. Why the human rights agenda was not advanced further in the WSIS process is the subject we consider next.

## Human Rights and the World Summit on the Information Society (WSIS)

First proposed by Tunisia at the ITU's 1998 Plenipotentiary Conference, the WSIS was endorsed by a U.N. General Assembly resolution in December 2001. Unlike previous U.N. summits, the WSIS was a two-phase event involving two summits and an elaborate preparatory process. The first phase included a series of preparatory committee meetings (hereafter referred to as PrepComs) and regional consultations begun in 2002 and concluded with a summit hosted by Switzerland in Geneva on December 10–12, 2003. The second phase included a series of PrepComs in 2004 and 2005 and concluded with a summit hosted by Tunisia in Tunis on November 16–18, 2005.

The WSIS process attracted hundreds of national and transnational CSOs from around the world that came together to form a broad civil society coalition. While these CSOs were quite heterogeneous in terms of their core missions and specific priorities in the WSIS, they were united in a desire to promote the inclusion of public interest and "people-centered" developmental objectives in the governments' negotiated outcomes. To facilitate dialogue and the development of shared positions on the many issues in play, coalition members launched over two dozen regional or thematic caucuses and working groups. In parallel, they established three peak organizations to coordinate the inputs from these groupings and the coalition's interface with governments, the private sector, and international organizations. These were the Plenary, an open forum of all interested civil society individuals and organizations, which served as the ultimate decision-making authority; the Bureau, which coordinated positions on procedural matters and represented civil society in consultations with the parallel governmental and private sector-bureaus; and the Content and Themes Group, which was responsible for coordinating collective inputs on substantive matters.[28] The Human Rights Caucus (HRC) was formed as part of this larger civil society coalition at the first PrepCom in July 2002, and served as the civil society focal point for organizations occupied with the human rights agenda of the information society.[29]

In WSIS Phase I, the HRC focused in particular on the intensive and extended negotiations over the Declaration of Principles and Plan of Action agreed upon at the December 2003 summit in Geneva.[30] The HRC called on governments not only to list internationally agreed human rights injunctions as overarching and guiding principles of these two agreements, but also to ensure that all their other provisions—on everything from trade, intellectual property, spectrum management, and Internet governance to development programs, national ICT regulation, labor rights, and beyond—were fully consistent with them. While the first of these objectives was at least partially realized, the second met with less success. In contrast, in WSIS Phase II, the HRC and everyone else involved in the process shifted focus from the broad terrain of GIS issues to a narrower agenda of unresolved negotiation topics: Internet governance, development financing, and WSIS follow-up and implementation.

The work of the HRC can be divided into influencing the official negotiations and influencing civil society itself. On the second track, one of the contentious issues between HRC and other CSOs concerned a right to communicate, promoted as a new human right by the Communication Rights in the Information Society (CRIS) campaign.[31] Different rationales were expressed in support of such a right, which addresses a concern that the media are becoming increasingly homogenized and commercialized, and that minority, dissenting, or local voices are being excluded from decision-making processes due to a lack of information and access to the means of communication.

The idea of a right to communicate bears a heavy historical burden. It was at the center of an international diplomatic battle known as the New World Information and Communication Order (NWICO), which took place at UNESCO from 1973 to 1985, and which resulted in both the United States and the United Kingdom withdrawing from UNESCO. In short, the United States and others saw NWICO as a disguise for nondemocratic states to restrict freedom of expression, especially press and other media freedom, while the other side claimed that media should be under stricter (state) control, and that media concentration should be limited, in order to allow for a more pluralistic flow of information. At the onset of WSIS, organizations that had been involved in NWICO and newcomers gathered around the CRIS campaign, this time not calling for a state- or industry-led effort to create new global orders, but for democratization of media and communication.

However, the call for a new human right was opposed by a number of human rights groups. These argued that broader access to media and communication could be realized by enforcing existing human rights.

Furthermore, the broadly defined right to communicate could potentially harm core freedom provisions of UDHR Article 19. It was stressed by Article 19, a London-based CSO, that the right to freedom of expression is recognized to include positive state obligations. Thus, freedom of expression includes the right to diverse, pluralistic media and equitable access to the means of communication, as well as to the media. In addition, among related provisions of UDHR are the right to practice and express one's culture, the right to participate in public decision-making processes, and privacy rights, including the right to communicate anonymously.[32] In sum, enforcement of these provisions could provide for democratization of media and communication, the concerns of the CRIS campaign. The debate on this within WSIS CSOs was resolved by the end of WSIS Phase I, and there is now a more or less explicit agreement that the claim to a right to communicate need not invent new legal standards, but should, rather, call for enforcement of existing human rights standards.[33]

Another sore topic within civil society was the linkage between human rights and development. In the process of finalizing the civil society declaration for the Geneva Summit,[34] a number of organizations claimed that the issue of development (poverty reduction and economic and social development) was to take priority over human rights, thus insisting that the CS declaration should not be opened with the human rights language. This perspective presupposes a distinction between development and human rights rather than recognizing that the two are intimately related. The debate is also a reminder of the fact that a number of civil society organizations do not see human rights as the normative foundation for any society, independent on the level of development, but rather as something secondary to issues of development. On the other hand, many civil society organizations, especially from northern countries, demonstrated a more restricted understanding of human rights by focusing solely on civil and political rights—if not only freedom of expression and privacy.

In relation to the official negotiations, a core challenge for all CSOs involved in WSIS Phase I was to work with like-minded governments to give the DP a people-centered orientation, thus shifting the focus from infrastructure to people. HRC and its supporters had two objectives in particular: to establish links to the International Bill of Human Rights as overarching guiding principles, and to get treatment of specific ICT issues to incorporate HR-friendly language.

The aim of having explicit reaffirmation of human rights in the DP was realized only in the last days before the Geneva Summit; however, it was still unresolved whether all governmental delegations would agree to a reference to the Universal Declaration of Human Rights in the opening paragraphs of the DP. In the end this was resolved after strong pressure especially from the Western group of countries, but the struggle remains a reminder of the (low) level of state ambition when it comes to human rights and WSIS. Since formal commitment to human rights treaties is in place in most countries, it is ironic that a U.N. summit spends hours of plenary debate on whether it can agree to refer to the Universal Declaration of Human Rights in its political declaration. The aim of having the official declaration present a people-centered vision for the GIS was realized, to a lesser extent, which was part of the reason why CSOs decided, in November 2003, to stop providing input to the official process, and instead concentrate on developing their own civil society declaration for the Geneva Summit. "It is not about Digital but about Dignity," civil society stated at its press conference in November 2003.[35]

The HRC also fought to get specific ICT issues to incorporate HR language. The human rights provisions in play concerned in particular freedom of expression, the right to privacy, freedom of assembly and association, procedural rights and the rule of law, the right to participate in public decision-making processes, the right to development, and the principle of nondiscrimination, both as a general overarching principle and in relation to gender and minorities. All of these are issues which are covered in this volume.

The Caucus spent many sessions arguing that the current challenge is to address and improve the specific areas in which ICT can help realize human rights. The specific right which attracted most attention in WSIS, on a number of different but related themes, was freedom of expression. The baseline was to reaffirm respect for freedom of expression, as laid down in UDHR, in the WSIS documents. However, as mentioned above, freedom of expression entails positive state obligations. Thus HRC and other CSOs raised a much broader agenda of empowering people, not least vulnerable groups and regions, to actually be able to participate in the GIS, in order to have their human rights realized more effectively. The points raised included infrastructure, especially global inequalities in access and cost schemes, and, more generally, questions around freedom and control: Who owns and controls the information resources? Who has resources to participate in the GIS? And how are commercial or state interests balanced against the public interest and the public domain of knowledge? In the end, full reference to UDHR Article 19 was included in the DP after strong lobbying efforts from many CSOs, especially press and other media organizations. The broader debate, touching upon existing regimes of information ownership and control, was never taken up in the official negotiations.

Another specific right that was addressed time and again, and that has specific importance in an online environment, was the right to privacy. Despite the crucial role of privacy standards to guide the collection, access, and use of personal information, the DP contains only a minor reference to privacy. During WSIS, the HRC and the Privacy and Security Working Group of civil society time and again expressed their concern with the strong focus on national and international security and criminal use of ICTs vis-à-vis a state commitment to respect and protect civil liberties such as privacy.[36] Furthermore, the Geneva Summit itself presented a number of privacy violations, such as radio frequency identification device (RFID) tagging of participants without prior notice, and without any privacy policy on the retention, use, disclosure, and deletion of the personal information being collected.

The right to freedom of assembly and association was brought up in relation to labor rights in the GIS, but was not included in the DP. Likewise, the right to political participation was mostly addressed in relation to the Internet governance debate of WSIS Phase II, but often not with explicit human rights reference. On the issue of procedural rights and the rule of law, much debate evolved around the notion of an "enabling environment." In the DP it is stated that the regulatory framework is expected "to reflect national realities," which to many ICT regulators means a business-friendly environment subject to local conditions, but which from a human rights perspective has different connotations since "national realities" are often used to circumvent the obligations of states according to the human rights treaties they have ratified. Despite the many interventions from the HRC on this issue, the language was kept in the final documents. The case is illustrative of the disjuncture between HR thinking and ICT policy thinking and the lack of cross-cutting reference points that are needed if ICT policymakers are to integrate HR standards in their policy formulation.

Cross-cutting themes such as nondiscrimination, including women's rights and minority rights, were advocated by a number of civil society groups, including the HRC, but were not addressed to any major extent in the final documents. The same goes for the right to development, though much of the language in the DP speaks to the need for development and for bridging digital divides.[37]

At the end of WSIS Phase I, the HRC proposed a specific follow-up mechanism for human rights and the GIS. Supported by the civil society Plenary, and the International Symposium on the Information Society, Human Dignity and Human Rights,[38] HRC proposed to establish an Independent Commission on the Information Society and Human Rights. This commission should be composed of qualified experts with a broad geographical representation to monitor state practices and policies in order to advance compliance with human rights in the GIS. At the time of writing, no WSIS follow-up mechanism focusing on human rights in the GIS exists.[39]

In sum, the main result of WSIS Phase I was human rights damage control. The DP in the end included reference to human rights as overarching principles, and to a few other central rights. However, the broad range of issues that CSOs tried to raise, and that is reflected in the civil society declaration, were not included in the official negotiations. As we shall see below, WSIS Phase II was essentially different in this regard.

After the Geneva Summit in December 2003, everyone involved in the WSIS process shifted focus. The broad range of GIS issues covered in Phase I was replaced by a narrower agenda of unresolved negotiation topics in Phase II. These topics concentrated on Internet governance, development financing, and WSIS follow-up and implementation.

Internet governance was by far the most heatedly contested focus of the Phase II deliberations. The WSIS process fundamentally transformed the global debate on this topic in a number of important respects. In particular, it brought to a head the profound disagreement between the United States and many other governments and stakeholders concerning U.S. control over the root zone file at the apex of the domain name system, and—via contractual relationships—over the Internet Corporation for

Assigned Names and Numbers (ICANN), which is responsible for setting global rules regarding Internet identifiers. This and related conflicts are unresolved at the time of writing, have been covered elsewhere, and hence need not be delved into here.[40] Rather, two points of direct concern to the role of human rights considerations in WSIS are more pertinent.

First, the WSIS process resulted in a fundamental rethinking of the character and scope of Internet governance. Previously, the standard practice had been to equate the term "Internet governance" with the social organization of Internet identifiers and the root server system and, by extension, the functions performed by ICANN. This narrow vision overlooked the fact that there are various internationally shared private- and public-sector principles, norms, rules, procedures, and programs that shape both the Internet's infrastructure (physical and logical) and use for communication and commerce. But as the WSIS discussions progressed, participants began to converge around the need for a broader, holistic conception that could encompass the full range of Internet governance mechanisms and facilitate their systematic evaluation and coordinated improvement. This demand would be met by a pair of reports issued in July 2005 by the U.N. Working Group on Internet Governance (WGIG). A multistakeholder group appointed by U.N. Secretary-General Kofi Annan in November 2004, the WGIG developed a broadly framed "working definition" of Internet governance that was subsequently embraced by governments and other stakeholders. The effect of this shift was to put on the table a broad range of governance mechanisms and issues, including those pertaining to freedom of expression versus content regulation, privacy, "information security" and network security, intellectual property, international trade, technical standardization, and other matters.[41]

Second, and in consequence, the new understanding significantly increased the number of contact points between human rights standards and Internet governance policies and programs. As such, human rights received greater attention in the Internet governance discussions of Phase II than they had in those of Phase I. For example, human rights standards were invoked in the WGIG's internal debates, and the group's main report noted that "Measures taken in relation to the Internet on grounds of security or to fight crime can lead to violations of the provisions for freedom of expression as contained in the Universal Declaration of Human Rights and in the WSIS Declaration of Principles." The report also decried the lack of fully enforceable international standards on privacy protection.[42] Similarly, the WGIG's background report, which, unlike the main report, was not a fully agreed consensus document, made two specific references to human rights:

- There may be difficulties in reconciling the protections granted in Human Rights conventions and treaties with actions taken to combat criminalized behaviour;
- Privacy, a fundamental human right according to Article 12 of the Universal Declaration of Human Rights, becomes even more important over the Internet, where the intrinsic nature of the Internet makes it possible to effectively track an individual in cyberspace and use information about him/her illegally or without authorization. Threats to personal privacy increase the mistrust towards the Internet.[43]

In addition, during the open PrepCom debates, the HRC made several interventions noting that Internet governance has significant human rights dimensions and that the relevant international legal protections needed to be applied and enforced. Human rights principles also were mentioned from time to time by governments in relation to Internet governance, which was a new development. At the time of writing, governments also have tentatively agreed on the following statement, which represents progress from Phase I: "We affirm that measures undertaken to ensure Internet stability and security, to fight cybercrime and to counter spam, must protect and respect the provisions for privacy and freedom of expression as contained in the relevant parts of the Universal Declaration of Human Rights and the WSIS Declaration of Principles."[44]

A common feature of WSIS Phases I and II was the debate around Tunisia as WSIS II host country. The initial idea of holding a U.N. summit on the information society came from Tunisia, which is often overlooked in the debate. In terms of indicators of Internet use by the population, and thus from a strict infrastructure point of view, Tunisia as host country was not necessarily a bad choice. However, when addressing the summit from a broader societal and human rights perspective, Tunisia as the second host country was at best ironic, at worst an insult for the many victims and human rights organizations that have time and again pointed to the human rights violations in the country, including blocking of Web sites, police surveillance, press censorship, and imprisonment of individuals for their opinions.

The Human Rights Caucus pointed to the problems of having Tunisia as the second host country early on, and was, together with many other civil society groups, subject to continuous harassment, obstruction of meetings, and infiltration of various WSIS mechanisms, such as the CS Selection Committee (selection of speakers for the summit), especially in the second phase. The strategy pursued by the Caucus was not to boycott the Tunisia Summit nor keep silent on the human rights problems in the country,[45] but to act from inside the process, raise awareness among CSOs and governments, intensify the international spotlight, and give maximum support to the independent Tunisian NGOs. Initiatives in support of this strategy included a number of fact-finding missions to Tunisia; one initiated by human rights groups, others by a coalition of press organizations active around WSIS; an appeal signed by more than 100 CSOs to U.N. Secretary-General Kofi Annan; and, at the time of writing, organization of a Citizens Forum—a side event to the summit. This will be a space in which civil society actors from all over can meet and debate in solidarity with the independent Tunisian NGOs.[46]

## Overview of the Book

The book is structured into three parts. The first part addresses information society issues related to freedom of expression, access to information, and privacy protection. Generally speaking, the themes covered in this section represent some of the issues that have been most contested since about 1995, and the areas where most human rights battles have taken place in relation to the GIS. In terms of linking human rights with the GIS, it is thus the most advanced debate covered in this book. The second part focuses on freedom of association, participation, and procedural protections. The rights covered in this section have a stronger procedural element, and have not received the same level of attention. However, they are increasingly evoking interest, not least in relation to the debate around international cooperation—for instance, in the field of so-called cybercrime and in relation to the WSIS Internet governance debate, in which the role of various stakeholders, democratic legitimacy, and the rule of law surfaced time and again. The third part, on equal treatment and development, is the least developed part within the GIS framework, and though many would recognize and praise the standards at a general level, there is still a long way to go before issues of nondiscrimination and equal treatment are mainstreamed into global ICT policy thinking, not to mention the right to development.

## Part I: Freedom of Expression, Access to Information, and Privacy Protection

In chapter 1, Rikke Frank Jørgensen (RFJ) examines the principles behind the right to freedom of expression and discusses some of the current challenges to this right in the GIS. The right is laid down in the UDHR Article 19 and CCPR Article 19, and has been reiterated and amplified in a variety of subsequent international instruments. The challenges addressed in the chapter include lack of access, privatized censorship, filters and other means of restricting online content, and regulation of Internet service providers. Many of the issues were hardly addressed within the official WSIS debates because they touch upon established systems of power and ownership; thus it is easier to speak of infrastructure than to speak of censorship, she argues. RFJ suggests some principles for effective protection of freedom of expression in the GIS, such as to assure that relevant qualifications are supported in the curricula of primary and secondary schools, to develop indicators to measure compliance of national regulation with freedom of expression standards, and to conduct reviews of national legislation and practice.

In chapter 2, David Banisar (DB) addresses citizens' right to access public information. The right is part of freedom of expression (UDRH Article 19 and CCPR Article 19), and has been transposed into national law in a large number of countries over the last years. With a number of national examples DB illustrates how the years since 1995 have seen an explosion in laws promoting legal rights to public information. Today, nearly sixty countries have adopted freedom of information laws, and another forty are currently reviewing proposals; over half the world is making their government more open. However, there are still considerable barriers to obtaining crucial information in many countries, and efforts to expand citizens' participation in governance have not been adequately developed. Developing a culture of openness is an evolutionary process, in which both governments and civil society must change, argues DB, who also looks at the development of electronic government and how that might affect a culture of openness.

In chapter 3, Kay Raseroka (KR) analyzes another aspect of freedom of information (UDHR Article 19 and CCPR Article 19): the role of libraries in providing information access, especially in developing countries. In the chapter, KR debates the challenges and opportunities offered by ICTs to extend communication systems of nonreading cultures through the use of libraries. The majority of the populations in the developing world rely on people-centered information networks and trust relationships for exchange of information and sharing of knowledge; hence the information society vision must reflect these social realities. The Botswana Vision 2016 pilot project, in which elders share local culture stories with rural primary school children in their mother tongue, is used as an example of how local content creation can be nurtured, and access to information improved, by breaking down cultural barriers in intergenerational information exchange. As part of the project, computers and software are provided, since it is envisaged that ICTs will serve the children in learning to word-process their stories as part of learning to use the keyboard as a tool for writing. The project has demonstrated that it is both challenging and rewarding when libraries engage with communities in the emerging information society, argues KR.

In chapter 4, Robin Gross (RG), focuses on access to knowledge and the development of a public domain of knowledge vis-à-vis intellectual property rights regimes. The rights most often invoked in this discussion are freedom of expression (UDHR Article 19 and CCPR Article 19) and the right to enjoy your own culture, including an author's right to protection (UDHR Article 27 and ESCR Article 15). RG examines the clashes between freedom of expression guarantees (the public) and intellectual property rights, which is currently one of the most controversial battlefields in the GIS. The increase in copyright holders' rights has come at the expense of the public's rights to communicate freely, argues RG, and illustrates her point with a number of current examples, such as digital rights management schemes, design of DVD players, Peer-2-Peer software, the U.S. Digital Millennium Copyright Act, the EU Copyright Directive and the related Enforcement Directive, plus WTO's Trade Related Aspects of Intellectual Property Rights Agreement. According to RG, the current trend is to impose the U.S. copyright agenda on the rest of the world, resulting in a one-way flow of ideas from the North to the South—a form of "information age colonialism." In response, RG recommends some principles for creating balanced communication rights in a digital world.

In chapter 5, Gus Hosein (GH) examines one of the most directly affected rights in the digital era: the right to privacy. The right is laid down in UDHR Article 12 and CCPR Article 17, and has been reiterated and amplified in a variety of subsequent instruments, especially at the EU and OSCD level. GH starts by defining privacy, tracing its historical roots, and presenting the various dissenting views on privacy. After having outlined the legal and regulatory landscape, GH illustrates a number of current threats to privacy, such as mandatory retention of communication data, online tracking, exchange of passenger data, profiling systems, and use of biometrics in passports and identity cards, which is then combined with central databases. The current tendency toward still more invasive measures is alarming since privacy is a necessary foundation for an open and free information society, he argues. Without an adequate grounding in the politics of privacy, information society politics, as they manifest themselves in WSIS and other forums, may result in grave errors that will take years to reverse, GH concludes.

**Part II: Freedom of Association, Participation, and Procedural Protections**
In chapter 6, Charley Lewis (CL) addresses the right to freedom of assembly and association, laid down in UDHR Article 20, CCPR Article 21, and CCPR Article 22. With examples from Zimbabwe, Chiapas, and Seattle, CL illustrates how since the mid-1990s the development and spread of ICTs has fundamentally altered both the spaces and channels through which individuals and organizations interact, mobilize, and assemble in the face of government repression. Departing in the case of the Congress of South African Trade Unions, CL discusses the role that ICTs have played in strengthening the ability of unions to enforce their right to freely assemble and associate, and how ICTs have more practically changed the way unions work. Also, new means of blocking, limiting, or monitoring online activities are debated, and it is stressed that these restrictions are carried out both by regimes with a bad human rights record and by countries which are considered bastions of democracy and freedom.

In chapter 7, Hans Klein (HK) discusses the right to political participation, as laid down in UDHR Article 21 and CCPR Article 25, in the GIS.

HK starts by outlining the foundations for the right to political participation and next considers its relevance to the information society, depending on whether this is understood as an evolved version of the existing society or whether it constitutes a novel and distinct society in its own right. Using the free software movement and ICANN as cases, HK debates two settings for public affairs that create problems of participation in the GIS. A solution may require rethinking of the public–private distinction that lies at the core of the liberal state, in order for citizens' rights to be attached to private institutions, he argues. The alternative would be to bring new forms of political authority under existing governmental institutions, concludes HK.

In chapter 8, Meryem Marzouki (MM) debates procedural rights such as fair trial, presumption of innocence, effective remedy, and equality before the law, as laid down in UDHR Articles 7, 8, 10, 11, and CCPR Articles 2, 14, 15, and 26. MM argues that procedural rights are often overlooked in the information society context, though they present necessary conditions for the realization of the rule of law and thus for the effective enjoyment of all human rights. Furthermore, these rights have been particularly challenged by recent regulatory and legislative processes. With examples, such as the Council of Europe's Cybercrime Convention, the U.S. Patriot Act, French antiterrorism legislation, and EU privacy regulation, she argues that the recent trend has been to weaken the role of the judiciary, while extending the prerogatives both of the police and of private parties. Furthermore, there is a tendency for states to increase their monitoring powers over citizens without ensuring the necessary procedural safeguards. In the name of a war against terrorism, states are increasing their surveillance over citizens, and human rights, the rule of law, and basic democratic principles are paying the price, MM concludes.

### Part III: Equal Treatment and Development

In chapter 9, Mandana Zarrehparvar (MZ) focuses on the right to be protected against any form of discrimination or hate incitement in the GIS. The right is laid down in UDHR Article 2, CCPR Article 2, ESCR Article 2, and a large number of international instruments. MZ explores the different ways in which discrimination manifests itself in the GIS, and suggests that more attention be paid to two dilemmas: the backlash against any commitment to combat racism or any other form of intolerance through the Internet, and discrimination through lack of access to technology and means of communication. The structure of the Internet, its pervasiveness, and the possibility it affords for anonymity have made cyberspace a playground for those who wish to spread hateful propaganda and incite to hate and violence, she argues. The response should be to apply the principle of nondiscrimination as stipulated in the different human rights instruments and use this for stronger enforcement, while ensuring respect for freedom of expression. Regarding access to ICTs, information often has its source in the majority, and thereby excludes the minorities, MZ argues. She examines access to ICTs within the scope of public goods and services, and argues that it is the positive obligation of the state to guarantee the effective right to access to these goods and services for everyone, without distinction.

In chapter 10, Heike Jensen (HJ) continues the issue of discrimination (UDHR Article 2, CCPR Article 2, ESCR Article 2) with an examination of women's human rights as laid down in the Convention on the Elimination of All Forms of Discrimination Against Women (CEDAW) and a number of additional instruments. HJ uses existing articulations of women's human rights as a lens to focus on the challenges women face in the information society. This is done using the dimensions of ICTs as tools, ICTs as careers, and ICT ideology. With regard to ICTs as tools, it is argued that strong policy measures are required if ICTs are to be tools for the promotion of women's rights. Most ICT decisions, be they concerned with infrastructure, networks, tariffs, regulation, or licensing, need specifically to take into account the situation particularly of women in the South, rural and poor women, and to promote their right of inclusion. Looking at ICTs as career options, the point is made that while women's occupations in the ICT field constitute new opportunities for employment, they have generally been characterized by low pay and low appraisal, repetitiveness of duties, and limited career opportunities. Finally, with regard to the underlying ideology, HJ argues that what is now canonized as information is heavily indebted to the positions of dominance and control under which it is produced. Thus, since most information is produced in a reality where women do not participate on the same footing as men, it is not representing the perspectives and knowledge of women.

In chapter 11, Birgitte Kofod Olsen (BKO) looks at the specific challenges posed to minority rights by the information society. The right to minority protection is not laid down in the UDHR but is found in CCPR Article 27 and subsequent international instruments. BKO maps the traditional minority protection and argues that the challenges posed by the development in society toward increased communication and interaction, mobility and migration, as well as cultural, ethnic, and linguistic diversity, make it necessary to address minority rights, issues, and conditions in a new perspective. One major challenge and focal point will be to strike the balance between self-determination within a minority group and adequate safeguard mechanisms for external protection against restrictions on the rights of members of minorities set up by internal regulation within the minority group. Thus, the principle of pluralism should be applied in order to ensure that cultural life, religious practice, communication, and interchange of information in minority languages on minority and other issues are not restricted or in other ways interfered with in a way which is not compatible with international human rights norms and standards, BKO concludes.

In chapter 12, Ran Greenstein (RG) and Anriette Esterhuysen (AE) target the right to development. A right to development is not included as such in the International Bill of Human Rights, but is laid down in the subsequent Declaration on the Right to Development, which has been subject to much controversy. In the chapter, RG and AE start by outlining the right to development and its relationships to inequality within and between countries, and to collective versus individual rights. The notion is then linked to information and communications for development, including how this might be integrated into the broader discussion of human rights in the information society. Digital exclusion, or the "digital divide"—referring to unequal distribution of and access to ICTs—cannot be seen in isolation, since it is in fact a mapping of new asymmetries onto the existing grid of social divides, the authors argue. Accordingly, one of the most important challenges is to identify the main obstacles to development—whether social, political, or technological—and outline a way of overcoming these in the specific context of the information society, RG and AE conclude.

## Conclusion

The WSIS process shifted the rhetoric around the GIS from infrastructure to a much broader human rights focus, and an increasing number of actors within governments, industry, and civil society have started to address ICT issues within a human rights framework. As such the WSIS process initiated the first holistic assessment of GIS issues, catalyzed CS coalition development, and promoted collective learning and institutionalization.[47] It also represented the first real encounter between human rights advocates and issues and the broad GIS agenda. The challenges now are to sustain the momentum by building a coalition that can carry this agenda forward in the post–WSIS world. This will be an operationally demanding task since, in the absence of the interorganizational focal point the WSIS provided, GIS issues will once again be addressed primarily within a wide and heterogeneous array of institutional environments. It also will be conceptually challenging; as the HRC experience in WSIS demonstrated, there is a pressing need for analyses that flesh out the linkages between human rights principles and the GIS, and that translate these principles into specific policy requirements on the full range of issues. Without compelling arguments along these lines, it will be difficult to convince ICT policy makers specializing on any of the many ICT issues that engagement with human rights organizations and issues is relevant and necessary.

While the importance of international human rights standards for the GIS was raised in the WSIS process, the debates therein really just scratched the surface. Carrying the human rights agenda forward will require sustained, interdisciplinary analysis of and a globally inclusive, multistakeholder dialogue on, the interpretation and application of these standards to the full array of issues raised by the GIS. The participants in this project hope that this volume can contribute to the development of that analysis and dialogue.

## Notes

1. For overviews, see William J. Drake, "Communications," in P. J. Simmons and Chantal de Jonge Oudraat, eds., *Managing Global Issues: Lessons Learned* (Washington, DC: Carnegie Endowment for International Peace, 2001), pp. 25–74, also at www.ceip.org/files/pdf/MGIch01.pdf; and William J. Drake, "Introduction: The Global Governance of Global Electronic Networks," in William J. Drake and Ernest M. Wilson III, eds., *Governing Global Electronic Networks: International Perspectives on Policy and Power* (Cambridge, MA: MIT Press, 2006).

2. For illustrative discussions, see Jamie Frederic Metzl, "Information Technology and Human Rights," *Human Rights Quarterly* 18 (November 1996): 705–746; David L. Richards, "Making the National International: Information Technology and

Government Respect for Human Rights," in Juliann Emmons Allison, ed., *Technology, Development, and Democracy: International Conflict and Cooperation in the Information Age* (Albany: State University of New York Press, 2002), pp. 161–186; the essays in Steven Hick, Edward F. Halpin, and Eric Hoskins, eds., *Human Rights and the Internet* (New York: St. Martin's Press, 2000); and Association for Progressive Communications (APC), *ICT Policy: A Beginner's Handbook* (Johannesburg: APC, 2003), which includes a number of global examples on the linkage between the Internet, ICT regulation, and human rights.

3. For key examples of these initiatives, see the Web site of the Global Internet Liberty Campaign, a coalition of human rights and civil liberties NGOs, www.gilc.org; the global censorship report *Silenced*, by Privacy International (PI) and GreenNet Educational Trust (London: PI/GreenNet Educational Trust, 2003); the annual survey *Privacy and Human Rights*, by Electronic Privacy Information Center (EPIC) and Privacy International (Washington, DC: EPIC/PI, 2004); Human Rights Watch, www.hrw.org/doc/?t=internet?; and the annual report by Reporters Without Borders, *The Internet Under Surveillance: Obstacles to the Free Flow of Information Online—2004 Report* (Paris: Reporters Without Borders, 2004). For a scholarly and empirical assessment of Internet restrictions in authoritarian and semi-authoritarian countries, see Shanthi Kalathil and Taylor C. Boas, *Open Networks, Closed Regimes: The Impact of the Internet on Authoritarian Rule* (Washington, DC: Carnegie Endowment for International Peace, 2003).

4. For example, the U.N. Commission on Human Rights adopted Resolution 1986/9, "On the Use of Scientific and Technological Development for the Promotion and Protection of Human Rights and Fundamental Freedoms," which calls upon states to "make every effort to utilize the benefits of scientific and technological developments for the promotion and protection of human rights and fundamental freedoms." On this and other examples, see Cees J. Hamelink, "Human Rights for the Information Society," in Bruce Girard and Seán ó Siochrú, eds., *Communicating in the Information Society* (Geneva: U.N. Research Institute for Social Development, 2003), pp. 121–163.

5. Detailed information is available at the Human Rights Caucus's Web site: www.iris.sgdg.org/actions/smsi/hr-wsis/.

6. Chris Brown, "Universal Human Rights: A Critique," in Tim Dunne and Nicholas J. Wheeler, eds., *Human Rights in Global Politics* (Cambridge: Cambridge University Press, 1999), p. 103.

7. For particularly helpful overviews of the historical development of human rights, see Jack Donnelly, *Universal Human Rights in Theory and Practice*, 2nd ed. (Ithaca, NY: Cornell University Press, 2003); and Paul Gordon Lauren, *The Evolution of International Human Rights: Visions Seen*, 2nd ed. (Philadelphia: University of Pennsylvania Press, 2003).

8. Quoted in Christian Tomuschat, *Human Rights: Between Idealism and Realism* (Oxford: Oxford University Press, 2003), p. 22.

9. William Korey, *NGOs and the Universal Declaration of Human Rights: "A Curious Grapevine"* (New York: Palgrave, 1998), p. 2.

10. In this vein, Andrew Moravcsik has argued that newly established democracies were the chief proponents of strong human rights agreements because they wanted to use international commitments to bind future governments. In contrast, the United States and United Kingdom joined with authoritarian and totalitarian states in opposing compulsory, enforceable human rights commitments. See Moravcsik's "The Origins of Human Rights Regimes: Democratic Delegation in Postwar Europe," *International Organization* 54 (Spring 2000): 217–252. This may explain the dynamics of the strong European system, described below, but at the global level it would be the looser framework supported by the United States and Soviet Union that would prevail.

11. See Charter of the United Nations, www.un.org/aboutun/charter.

12. Dinah L. Shelton, "Human Rights," in P. J. Simmons and Chantal de Jonge Oudraat, eds., *Managing Global Issues: Lessons Learned* (Washington, DC: Carnegie Endowment for International Peace, 2001), p. 439.

13. Quotes in the above paragraphs are from the Universal Declaration of Human Rights, at www.udhr.org/UDHR/default.htm. The original, gendered language referring to "his" rights has been modified in the above text.

14. These and related considerations pose significant challenges for human rights advocacy. For a discussion, see Kenneth Roth, "Defending Economic, Social and Cultural Rights: Practical Issues Faced by an International Human Rights Organization," *Human Rights Quarterly* 26 (February 2004): 63–73.

15. Tomuschat, *Human Rights,* p. 39.

16. Asbjørn Eide has become known as the originator of the tripartite terminology in the slightly different version of obligations to *respect, protect,* and *fulfill,* which he originally introduced in 1987 when he served as the special rapporteur to the U.N. Subcommission on Human Rights.

17. For a critical discussion on the tripartite typology and ESCR, see Ida Elisabeth Koch, "Dichotomies, Trichotomies, or Waves of Duties?" in *Human Rights Law Review* 5 (1) (2005): 81–103, also at http://hrlr.oxfordjournals.org/cgi/content/full/5/1/81.

18. Ibid, p. 84.

19. The Commission on Human Rights has established an open-ended working group to consider options regarding the elaboration of an optional protocol to the International Covenant on Economic, Social, and Cultural Rights. Information on the working group is available at: www.ohchr.org/english/issues/escr/group.htm.

20. A new international Convention on the Protection and Promotion of the Rights and Dignity of Persons with Disabilities is currently being negotiated, as a follow-up to General Assembly resolution 56/168 of December 19, 2001. The draft convention is available at www.un.org/esa/socdev/enable/documents/chairtext.DOC.

21. For illustrations of these dynamics with respect to development, see Hans-Otto Sano, "Development and Human Rights: The Necessary but Partial Integration of Human Rights and Development," *Human Rights Quarterly* 22 (August 2000): 734–752; Brigitte I. Hamm, "A Human Rights Approach to Development," *Human Rights Quarterly* 23 (November 2001): 1005–1031; and Arjun Sengupta, "On the Theory and Practice of the Right to Development," *Human Rights Quarterly* 24 (November 2002): 837–889.

22. Stephen D. Krasner, "Structural Causes and Regime Consequences: Regimes as Intervening Variables," in Stephen D. Krasner, ed., *International Regimes* (Ithaca, NY: Cornell University Press, 1983), p. 1.

23. For early and groundbreaking discussions, see John Gerard Ruggie, "Human Rights and the Future International Community," *Daedalus* 112 (Fall 1983): 93–110; and Jack Donnelly, "International Human Rights: A Regime Analysis," *International Organization* 40 (Summer 1986): 599–642. For more recent treatments, see Andrew Moravcsik, "The Origins of Human Rights Regimes: Democratic Delegation in Postwar Europe," *International Organization* 54 (Spring 2000): 217–252; and the essays in Thomas Risse, Stephen C. Ropp, and Kathryn Sikkink, eds., *The Power of Human Rights: International Norms and Domestic Change* (Cambridge: Cambridge University Press, 1999).

24. "Legalization" is a concept employed by some political scientists in assessing international institutions. It comprises three dimensions along which institutions vary: the *obligations* undertaken by states and other actors to be legally bound to rules or commitments and subject to the scrutiny of international and (often) domestic law; the *precision* of the rules involved; and the *delegation* to third parties of authority to implement, interpret, and apply the rules; to resolve disputes; and, in some cases, to formulate new rules. For a discussion, see Kenneth W. Abbott, Robert O. Keohane, Andrew Moravcsik, Anne-Marie Slaughter, and Duncan Snidel, "The Concept of Legalization," in Judith Goldstein, Miles Kahler, Robert O. Keohane, and Anne-Marie Slaughter, eds., *Legalization and World Politics,* a special issue of *International Organization* 54 (Summer 2000): 401–419.

25. For a global overview of NHRIs, see www.nhri.net, which is a platform for national human rights institutions jointly provided by the U.N. Office of the High Commissioner for Human Rights and the Danish Institute for Human Rights. For a discussion on the role of NHRIs, see Morten Kjærum, "National Human Rights Institutions Implementing Human Rights," in Morten Bergsmo, ed., *Human Rights and Criminal Justice for the Downtrodden: Essays in Honour of Asbjørn Eide* (Leiden: Martinus Nijhoff, 2003), pp. 631–653.

26. "An epistemic community is a network of professionals with recognized expertise and competence in a particular domain and an authoritative claim to policy-relevant knowledge within that domain or issue-area. Although an epistemic community may consist of professionals from a variety of disciplines and backgrounds, they have (1) a shared set of normative and principled beliefs, which provide a value-based rationale for the social action of community members; (2) shared causal beliefs, which are derived from their analysis of practices leading or contributing to a central set of problems in their domain and which then serve as the basis for elucidating the multiple linkages between possible policy actions and desired outcomes; (3) shared notions of validity—that is, intersubjective, internally defined criteria for weighing and validating knowledge in the domain of their expertise; and (4) a common policy enterprise—that is, a set of common practices associated with a set of problems to which their professional competence is directed, presumably out of conviction that human welfare will be enhanced as a consequence." Peter M. Haas, "Introduction: Epistemic Communities and International Policy Coordination," in Peter M. Haas, ed., *Knowledge, Power and International Policy Coordination,* a special issue of *International Organization* 45 (Winter 1992): 3.

27. The Human Rights & Business Project of the Danish Institute for Human Rights develops concrete tools and training material on how companies can live up to human rights standards. Information is available at www.humanrightsbusiness.org/.

28. For an overview of the WSIS civil society organizations with contact details for the various groups, see www.wsis-cs.org/caucuses.html. For a collection of articles on the various steps of the WSIS process, from a civil society perspective, see www.worldsummit2005.org.

29. Members, documents, archives, and other materials of the Human Rights Caucus are available at http://www.iris.sgdg.org/actions/smsi/hr-wsis/.

30. See World Summit on the Information Society, *Declaration of Principles—Building the Information Society: A Global Challenge in the New Millennium,* WSIS-03/GENEVA/DOC/4-E, December 12, 2003, www.itu.int/wsis/docs/geneva/official/dop.html, and its *Plan of Action,* WSIS-03/GENEVA/DOC/5-E, December 12, 2003, www.itu.int/wsis/docs/geneva/official/poa.html.

31. For an analysis of the CRIS campaign by one of its founders, see Seán ó Siochrú, "Communication Rights," in *Word Matters—Multicultural Perspectives on Information Societies.* Caen: C&F editions, 2005.

32. Article 19, *Statement on the Right to Communicate by Article 19 Global Campaign for Free Expression* (London: Article 19, 2003), also available at www.itu.int/dms_pub/itu-s/md/03/wsispc2/c/S03-WSISPC2-C-0095!!PDF-E.pdf.

33. This was stressed during the World Forum on Communication Rights, organized by, among others, the CRIS campaign and the Human Rights Caucus as a side event of the Geneva Summit.

34. WSIS, Civil Society Plenary, *Shaping Information Societies for Human Needs*, adopted in Geneva, December 8, 2003, www.itu.int/wsis/docs/geneva/civil-society-declaration.pdf.

35. At the end of PrepCom 3a in November 2003, civil society representatives issued a critical statement on the state of affairs in the official negotiations, and published civil societies benchmarks for the Geneva Summit; see www.worldsummit2003.de/download_en/CS-Essential-Benchmarks-for-WSIS-14-11-03-final.rtf.

36. The potential use of ICTs by criminals and the new threats to international stability have been emphasized all through the WSIS process, not least by the U.S. and European delegations, which have promoted the Council of Europe Cybercrime Convention as a model for future global cooperation and agreement in this field.

37. For a human rights assessment of WSIS, see Meryem Marzouki and Rikke Frank Jørgensen, "A Human Rights Assessment of the World Summit on the Information Society," in *Information Technologies and International Development* 1 (3–4) (special issue, "The World Summit in Reflection: A Deliberative Dialogue on the WSIS") (Summer 2004): 86–88; and Rikke Frank Jørgensen and Meryem Marzouki, "Human Rights: The Missing Link," in *Visions in Process II—The World Summit on the Information Society* (Berlin: Heinrich Böll Foundation, 2005). For a collection of key documents from WSIS Phase I, see Electronic Privacy Information Center (EPIC), *The Public Voice: WSIS Sourcebook* (Washington, DC: EPIC, 2004).

38. International Symposium on the Information Society, Human Dignity and Human Rights, Statement on Human Rights, Human Dignity and the Information Society, www.pdhre.org/wsis/statement.doc.

39. It should be noted that the Council of Europe has taken the HR/GIS agenda on board and in May 2005 adopted a "Declaration of the Committee of Ministers on Human Rights and the Rule of Law in the Information Society," CM (2005) 56 final, available at www.bka.gv.at/Docs/2005/6/1/COE-minister13052005.pdf.

40. See, for example, the essays in William J. Drake, ed., *Reforming Internet Governance: Perspectives from the UN Working Group on Internet Governance* (New York: United Nations Information and Communication Technologies Task Force, 2005), www.unicttaskforce.org/.

41. The working definition is "Internet governance is the development and application by Governments, the private sector and civil society, in their respective roles, of shared principles, norms, rules, decision-making procedures, and programmes that shape the evolution and use of the Internet." See *The Report of the Working Group on Internet Governance* (Geneva: United Nations, 2005), p. 4. For a significantly more extended discussion of the issues, including the definition, see *The Background Report of the Working Group on Internet Governance* (Geneva: United Nations, 2005), both at www.wgig.org. William Drake was a member of the WGIG and drafted the material definition and related material. For a discussion of the need for such a definition

and other matters, see William J. Drake, "Reframing Internet Governance Discourse: Fifteen Baseline Propositions," in Don MacLean, ed., *Internet Governance: A Grand Collaboration* (New York: United Nations Information and Communication Technology Task Force, 2004), pp. 122–161. Also published as a working paper of the Social Science Research Council's Research Network on IT and Governance, 2004; see www.ssrc.org/programs/itic/publications/Drake2.pdf.

42. *The Report of the Working Group on Internet Governance*, p. 7.

43. *The Background Report of the Working Group on Internet Governance*, pp. 34 and 36.

44. See World Summit on the Information Society, "Chair of Sub-Committee A (Internet Governance), Chapter Three: Internet Governance Chair's Paper (After Fourth Reading)," WSIS-II/PC-3/DT/10 (Rev. 4)-E, September 30, 2005, p. 6, www.itu.int/wsis/docs2/pc3/working/dt10rev4.doc.

45. On October 14, 2005, the U.N. special rapporteur on the right to freedom of opinion and expression urged the Tunisian government to unconditionally release persons imprisoned for exercising freedom of expression. The statement is available at www.unhchr.ch/huricane/huricane.nsf/view01/4247E1D7DA2A9950C125709A 0054AF1D?opendocument.

46. Details of actions taken by the Human Rights Caucus on Tunisia may be found at: www.iris.sgdg.org/actions/smsi/hr-wsis/tunis.html.

47. On the dynamics of collective learning, see William J. Drake, "Collective Learning in the World Summit on the Information Society," in Daniel Stauffacher and Wolfgang Kleinwächter, eds., *The World Summit on the Information Society: Moving from the Past into the Future* (New York: United Nations Information and Communication Technology Task Force, 2005), pp. 135–146. Also published as CPSR Working Paper no. 2, www.cpsr.org/pubs/workingpapers/2/Drake.

# I  Freedom of Expression, Access to Information, and Privacy Protection

# 1 The Right to Express Oneself and to Seek Information

Rikke Frank Jørgensen

Freedom of expression and access to information was one of the most debated rights during the negotiations leading up to the World Summit on the Information Society held at Geneva in December 2003, and at Tunis in November 2005. This right was praised by some as the very core of the information society, and accused by others of being a merely formal standard with little practical reality in a world where the majority of the population does not have access to information technology and in which the "communication sphere" is dominated by Western/American culture and content, media concentration, and the English language.

In this chapter I will examine the spirit and ideas behind the right to freedom of expression, and discuss the potentials, challenges, and effective implementation of the right within the framework of the information society. The focus is biased toward Europe and the legal protection of freedom of expression spelled out in the European Convention on Human Rights. I will, however, try to give a more global perspective as well, and at the end of the chapter I have included a global overview of Internet access, regulation, and restrictions.

## Background and Spirit of Freedom of Expression

Freedom of expression is a fundamental human right that draws on values of personal autonomy and democracy. It is closely connected to freedom of thought and is a precondition for individuals' self-expression and self-fulfillment. The European Court of Human Rights has described freedom of expression as one of the essential foundations of a democratic society, one of the basic conditions for its progress and for the development of every man.[1] Since the ideas put forward during the Enlightenment, freedom of expression has been one of the fundamental human rights, and it has taken its place in all major international instruments protecting human rights.

Though freedom of expression is not specifically mentioned in the U.N. Charter, its importance was recognized from the very beginning of the United Nations. In its first session in 1946, the U.N. General Assembly stated: "Freedom of information is a fundamental human right and is the touchstone of all the freedoms to which the United Nations is consecrated."[2] Further, a conference on freedom of information was convened at Geneva in 1948 with the purpose of laying down an information policy for the United Nations. The conference adopted a draft convention on freedom of information, but the convention never came into place due to an unresolved conflict between the Western countries, arguing for a free flow of information, and the Soviet Union, arguing for a balanced flow of information. The Geneva conference, however, provided the text for Article 19 of the Universal Declaration of Human Rights, which was adopted by the Human Rights Commission at its third session in 1948, by 13 votes to 4.[3]

Freedom of expression is a typical "first generation" human right with individual emphasis, though it also carries strong societal implications. The point of departure is the protection of the individual from outside intervention in order to form and express opinions freely, without outside threats. In the Western world, one can speak of two main traditions for freedom of expression, originating from the French Revolution and its American counterpart. Whereas the European tradition has more emphasis on the protection of the rights of others, the U.S. tradition is more absolute.[4] One of the shortcomings of the classical liberty approach is the lack of emphasis on the structures and conditions that shape the public sphere, in which communication takes place. De facto restrictions on freedom of expression do not necessarily take the form of direct censorship, but can also be structured as self-censorship, institutional and/or social constraints, or merely lack of access to communication technology.[5] One could therefore argue that the regulation of the structures of communication have at least as much impact on communication as do direct measures aimed at specific content, which is an important point not least in light of the information society and the (lack) of access to its communicative sphere by a majority of the world's population.

## The Freedoms Protected

The right to freedom of expression is provided for in the Universal Declaration of Human Rights, Article 19; the International Covenant on Civil and Political Rights, Article 19; the American Convention on Human Rights, Article 13; The African Charter on Human and People's Rights, Article 9; and the European Convention on Human Rights, Article 10. The freedoms included in the right to freedom of expression are the following:

- Freedom to hold opinions   which implies that the state must not try to indoctrinate its citizens or make distinctions between those holding various specific opinions. The freedom gives citizens the right to criticize the government and to form opposition.[6]
- Freedom to impart information and ideas   which gives citizens the right to distribute information and ideas through all possible lawful sources.
- Freedom to receive information   which includes the right to gather information and to seek information through all possible lawful sources.[7]
- Freedom of the press   which is not explicitly mentioned, but has been emphasized in several cases in which the European Court of Human Rights has put strong emphasis on the public's right to know.[8]
- Freedom of radio and TV broadcasting   to which freedom of expression also applies.[9]

These freedoms are not unlimited, but restrictions must follow international human rights standards: they must be prescribed by law, must serve legitimate aims, and must be considered necessary in a democratic society. If these conditions are not fulfilled, a limitation on freedom of expression will amount to a violation of international human rights standards.

Looking at the case law on freedom of expression from the European Court on Human Rights, a few points are worth emphasizing. The first concerns the scope of the content protected. In an important judgment from 1976, the Court stressed the pluralism of expressions protected: "it is applicable not only to information or ideas that are favorably received or regarded as inoffensive or as a matter of indifference, but also to those that offend, shock or disturb the state or any sector of the population. Such are the demands of that pluralism, tolerance and broadmindedness without which there is no democratic society."[10] The broad content protection is crucial because freedom of expression is by its very nature a protection of minorities' or dissenters' voicing of their opinions—thus, the legitimate right of the minority to oppose the majority. Another important concept, not least in the light of the Internet's borderless nature, is the term "regardless of frontiers." The phrase indicates that the state shall admit information from beyond the frontiers of the country, to be both imparted and received, subject to the possible restrictions mentioned above.[11]

## Freedom of Expression Challenges in the Information Society

### The Same Level of Protection Applies

The U.N. special rapporteur on the promotion and protection of the right to freedom of opinion and expression has stressed the Internet's effect on freedom of expression and emphasized its potential for bringing out dissenting voices and shaping the political and cultural debate.[12] According to the special rapporteur, the Internet is inherently democratic, and online expressions should be guided by international standards and be guaranteed the same protection that is given to other forms of expression.[13] Also, the Declaration of Principles from the World Summit on the Information Society at Geneva (2003) reaffirms that freedom of expression in the information age is protected according to the human rights standards already agreed upon. Despite this formal commitment to uphold freedom of expression, there are a number of challenges when transposing rights of expression to the information society.

The Internet's potential for enhancing freedom of expression is linked to the displacement of certain architectures of control.[14] The single-purpose network of telephones and the one-to-many architecture of mass media are supplemented by an architecture in which every individual can participate. Cyberspace therefore holds the potential for a greater diversity of opinions and expressions as they actually exist in society, thus strengthening the public discourse and sphere. This potential is illustrated by a number of cases where individuals and organizations use e-mail, Web sites, newsgroups, and so on to disseminate information, find like-minded, persons, meet in online spaces, mobilize, and search for information despite state censorship, lack of resources, or closure of traditional media.[15]

Since the 1990s there has been a broad variety of attempts to regulate cyberspace. It is important to note that Internet regulation does not arise from a legal vacuum; most of the legal issues are subject to regulation or can be resolved by deduction from existing rules.

Seen from a human rights perspective, the major areas of Internet regulation so far have been privacy, freedom of expression, and freedom of information. Privacy issues have concentrated on how to ensure the privacy of personal data and of communications in a climate with strong emphasis on counterterror and state security measures. The freedom of expression issues have focused on how to secure freedom of information *and* the right of creators, and how to protect the standards of freedom of expression in a context that increasingly calls for control not only of illegal but also of so-called harmful content.

Below I will give an overview of some of the current challenges facing freedom of expression.[16]

### Access to the Public Sphere

Since the effective implementation of freedom of expression requires citizen's access to express opinions and to seek information in the public sphere,[17] access to the Internet is crucial. Currently, one of the biggest challenges is to ensure that the exclusive character of the information society is replaced by inclusiveness. The current lack of access for a majority of the world's population, often referred to as the digital divide, is at the same time a cause and a consequence of the unequal distribution of wealth and resources in the world. It is defined along lines of poverty and lack of infrastructure and development at all levels, including health and education, and must be understood and addressed within this more general political context. However, bridging the digital divide and providing infrastructure is only the first step. De facto access in order to communicate and to participate in the public sphere, whether online or offline, requires development at many levels and must include democratic, economic, and social development; literacy; and pricing schemes etc. in order to make access to the global public sphere and to democratic participation a real option for a majority of the world's population.

If we acknowledge access to the Internet as an important condition for democratic participation and development—for exercising freedom of expression—it is reasonable to argue for a positive state obligation not only to protect online expressions but also to secure individuals' access to the Internet. The positive state obligation could be to ensure Internet access in all local communities, as has been the case in Denmark, where the local public libraries, as part of their public service, are obliged to provide free Internet access.[18] Other recent examples of new access models include wireless solutions, which increasingly are being used to provide low-cost access at the community level.[19]

### Information Access and Ownership of Knowledge

The system of knowledge ownership, including patents, copyrights, and trademarks, is another topic closely related to the discussion of effective implementation of freedom of expression. Access to information (to use, share, and distribute) is closely related to ownership of information, and is seen by many to be the most crucial regulatory battle at this time.[20] The challenge and balance to be established involve maximizing access and use of knowledge, encouraging creativity as widely as possible, and, at the same time, ensuring protection of authors and creators. Since 2000, the United States and Europe have enacted legislation[21] that gives the industry freedom to undermine traditional fair use limits to copyright—for instance, by prolonging the time that content stays out of the public domain. Copyright protection is also increasingly becoming a censorship issue; content is being removed by Internet service providers through fear of liability or through end user license agreements whereby users must acquire permission to publish criticism or reviews of the software.

Another aspect relates to the disputed practice of patenting software, which at the moment is subject to a heated battle among the European Parliament, civil society groups, and the European Commission. One of the issues at stake is the claim that patenting of software elements will have damaging effects on creativity and the free flow of information. Compared with the physical world, software represents cultural products (such as books), and as such is protected by copyright law. However, if the ownership regime is expanded to allow the patenting of specific software elements—as proposed and supported by a number of EU member states—this could be seen as equivalent to allowing the patenting of the ideas contained in a book, and would pose a radical change to the current ability to use and build on other people's ideas and thoughts, as long as copyright is protected. Since the topic is covered separately in this book, I will not go into greater detail here.

The system of knowledge ownership touches the very core of our information society, and thus how we envision an expanding public domain—as our common reservoir of knowledge—as well as use of the digital age to strengthen our means to access and benefit from this information and knowledge. The Berlin Declaration, produced by a number of civil society groups,[22] is one example of an alternative compensation model that seeks to reestablish the balance between fair use and fair compensation through a system built on collectively managed online rights. Another example is the Creative Commons (CC) project, founded in 2001. Creative Commons is a nonprofit that has developed a set of licenses which creators can use to mark the conditions under which their content can be copied, distributed, and shared, using "human readable," "lawyer readable," and "machine readable" code, thereby offering more flexible copyrights for creative work. Currently more than 5 million Web pages are licensed under Creative Commons.[23]

### Restrictions on Information and Communication Content

One of the cherished characteristics of the information society is the enhanced possibility of voicing opinions and seeking information globally. In the physical world people encounter only a limited degree of communications because of physical and geographical limits, whereas on the Internet they can express and access a broad array of information irrespective of national boundaries, and be informed and disturbed accordingly. This has led to direct censorship in some countries, in the form of banning or blocking of information, and to more subtle "protective" measures in other countries, often in the form of rating or filtering.

Legal and political attempts to regulate content take many forms, depending on the national context. Measures include regulation of Internet service providers, strict licensing schemes, and national laws regulating speech and publications. One of the threats to online (as well as offline) freedom of expression is the way notions such as "indecent" and "harmful" are transposed into national legal standards that vary according to the local context and political regime, providing space for content restrictions that do not comply with international freedom of expression standards.[24] According to the international human rights standards, governments are allowed to restrict freedom of expression to protect certain interests, such as national security or public morals, but any restriction must be subjected to strict scrutiny, which includes inquiry into the aim of the restriction, the seriousness of the threat, and whether there are alternative and less restrictive means of protecting that interest. As illustrated by a number of studies and cases, many laws and practices around the world do not comply with these standards.[25]

### Which Jurisdiction Applies?

Another challenge relates to the borderless nature of the Internet, and to ensuring that the protection of legal standards in one country does not infringe on the freedoms of citizens in another country or state. In an important judgment from 1996 on the U.S. Communication Decency Act (CDA),[26] the Court stressed the Internet's global character, and the undue infringement on online speakers if they were to comply with the standard of the community most likely to be offended by the expression. Internet speakers cannot be required to speak according to the standards of the community with the lowest common denominator, since they have no means of restricting their expression from entering any community in the global public sphere. On the Internet you potentially speak to a world audience.

Following the argument of the CDA judgment, online speakers or service providers can reasonably be expected to comply only with the laws of the jurisdiction where they are physically located. However, recent court decisions have considered content from Web sites located on servers in other countries to be subject to their national jurisdiction, thereby placing individuals and service providers in a situation where they have to comply with laws of other countries in addition to their own national laws—for instance, if the content is targeting a specific national audience[27] or following the principle of the application of the law where damage occurs. One example of the latter is the European Commission's draft proposal for a Council regulation on the law applicable to noncontractual obligations (known as Rome II). Rome II includes treatment of claims involving defamation, advertising, intellectual property rights, and product liability, and promotes the principle of the application of the law where damage occurs. The draft has been criticized by a number of organizations that have asked for a reexamination and clarification of aims and consequences.[28] The tendency to subject content to restrictions under other national jurisdictions might pose de facto restrictions on online freedom of expression, and proposed regulations have to be assessed carefully for compliance with human rights standards.

### Self-Regulation and the Role of Internet Service Providers

Another crucial point with regard to Internet communication is the role and responsibility of Internet service providers. Discussions on censorship are usually focused on governments as the main actors. However, in cyberspace the control of access and the protection of freedom of expression are—contrary to the physical world—somewhat in the hands of commercial parties, the Internet service providers (ISPs). This gives Internet service providers a "statelike" power over public sphere communication and challenges the freedoms that human rights are meant to protect. It also raises the question of how far the state's positive obligation goes toward protecting individuals from interference by third parties. The discussion on the role and regulation of Internet service providers has evolved since the 1990s and is closely related to whether the Internet is perceived as a broadcast medium, a library, or a public space (plus additional variations of the three models).

The first conception results in a legal situation where Internet service providers must take responsibility for all content hosted on their servers, as in a traditional broadcast medium, a direction followed in some North African countries. The library analogy gives Internet service providers the role of secondary publishers with a certain responsibility for monitoring the content within their area. Finally, perceiving the Internet as a content-neutral public space shifts responsibility to the content provider, and in this case the Internet service provider is perceived as a common carrier, which is the case in the United States and a number of European countries.[29] The examples illustrate how the analogies consciously or unconsciously transposed from the physical world influence the way we seek to regulate the Internet.

Seen from a freedom of expression perspective, it is important to uphold that Internet communication is protected by international human rights standards; hence the ability to communicate in this public space should not be restricted by commercial parties without a judiciary or democratic mandate, but should be protected by the state. A related tendency concerns the state encouragement of Internet service providers to self-regulate. Private parties' self-regulation potentially involves privatized censorship, in which Internet service providers restrict individuals' freedom of expression by removing content through fear of liability, or by demanding a certain "decency" standard of their customers (for instance, through customer contracts). In Europe the discussions have evolved around "notice and take-down procedures," which are attempts to standardize procedures for when and how Internet service providers must notify users and take down content as a follow-up to the E-commerce Directive. So far the attempts to develop standardized procedures have failed, since citizens, service providers, and copyright holders have not been able to agree on the exact meaning of terms such as "expeditiously" and "apparently illegal," and since there is a growing awareness that ISPs should not play the role of the judiciary.[30]

### Media Concentration

A different but related development concerns the growing concentration of media ownership and the merger of media and telecommunication companies. Traditional players in media—publishers and broadcasters—are increasingly being joined by partners from the telecommunication sector and from the ICT industry. Some of these new alliances bring together information carriers and content providers (media industry), which gives private parties increasing power to combine control of access with control of content. Since access to express oneself is crucial for freedom of expression to have practical effect, it is important to ensure that the current tendency does not lead to a situation where media and telecommunication monopolies determine individuals' access to communicate and to express opinions in the public sphere of the Internet.[31] The issue of media concentration is politically sensitive and involves strong commercial interests, which is probably one main reason why it was barely touched upon within the WSIS context. However, it was raised by civil society groups, not least the CRIS (Communication Rights in the Information Society) Campaign, initiated by a number of media and social justice organizations.[32]

### Restrictions on Freedom of Information

Freedom of expression covers not only protection of the right to express opinions but also freedom of information.[33] Freedom of information is the right to search freely among all publicly available information and to receive all information that others are willing to communicate.[34] The freedom should ensure that there are no restrictions imposed on a person who wishes to receive information from someone who wishes to communicate that actual information.[35] Further, it should ensure that the individual can use any technical means in the search for information.[36] The freedom to seek and receive information from any public source must not be hindered, unless legitimate and proportionate restrictions can be raised in accordance with international human rights standards.

However, there are de facto a number of ways that governments around the world restrict citizens' access to information. Some of the more well-known cases include state-enforced filtering software that blocks access to unauthorized content, so that only state-approved content is available, or blocking of access to certain categories of information through blacklisting of Web sites. Other examples include extensive state surveillance, which often leads to self-censorship.[37] The censorship debate is typically targeting countries such as Cuba, China, Singapore, and Saudi Arabia for state censorship and imprisonment of Internet publishers. However, countries such as the United States and Denmark are using filtering software at public access points, and thus are also restricting means to seek information freely on the Internet. In the United States, filters at public libraries are now a condition for receiving state funding,[38] and in Denmark a number of public libraries have installed filters to protect users from harmful but legal content.[39]

In Europe, a filter-related discussion has concentrated on rating schemes, whereby Web content would be required to be rated (i.e., categorized in terms of metastandards on decency) in order to facilitate and effectuate filtering. As a consequence, only rated content would be searchable for users of the Internet. However, given the premise that the Internet is a public sphere, the demand that users categorize their content/expressions according to a metastandard of decency would be a very radical demand. "Is this expression very harmful, partly harmful, or not harmful at all?" "Does this discussion involve indecent language to a small, medium, or large degree?" Rating goods and services is natural within a commercial sphere, but when viewed from a public sphere perspective, it would be asking people to declare their "speak" as a precondition for speaking. Since an important element of freedom of expression is the individual's right to express herself without arbitrary restrictions, having to declare your "speak" as a requirement for speaking would mark a significant restriction on this freedom. The discussion on the use of rating and filtering schemes is ongoing, and its results and consequences for online freedom of expression remain to be seen.[40]

## The Potential and the Principles for Effective Implementation

Since the 1990s many have praised the Internet's potential for strengthening freedom of expression by giving practical reality to the vision of a world where people can freely speak their minds and access information. And no doubt access to information and to communication technology is empowering. The ability to communicate or to access a needed piece of information can be the decisive factor in taking action. As such it is a premise for development both at a personal level and at the level of society. Access to information is also important to democratic participation and control, for people to take active part in local, regional, or global society.

As I have tried to outline above, the challenges facing freedom of expression at this particular point in time are many. Often the discussions stop at the digital divide, and however important this problem is, there is a whole range of other problems and politics involved as well. Problems that are difficult because they require political will to readdress established systems of power, ownership, and money (for instance, related to copyright, trade, or media regimes), and because it's easier to speak of rolling out infrastructure than to speak of censorship or surveillance, or to address discrimination against regions, languages, and vulnerable groups.

In the context of the information society, freedoms—freedom to access information, freedom from surveillance, or freedom to express opinions—are tied to both local and global structures. It is therefore crucial that national, regional, and international regulations respect and enforce human rights standards, which are by their very nature universal standards. We must not forget that for freedom of expression to be more than a principle, people must have real and de facto means of expressing themselves, communicating, and seeking information. This requires effective protection of freedom of expression in a number of areas. Below I have listed some of the principles and actions that might help enforce freedom of expression in the information society.

## Principles and Possible Actions for Effective Implementation of Freedom of Expression in the Information Society

• Establish low-cost and nonfiltered Internet access, not least in marginalized regions

• Include education in the use of technology, information search, and communication and collaboration in an online environment in the curricula of primary and secondary schools

• Mainstream information society priorities, such as strengthening of information access and building of communicative capacity, in development programs and priorities

• Establish agreements and actions to ensure the continuous development of a diverse and strong public domain of information

• Develop indicators to measure the compliance of national regulations with human rights standards

• Conduct international review of national regulations to ensure that relevant legislation and policies are in compliance with human rights standards

• Mainstream information society issues in existing monitoring mechanisms, such as the monitoring committees of U.N. treaty bodies, the special rapporteurs, and other relevant mechanisms, within the office of the U.N. high commissioner for human rights

### Appendix 5.1
### Global Overview of Internet Access, Regulation, and Restrictions

| Region | Access | Regulations/Legislation | Restrictions/Censorship |
| --- | --- | --- | --- |
| Africa | Less than 0.01 percent of the population has access to the Internet Slow reform and liberalization of the telecommunication sector | ICT policies that stress the importance of online freedom of expression for economic development Antiterror legislation has provided increased state power to monitor communication Laws holding ISPs liable for content in some of the countries | Extreme poverty and lack of access Culture of self-censorship/hostile environment |

**Appendix 5.1**
(continued)

| Region | Access | Regulations/Legislation | Restrictions/Censorship |
|--------|--------|-------------------------|-------------------------|
| Asia | Growth of access, particularly in urban centers | Political recognition of the importance of the Internet for economic, political, and social progress Post–9/11 legislation increasingly restricts online content considered unacceptable or harmful | Still lack of access, in especially rural areas State censorship in many legal and technical forms |
| Europe | High level of access, especially in northern Europe Increasing consolidation and cross-ownership in the privatized telecom sector | EU and Council of Europe regulation/ protection in place for freedom of expression (and privacy); however, since 9/11 increased pressure on freedom of expression ISPs in principle not held liable for content | Lack of access, especially in southern and eastern Europe Some self-regulation by ISPs and some filters on public computers |
| Latin America | High level of access in (urban) areas of Brazil, Mexico, and Argentina; lower in other (rural) areas and countries Telecommunication sector mostly privatized, with universal access obligation | Constitutional protections for freedom of expression (and privacy) in place in most countries Special rapporteur for freedom of expression No law on ISP liability | Lack of access, especially in rural areas No specific restrictions on use of the Internet Mandatory filters at public access points in some countries |
| Middle East | Still relatively limited access in many countries; 2.2 percent of the population has access to the Internet Relatively weak telecommunication infrastructure | State ownership or strict laws on media in general A few states have permitted a more liberal approach to Internet regulation than is permitted other media | Media controlled and closely monitored by government Direct censorship by state; culture of self-censorship |

**Appendix 5.1**
(continued)

| Region | Access | Regulations/Legislation | Restrictions /Censorship |
|---|---|---|---|
| North America | Highest level of access after Scandinavia Cheap and liberalized telecommunication infrastructure | Long tradition of strong constitutional protection of civil rights Since 9/11, strong pressure on freedom of expression and privacy. Several more restrictive laws introduced Increase in exceptions to freedom of information | Use of filters at public schools and libraries is mandatory in the United States in order to receive state funding No state filtering or blocking in Canada |

Source: Regional reports presented in Privacy International and GreenNet Educational Trust (2003).

**Notes**

1. *Handyside* judgment (1976), para. 23.

2. U.N. Resolution A/RES/59(1), para. 1.

3. See U.N. document E/800, appendix.

4. See Juhani Kortteinen, Kristian Myntti, and Lauri Hannikainen, "Article 19," in Alfredsson and Eide (1999) for an elaboration on the freedom of expression traditions.

5. Ibid., 395.

6. Certain positions have inherent limitations on the right to express opinions (e.g., civil servants and prisoners).

7. The Universal Declaration of Human Rights, Art. 19, and the International Covenant on Civil and Political Rights, Art. 19, specifically refer to the right to *seek* information.

8. The European Court of Human Rights has often stressed the public interest or public debate factor: for instance, in the *Sunday Times* case (1979), the *Lingens* case (1986), and the *Jersild* case (1994).

9. In Europe, for a long time the Commission (the instrument prior to the European Court of Human Rights) saw no incompatibility between state monopolies of radio and TV and the European Convention on Human Rights. However, in 1993

the European Court on Human Rights ruled on the Austrian radio monopoly case (*Informationsverein Lentia and others*), and concluded that a violation of Art. 10 existed. The issue is also mentioned in the International Covenant on Civil and Political Rights, General Comment 10: "Effective measures are necessary to prevent such control of the media as would interfere with the right of everyone to Freedom of Expression" (UNHCHR 1983:1).

10. Handyside judgment (1976), para. 23.

11. For judgments concerning the imparting and receiving of information from abroad, see *Groppera Radio AG and others* (1990) or *Autronic AG* (1990), both from the European Court on Human Rights.

12. UN Report E/CN.4/2000/63.

13. Ibid.

14. The link between code and law of cyberspace is described in Lessig (1999).

15. See, e.g., Privacy International and GreenNet Educational Trust (2003); Reporters Sans Frontières (2004); Electronic Privacy Information Center (2003); Human Rights Watch (1996).

16. See appendix 5.1 for a global overview of Internet access, regulation, and restrictions.

17. "The public sphere of civil society stood or fell with the principle of universal access. A public sphere from which specific groups would be eo ipso excluded was less than merely incomplete; it was no public sphere at all" (Habermas 1989, 85).

18. The duty to provide free Internet access in public libraries was appended to the Danish Library Act in 2000.

19. A project such as the Wireless Road Show is an example of on-the-ground training in how to build low-cost connectivity. The wireless networks are constructed using a license-exempt spectrum and are based on open technology and free software. See http://thewirelessroadshow.org/.

20. In his opening address at the WSIS Prepcom2 on Feb. 17, 2003 in Geneva, Lawrence Lessig, professor of law at Stanford University, urged governments to fight the current U.S. and European tendency to expand intellectual property right regimes.

21. The 1998 U.S. Digital Millennium Copyright Act (DMCA) and the 2002 European Union Copyright Directive (EUCD).

22. The Berlin Declaration on Collectively Managed Online Rights, June 2004.

23. For more information, see http://creativecommons.org.

24. A country-based survey on national legislation is in Privacy International and GreenNet Educational Trust (2003). Examples from the report include the following: Morocco bans criticism of the monarch and of "offensive reporting" by journalists; China bans "subversive speech"; Australia regulates speech that is "unsuitable" for minors; Egypt regulates, among other things, speech that discusses "taboo issues" and "human rights violations," whereas the European Convention on Human Rights speaks for the "protection of public morals."

25. See, for instance Privacy International (2003); Reporters Sans Frontiers (2004); Electronic Privacy Information Center (2004); Human Rights Watch (1996); Global Internet Liberty Campaign (1998).

26. The CDA sought to impose criminal penalties on anyone who used the Internet to communicate material that, under contemporary community standards, would be deemed patently offensive to minors under eighteen years of age. The law was passed by the U.S. Congress in Jan. 1996, but was ruled unconstitutional by the District Court for the Eastern District of Pennsylvania in June 1996 and by the U.S. Supreme Court in June 1997.

27. Examples of this are the 2000 French Yahoo case (Tribunal de Grande Instance de Paris) and the 2002 Australian *Gutnick* case. Within the European Union there is a tendency toward mutual recognition in Web cases, implying that the lowest legal standards in any EU country become EU practice, as is currently the case with the Intellectual Property Enforcement Directive adopted in Mar. 2003.

28. See, e.g., http://www.iccwbo.org/law/jurisdiction/rome2/.

29. The 2000 European Commission E-commerce Directive operates with limited liability, stating that ISPs are not to be held liable unless they become aware of illegal content and fail to take action. There is, however, a legal gray zone surrounding the notification procedure that is currently being transposed to the national level as EU member states implement the E-commerce Directive.

30. The most comprehensive European initiative has been the research program (Rightswatch) carried out by the European Commission. See Sjoera Nas, "The Future of Freedom of Expression Online: Why ISP Self-regulation Is a Bad Idea," in OSCE (2003), 165–172.

31. See Hamelink (2000), chap. 6.

32. For more information see http://www.crisinfo.org/.

33. An important aspect of freedom of information concerns the right to gain access to public information. Since this is covered in the chapter on the right to information, it will not be covered here.

34. Eggen (1994), 63.

35. Ibid. The principle was affirmed in the *Gaskin* case (1989), para. 52; and the *Leander* case (1987), para. 74.

36. *Autronic AG* case (1990), para. 47.

37. See Privacy International/GreenNet (2003), 12–19, for an elaboration on the various means and mechanisms for restricting access to information.

38. This was enforced through the Children Internet Protection Act (CHIPA), which was passed by the U.S. Congress in December 2000.

39. According to a survey published in Sep. 2003, 14 out of 224 public libraries in Denmark have installed filters. See Pors (2003).

40. For a more elaborate discussion on this, see Jørgensen (2001).

**References**

Alfredsson, Gudmundur, and Asbjørn Eide, eds, *The Universal Declaration of Human Rights*, The Hague: Martinus Nijhoff, 1999.

Eggen, Kyrre, *Vernet om ytringsfriheten etter art. 10 i Den europeiske menneskerettighets-konvensjon* (The Protection of Freedom of Expression in Article 10 in the European Convention of Human Rights), Oslo: Oslo University Press, 1994.

Electronic Privacy Information Center and Privacy International. *Privacy & Human Rights*. Washington, DC: EPIC, 2004.

Global Internet Liberty Campaign (GILC). "Regardless of Frontiers," Washington, DC: Center for Democracy and Technology, 1998.

Habermas, Jürgen. *The Structural Transformation of the Public Sphere*. Oxford: Polity Press, 1989.

Hamelink, Cees J. *The Ethics of Cyberspace*. London: Sage, 2000.

Human Rights Watch. "Silencing the Net." *Human Rights Watch* 8, no. 2 (1996).

Jørgensen, Rikke Frank. "Freedom of Expression on the Internet." EMA thesis, Raoul Wallenberg Institute, Stockholm, 2001.

Lessig, Lawrence. *Code and Other Laws of Cyberspace*. New York: Basic Books, 1999.

Organization for Security and Co-operation in Europe (OSCE). *Spreading the Word on the Internet*. Vienna: OSCE, 2003.

Pors, Niels Ole. "Notat om Filtre i danske folkebiblioteker," (Paper on Filters in Danish Public Libraries) Copenhagen, Sept. 27, 2003.

Privacy International and GreenNet Educational Trust. *Silenced*. London: Privacy International and GranNet Educational Trust, 2003.

Reporters sans Frontieres. *The Enemies of the Internet*. Paris: Reporters sans Frontieres, 2004.

United Nations Economic and Social Council. Report of the Special Rapporteur, Mr. Abid Hussain, Submitted Pursuant to Commission on Human Rights Resolution 1999/36. E/CN.4/2000/63. New York, 2000.

United Nations General Assembly. Resolution A/Res/59(1). 1st session. New York: United Nations, 1946.

United Nations High Commissioner for Human Rights. ICCPR General Comment 10: Freedom of Expression. New York, 1983.

United Nations Human Rights Commission. 3rd session. UN document E/800. New York: United Nations 1948.

World Summit of the Information Society (WSIS). Declaration of Principles. Geneva, 2003.

**European Court of Human Rights**

*Autronic AG* judgment. Series A, no. 178. May 22, 1990.

*Gaskin* judgment. Series A, no. 160. July 7, 1989.

*Groppera Radio AG and others* judgment. Series A, no. 173. Mar. 28, 1990.

*Handyside* judgement. Series A, no. 24. Dec. 7, 1976.

*Informationsverein Lentia and others* judgment. Series A, no. 276. Nov. 24, 1993.

*Jersild* judgment. Series A, no. 298. Sept. 23, 1994.

*Leander* judgment. Series A, no. 116. Mar. 26, 1987.

*Lingens* judgment. Series A, no. 103. July 8, 1986.

*Sunday Times* judgment. Series A, no. 30. Apr. 26, 1979.

**Other Courts**

High Court of Australia: *Dow Jones & Company Inc. v Gutnick*. Dec. 10, 2002.

Tribunal de Grande Instance de Paris. *International League Against Racism and Anti-Semitism (LICRA) and the Union of French Jewish Students (UEJF) v. Yahoo*. Nov. 24, 2000.

U.S. Supreme Court. *Attorney General of the United States et al. v. American Civil Liberties Union et al.* Case no. 96-511. June 26, 1997.

# 2 The Right to Information in the Age of Information

David Banisar

Freedom of Information is a fundamental human right and the touchstone for all freedoms to which the United Nations is consecrated.[1]

A popular government without popular information or the means of acquiring it is but a prologue to a farce or a tragedy, or perhaps both. Knowledge will forever govern ignorance: And a people who mean to be their own Governors, must arm themselves with the power which knowledge gives.

—James Madison (1822)

We live in the age of information. Computer and communications technologies have made available access to information at levels unprecedented in history. Governments are rapidly adopting these technologies and moving toward electronic government. They are increasingly recognizing, or being forced to recognize, that citizens have an inherent right to be informed of government activities and to participate in the development of policies that affect them.

Complementing this, the period since the 1990s has also seen an explosion of the legal "right to information." In the period from the fall of the Iron Curtain until now, over forty countries have adopted comprehensive national "right to know" laws that give to individuals and organizations a legal right to demand information on how the government is acting in their name. Today, nearly sixty countries have adopted these laws and another forty are reviewing bills or proposals—over half the world is making government more open. The right is also being incorporated into international law through a growing body of agreements and declarations.

This explosive growth has occurred mostly through the efforts of civic activists at the international, national, and local levels as they fight corruption and promote good government, free press, and accountability.

They are supported by foundations, international development organizations, and bodies such as the World Bank and IMF (which promote transparent budgeting).

## Benefits of the Right to Information

### Democratic Participation and Understanding

As recognized above by Madison, the right to know is essential for public participation. Democracy is based on the consent of the citizens, and that consent turns on the government's informing citizens about its activities and recognizing their right to participate. The public is truly able to participate in the democratic process only when they have information about the activities and policies of the government.

Public awareness of the reasons behind decisions can improve support and reduce misunderstandings and dissatisfaction. Individual members of Parliament are also better able to conduct oversight. Confidence in the government is improved if it is known that the decisions will be predicable. The New Zealand commission that led to the adoption of the far-reaching 1982 Official Information Act found "greater freedom of information could not be expected to end all differences of opinion within the community or to resolve major political issues. If applied systematically, however, with due regard for the balance between divergent issues [the changes] should hold narrow differences of opinion, increase the effectiveness of policies adopted and strengthen public confidence in the system."[2]

### Redressing Past Harms

In countries that have recently made the transition to democracy, right-to-information (RTI) laws allow governments to break with the past and allow society to better understand what happened, and the victims of abuses and their families to learn what happened. Almost all newly developed or modified constitutions include access to information from government bodies as a fundamental human or civil right. Over sixty countries now have constitutional provisions regarding access. They also often include provisions on a right to information on the environment and the right of individuals to access their personal files.

Following the transition to democracy, most Central and Eastern European countries adopted laws to regulate access to the files of the former secret police forces. In some countries, these files are made available to individuals so they can see what information is being held on them. In other countries, access to the files is limited to "lustration" committees to ensure that individuals who were in the previous secret services are barred from the current government or at least that their records are made public.[3] In the most far-reaching laws, such as those of Germany and the Czech Republic, there is broad access available to historians, the media, and the public.[4]

In Mexico, President Fox in 2002 ordered the declassification of all files on human rights abuses, so that families could find out what happened to their loved ones who disappeared. In the United States, Congress has enacted laws on the access to files relating to the assassination of President Kennedy (JFK Act)[5] and to Nazi and Japanese war crimes[6] held by government agencies, including the intelligence services. A law on human rights abuses by third countries is still being discussed. Both acts created review boards to collect and examine documents and decide on their release. Under the JFK Act, over 4 million pages were released, including thousands of previously classified records.[7] Over 8 million documents have been released under the war crimes laws. In the United States, the National Security Archive has made thousands of requests and has obtained information from the government on records relating to human rights abuses in Mexico, Peru, and Chile that have then been made available to the truth commissions in those countries.

## Improved Decision-Making Processes

RTI laws also improve how government bodies work. It has been found that decisions which will eventually be made public due to RTI laws are more likely to be based on objective and justifiable reasons. The New Zealand Law Commission found in 1997 that "the assumption that policy advice will eventually be released under the Act has in our view improved the quality and transparency of that advice."[8] The Australian Law Reform Commission and Administrative Review Council in 1997 found "the [Freedom of Information] Act has had a marked impact on the way agencies make decisions and the way they record information . . . [it] has focused decision-makers' minds on the need to base decisions on relevant factors and to record the decision making process. The knowledge that decisions and processes are open to scrutiny, including under the

Freedom of Information Act, imposes a constant discipline on the public sector."[9]

A significant use of RTI is in fighting corruption. RTI is considered a key tool in anticorruption measures because reasons for awarding contracts and other financial transactions must be documented and justified.[10] In India, the Mazdoor Kisan Shakti Sanghathan (MKSS), a grassroots social activist group, uses local right-to-know laws to obtain information on local public works projects. They then hold *jan sunwais* (public hearings) and read the files aloud to the community, thus revealing the amounts said to have been paid for school and road projects. Community members are then asked if the projects have been completed, and how much they were paid for their work. These hearings have revealed many instances in which actual payments were less than the amount that had been recorded as given to people who had died, or spent on projects never completed.

### Protecting Other Rights

RTI laws can improve the enforcement of many other economic and political rights. In Thailand, a mother whose daughter was denied entry into an elite state school demanded the school's entrance exam results. When she was turned down, she appealed to the Information Commission and the courts. In the end, she obtained information showing that children of influential people were accepted into the school even if they got low scores. As a result, the Council of State issued an order that all schools accept students solely on merit.[11] In India, the RTI laws are used to show that food vendors are not providing government-subsidized, low-cost food to impoverished citizens. This has resulted in substantial changes in the food distribution system to ensure that citizens are getting their food while vendors are getting adequate compensation.

Other laws, such as data protection acts, allow individuals to access records held by private entities. A right of access to and correction of personal files ensures that records on individuals are accurate and decisions are not based on out-of-date or irrelevant information. It also ensures that people can see what benefits or services they are entitled to and whether they are receiving the correct amounts. In South Africa, the private access provisions of the Promotion of Access to Information Act have been used against banks by individuals who want to know why their applications for loans are denied, by a minority shareholder to obtain records of a private company after he was denied access, to them, and by a historian who wanted to research how a private utility company operated during the apartheid era.

## History of the Right to Information

The right to information in order to make government accountable emerged in the revolutionary philosophies of the Enlightenment. In Sweden, the Freedom of the Press Act, which set the principle that government records were by default to be open to the public and granted citizens the right to demand documents from government bodies—the world's first Freedom of Information (FOI) Act—was adopted in 1766.[12]

European revolutionaries also recognized the need to make government officials accountable by allowing citizens access. The French Declaration of the Rights of Man called for access to information about the budget to be made freely available: "All the citizens have a right to decide, either personally or by their representatives, as to the necessity of the public contribution; to grant this freely; to know to what uses it is put."[13] The Netherlands' Declaration of Rights of Man (1795) states: ". . . everyone has the right to concur in requiring, from each functionary of public administration, an account and justification of his conduct."[14]

The founding fathers of the United States also recognized the power of the executive to control information as a means of limiting participation. In the Declaration of Independence, one of the complaints against British rule recognized how preventing open government and meetings undermined democratic activities:

He has called together Legislative Bodies at Places unusual, uncomfortable, and distant from the Depository of their Public Records, for the sole Purpose of fatiguing them into Compliance with his Measures.[15]

Few governments followed Sweden's lead in setting out a comprehensive right to information for their citizens, but there were some developments. In the United States, the state of Wisconsin adopted rules on public access to local government meetings and records in 1849, and Louisiana adopted its first Public Records Act in 1912.[16] In 1888, Colombia adopted the Code of Political and Municipal Organization, which allowed individuals to request documents held in government agencies and archives, unless release of these documents was specifically forbidden by another law. In many countries, legislatures began publishing their proceedings and making them open to the media and the public. Courts also began to open their doors.

It was following World War II, with the creation of the United Nations and international standards on human rights, that the right to information began to spread and countries began to enact comprehensive laws for access to government-held documents and information: Finland enacted its law in 1951; the United States enacted its Freedom of Information Act in 1966; Norway and Denmark in 1970; France and the Netherlands in 1978; Australia and New Zealand in 1982; and Canada in 1983.

The period since the mid-1990s has been the most active period of countries adopting freedom-of-information laws, with over two-thirds of the countries adopting their laws in that period. Today, RTI laws are found in all regions and continents.[17] Nearly all of the countries in the northern hemisphere have adopted comprehensive RTI acts, and the rest of the world is moving in the same direction. In Asia, India, Pakistan, Japan, Thailand, and South Korea have adopted laws, and a number of other countries are currently considering bills. Even in China, a few localities have adopted transparency laws, often in connection with electronic government. In South and Central America and the Caribbean, nearly a dozen countries have adopted laws, and almost every other country is currently considering them. In Africa, RTI is slowly emerging. South Africa adopted the Promotion of Access to Information Act, one of the most far-reaching laws, in 2000. In 2002, Angola adopted the Law on Access to Administrative Documents, based on the Portuguese law, and Zimbabwe has adopted a law that contains a section with the elements of a typical FOI law within a draconian censorship regime. Many other nations on the continent, including Uganda, Nigeria, Ghana, and Kenya, are currently considering similar acts.[18]

## Basic Elements of Right-to-Information Laws

Most national comprehensive RTI laws are broadly similar. The U.S. Freedom of Information Act has been the most influential model, and its structure of rights and exemptions has been widely copied. Canada's and Australia's national, provincial, and state laws have also been influential with countries that have the common law tradition. The following elements can be found in nearly every RTI law:

- A right of an individual, organization, or legal entity to be able to demand information from public bodies without having to show a legal interest
- A duty of the body to respond and provide the information; this includes mechanisms for handling requests and time limits for responding to requests
- Exemptions to allow the withholding of certain categories of information; these typically require that some harm to the national interest must be shown before information can be withheld and include the protection of national security and international relations, personal privacy, commercial confidentiality, law enforcement and public order, information received in confidence, and internal discussions
- Internal appeals mechanisms for requesters to challenge withholding of information
- External review of the withholding of information, including the setting up of an external body or the referral of cases to an existing ombudsman or the court system
- Requirement for government bodies to affirmatively publish some types of information about their structures, rules, and activities.

## Other Laws Providing Access to Information

Many countries—including Argentina, Australia, Canada, Germany, India, Japan, Mexico, Switzerland, and the United States—have adopted RTI laws at the provincial, state, and municipal levels. In Japan, nearly 3,000 local municipalities have adopted RTI ordinances since 1982. Often these laws lead to the adoption of a national law. They are also important testing grounds for innovative provisions that later appear in national laws.

There is a set of related laws on open meetings and participation, commonly known as sunshine laws. These laws, such as the U.S. Sunshine Act, require that government departments issue public agendas and hold open meetings of government officials to allow for public scrutiny. In Romania, the Law on Decisional Transparency in Public Administration requires that meetings of government bodies and information about pending activities of government bodies be automatically disclosed online and that citizens be invited to participate in decisions.[19] There is also a growing number of countries that have adopted these sunshine laws on the basis international obligations.

Finally, many other laws, such as administrative procedure acts and environmental, consumer, and data protection laws, often include provisions giving individuals the right to access information to protect their interests. Other laws require publication of information for public interest reasons, including laws on archives, statistics, elections and political parties, and the fight against corruption.

## Problems with Implementation of Freedom-of-Information Laws

The enactment of a freedom-of-information law is only the beginning. Developing a culture of openness is an evolutionary process that requires changes both in government bodies and in the public. Governments must change their internal cultures and realize that they are the caretakers of information for the public. Civil society and private persons must test governments and demand information.

There are problems in many countries. Governments often resist releasing information, causing long delays; courts uncut legal requirements; and users give up hope and stop making requests. In some countries, laws have been adopted but never implemented. In Panama, the government in 2002 enacted regulations that limited access to government records to those with a legal interest, even though the law did not require it. In Albania, there has been little use of the law because neither potential requesters nor government officials are aware of it. In Bosnia, one of the best-designed laws in the world is used only infrequently, in part because it was developed more by the international community than by local civil society. In Kosovo, the ombudsman said that he had not received a single complaint under the act.

In other countries, freedom of information laws are that in name only. The Zimbabwean Protection of Privacy and Access to Information Act sets strict regulations on journalists, and its access provisions are all but unused. In Serbia, the Milosevic-era Public Information Act was designed to restrict public information, not to promote it. In Paraguay, the Parliament adopted an FOI law in 2001 which restricted speech and was so controversial that media and civil society groups successfully pressured the government to rescind it shortly after it was approved.

These restrictions must be resisted. Civil society, the media, and other political actors must publicly criticize restrictions and conduct campaigns. Courts and ombudsmen must be asked to reject government decisions as being unjustified. Legislatures must step in and reverse changes, and amend or replace inadequate laws.

## The International Basis of RTI

There is a growing body of international agreements, treaties, resolutions, guidelines, and model bills promoting access to information as a human right and as key part of administrative law on issues such as environmental protection and the fight against corruption.

At its first session in 1946, the General Assembly of the United Nations recognized that "Freedom of information is a fundamental human right and is the touchstone of all the freedoms to which the United Nations is consecrated."[20] This was incorporated into the U.N. Declaration of Human Rights (1948) as Article 19, which states:

Everyone has the right to freedom of opinion and expression; this right includes freedom to hold opinions without interference and to seek, receive and impart information and ideas through any media and regardless of frontiers.

Since 1993, the U.N. special rapporteur on the promotion and protection of the right to freedom of opinion and expression to the Commission on Human Rights has advised that access to information is a part of freedom of expression. In his 1998 report to the Human Rights Commission, he stated:

The right to seek and receive information is not simply a converse of the right to freedom of opinion and expression but a freedom on its own . . . that the right to access to information held by the Government must be the rule rather than the exception. Furthermore, there must be a general right of access to certain types of information related to what may be called "State activity," for example, meetings and decision-making forums should be open to the public wherever possible.[21]

The 1992 U.N. Earth Summit's "Rio Principles" call for access to information on the environment held by public authorities in order to enhance citizens' participation in decision-making about environmental matters.[22] This was put into practice as the 1997 UN/ECE Convention on Access to Information, Public Participation in Decision-Making and Access to Justice in Environmental Matters (the Aarhus Convention), which requires that governments affirmatively make information available and engage citizens before making decisions on environmental issues. It has been signed by forty countries.[23] Over thirty countries have signed the 2003 Protocol on Pollutant Release and Transfer Registers, which requires governments to set up registers showing the amount of pollution being released into the environment by companies.[24] The U.N. Convention on Corruption calls for governments to make information available by "enhancing the transparency of and promoting the contribution of the public to decision-making processes; Ensuring that the public has effective access to information."[25]

RTI is also being widely recognized at the regional level. The Council of Europe (CoE) has been the most active regional body in developing the right to information. The CoE ministers issued a resolution in 1979 calling on member countries to adopt access laws. Since then, it has reiterated that recommendation several times and has assisted many countries in developing and implementing laws. In 2002, it issued detailed guidelines for member countries on developing access laws and is currently discussing development of the first international treaty on access to information.[26]

Article 10 of the European Convention on Human Rights (ECHR) provides for a right to freedom of expression similar to the Universal Declaration of Human Rights. In addition, while the European Court on Human Rights has never ruled directly that Article 10 provides for a right of access to information, it has found numerous times that other rights, such as the right of privacy for individuals (in Article 8), include a right to obtain records about oneself and provide for a positive obligation on governments to make information available about environmental hazards.

The basic treaties that make up the European Union include the right of EU citizens to access records created or held by EU bodies. The EU has also adopted two directives requiring national governments to allow access to environmental information laws, and other directives relating to privacy, the environment, human rights, and procurement that include provisions on rights of access.[27]

The Inter-American Commission on Human Rights first recommended in 1998 that countries adopt RTI laws[28] and is currently reviewing a case against Chile under Article 13 of the American Convention on Human Rights. In 2002 the Organization of American States recognized the need for nations to adopt RTI laws in the Inter-American Declaration of Principles on Freedom of Expression, and in 2003 issued a resolution stating that "access to public information is a requisite for the very exercise of democracy" and calling on member states to adopt appropriate laws.[29] In Africa, the African Commission on Human and People's Rights said in the 2002 Declaration of Principles on Freedom of Expression in Africa: "Public bodies hold information not for themselves but as custodians of the public good and everyone has a right to access this information."[30]

In 1980 the British Commonwealth issued a resolution encouraging its members to adopt access laws, and followed it with principles in 1999 and a model bill in 2003.[31]

International bodies and agreements are increasingly promoting freedom of information as a way to protect their interests. The 1999 Convention on the Rights of the Child recognized that children have a right to seek and impart information. The Convention on the Elimination of All Forms of Discrimination Against Women requires that women have access to educational and family-planning information. The 1992 Convention for the Protection of the Marine Environment of the North-East Atlantic requires that member states provide a right of access.

## Modernization and the Information Society

Another trend toward access to information is the increasing use of electronic government (e-government). Since the mid-1990s, e-government has been promoted as a way of providing a more efficient means of operating and a more responsive government. The most ambitious view of e-government is the development of tools and systems that allow citizens to participate in governance. Regardless of geography, they can comment and interact on government proposals, providing the government with information and insights to develop policies based on a broad range of viewpoints.

Interactive systems can be used to offer individuals the chance to comment on pending bills and consultations or on ongoing government policies. Online chats can allow ordinary citizens in diverse parts of a country to talk directly with key policy makers regarding ongoing projects and proposals.

This can also provide policy makers with easy access to relevant discussions before policies are set. There are various systems. They can be immediate interactive systems, Web-based Web logs, or mailing lists. In Finland, the www.otakantaa.fi project initiated by the Ministry of Finance has civil servants conducting conversations about issues in early states of preparation. Once a discussion is completed, a résumé of it is kept with the proposal as it is acted upon.

In 2003, an estimated 97 million Americans used the Internet to obtain information from government bodies, up from 40 million in 2000. As estimated 34 million used it to send comments to public officials.[32] It can also be used for implementation when government agencies are developing rulemakings.[33] The U.S. government has launched a comprehensive site for commenting on regulations at http://www.regulation.gov/.

### Electronic Government and RTI

Electronic government requires information as a prerequisite. In recognition of this, many national RTI laws now impose a duty on government agencies to routinely release certain categories of information on their Web sites. In Poland, each public body must create an online Public Information Bureau that is the primary means of accessing information under the Law on Access to Public Information. In Turkey, the main ministries have been very active in using electronic networks to make information available, encouraging users to submit requests and obtain status updates about their requests online.

Under the Estonian Public Information Act, national and local government departments and other holders of public information have the duty to maintain Web sites and post an extensive body of information on the Web, including statistics on crime and economics; enabling statutes and structural units of agencies; job descriptions of officials, their addresses, qualifications, and salaries; information relating to health or safety; budgets and draft budgets; information on the state of the environment; and draft acts, regulations, and plans, including explanatory memoranda. They are also required to ensure that the information is not "outdated, inaccurate or misleading."

The Council of the European Union automatically makes available many of the documents it creates, including any document released under its access regulations, in its electronic register. This has resulted in both improved access for citizens and efficiency gains by the Secretariat. As noted by the Council in its most recent annual report, "If the number of documents directly accessible to the public increases, the number of documents requested decreases."[34] The U.S. Electronic Freedom of Information Act of 1996 requires that each agency create electronic reading rooms and include regularly requested documents.

Many laws require that requesters be able to request information using electronic mail or Web-based forms. In Mexico, the Sistema de Solicitudes de Información (SISI) system, run by the Federal Institute for Access to Public Information (IFAI), provides for electronic filing of requests directed to federal bodies.[35] An agreement was recently signed to allow states to use the system for their requests. Another agreement was signed with the Federal Electoral Institute (FEI) to allow individuals to file requests from computers in FEI offices around Mexico. All requests, including those made orally or in writing, are entered into the system, which allows for easy automated monitoring of the processing of requests.

Many other laws require that government departments affirmatively publish information, including acts on public administration, consumer protection, the environment, court practices, and statistics. Other types of records of interest to consumers and consumer groups can be made available.

As noted above, dozens of countries have adopted pollution registers to allow citizens to learn about pollution released in their neighborhoods. South Korea and other nations have been using electronic procurement to make available information on government purchases, thus both increasing transparency and reducing corruption.

## Conclusion

The legal right of individuals to obtain information on their government's activities is an essential part of democracy. There has been substantial progress in adopting this right since the 1980s; over sixty countries have now adopted laws, and international bodies are routinely recognizing it as a human right. However, over half the world's governments do not recognize the right of their citizens to be informed of their activities, and there are still considerable barriers to obtaining crucial information in many countries. Furthermore, efforts to expand participation in governance have not been adequately developed.

Access to information is a precursor to the development of electronic governance. Without electronic access to information, there can be no real electronic government. Thus far, e-government has been limited more to providing services than interactive democracy, but the use of ICTs to improve governance is also increasing.

### Appendix 6.1   National Freedom-of-Information Laws

The following countries have adopted national comprehensive access-to-information laws. Not all laws have been implemented or are considered effective. For a review of these countries' laws, see David Banisar, "Freedom of Information and Access to Government Record Laws Around the World," at http://www.freedominfo.org/survey.htm.

Albania, Angola, Armenia, Australia, Austria, Belgium, Belize, Bosnia and Herzegovina, Bulgaria, Canada, Colombia, Croatia, Czech Republic, Denmark, Dominican Republic, Ecuador, Estonia, Finland, France, Georgia, Greece, Hungary, Iceland, India, Ireland, Israel, Italy, Jamaica, Japan, Kosovo, Latvia, Liechtenstein, Lithuania, Mexico, Moldova, The Netherlands, New Zealand, Norway, Pakistan, Panama, Peru, Poland, Portugal, Romania, Serbia, Slovakia, Slovenia, South Africa, South Korea, Spain, Sweden, Switzerland, Tajikistan, Thailand, Trinidad and Tobago, Turkey, Ukraine, the United Kingdom, the United States, Uzbekistan, Zimbabwe.

### Notes

1. U.N. General Assembly, Resolution 59(1), 65th Plenary Meeting, Dec. 14, 1946.

2. Committee on Official Information (Danks Committee), "Towards Open Government," General Report, Dec. 1980.

3. See Hungary, On the Screening of Holders of Some Important Positions, Holders of Positions of Public Trust and Opinion-Leading Public Figures, and on the Office of History, Act XXIII of 1994; Lithuania, Law on Registering, Confession, Entry into Records and Protection of Persons Who Have Admitted to Secret Collaboration with

Special Services of the Former USSR, no. VIII-1436, Nov. 23, 1999, As amended by no. VIII-1726, June 13, 2000.

4. "Act Regarding the Records of the State Security Service of the Former German Democratic Republic (Stasi Records Act) of 20 December 1991." *Federal Law Gazette* 1 (1991): 2272.

5. President John F. Kennedy Assassination Records Collection Act of 1992.

6. Nazi War Crimes Disclosure Act, Public Law 105–246; Japanese Imperial Government Disclosure Act of 2000, Dec. 6, 2000.

7. Final Report of the Kennedy Assassination Records Review Board, 1998.

8. Law Commission, "Review of the Official Information Act 1982," Report 40, Oct. 1997.

9. Australian Law Reform Commission, "Open Government: A Review of the Federal Freedom of Information Act 1982," Report 77 (1995).

10. See Transparency International, "Global Corruption Report 2003," available at http://www. globalcorruptionreport.org.

11. More details about the examples used in this article are available at David Banisar, "Freedom of Information and Access to Government Records Around the World," available at http://www.freedominfo.org/survey.htm, and at http://www.freedominfo.org/index.htm.

12. See Stephen Lamble, "Freedom of Information, a Finnish Clergyman's Gift to Democracy," *Freedom of Information Review* no. 97 (Feb. 2002): 2–8.

13. Available at http://www.yale.edu/lawweb/avalon/rightsof.htm.

14. Available at http://www.uni-kassel.de/~dippel/rmc_web/constitutions/NL-00-1795-01-31/translation_en/nl-nat-1795-I-31-t-en-112.html.

15. The Declaration of Independence, Action of Second Continental Congress, July 4, 1776.

16. "The Development of Public Access Law in Wisconsin," in *Tapping Officials' Secrets*, 4th ed. Washington, DC: Reporters Committee for Freedom of the Press, 2001.

17. See Banisar, http://www.freedominfo.org/survey.htm.

18. Countries throughout the world with pending efforts include Argentina, Azerbaijan, Bangladesh, Barbados, Bermuda, Botswana, Brazil, El Salvador, Ethiopia, Fiji Islands, Germany, Ghana, Guatemala, Honduras, Indonesia, Kenya, Lesotho, Macedonia, Malawi, Maldives, Montenegro, Mozambique, Namibia, Nepal,

Nicaragua, Nigeria, Papua New Guinea, Paraguay, the Philippines, Russia, Sri Lanka, Taiwan, Tanzania, Uganda, Uruguay, and Zambia. See the map of FOI laws and pending efforts at http://www.privacyinternational.org/issues/foia/foia-laws.jpg.

19. Law no. 52 of Jan. 21, 2003, regarding decisional transparency in the public administration.

20. Resolution 59(1), Dec. 14, 1946.

21. Abid Hussain, "Promotion and Protection of the Right to Freedom of Opinion and Expression," report of the special rapporteur, submitted pursuant to Commission on Human Rights resolution 1997/26, E/CN.4/1998/40 (Jan. 28, 1998); Ambeyi Ligabo, "The Right to Freedom of Opinion and Expression," report of the special rapporteur, United Nations Economic and Social Council E/CN.4/2004/62, Dec. 12, 2003.

22. "Rio Declaration on the Environment and Development," Principle 10, available at http://www.un.org/documents/ga/conf151/aconf15126-1annex1.htm.

23. Available at UN/ECE. http://www.unece.org/env/pp/.

24. See UN/ECE, "Protocol on Pollutant Release and Transfer Register," available at http://www.unece.org/env/pp/prtr.htm.

25. UN Convention on Corruption, Article 13, available at http://www.unodc.org/unodc/en/crime_convention_corruption.html.

26. Council of Europe, "Recommendation Rec(2002)2 of the Committee of Ministers to Member States on Access to Official Documents" (2002), available at http://cm.coe.int/stat/E/Public/2002/adopted_texts/recommendations/2002r2.htm.

27. European Parliament and the Council of 26, Directive 2003/35/EC (May 2003), providing for public participation in the drawing up of certain plans and programs relating to the environment; Directive 90/313/EEC (June 7, 1990) on the freedom of access to information on the environment.

28. Annual Report of the IACHR 1998, OEA/Ser.L/V/II.102, Doc. 6 rev., Chapter VII (Apr. 16, 1999).

29. AG/RES. 1932 (XXXIII-O/03), June 10, 2003.

30. African Commission on Human and People's Rights, Declaration of Principles on Freedom of Expression in Africa (2002). Adopted by the Commission at its 32nd Ordinary Session, Banjul, The Gambia, Oct. 17–23, 2002.

31. Commonwealth Secretariat, Freedom of Information Act, May 2003. Available at http://www.thecommonwealth.org/shared_asp_files/uploadedfiles/%7BAC090445-A8AB-490B-8D4B-F110BD2F3AB1%7D_Freedom%20of%20Information.pdf.

32. Pew Internet and American Life project, "How Americans Get in Touch With Government," May 24, 2004. http://www.pewinternet.org/pdfs/PIP_E-Gov_Report_0504.pdf.

33. See Robert D. Carlitz and Rosemary W. Gunn. "Online Rulemaking: A Step Toward E-Governance," *Government Information Quarterly* 19 (2002): 389–405.

34. See http://register.consilium.eu.int/pdf/en/03/st06/st06353en03.pdf.

35. Available at http://www.informacionpublica.gob.mx/.

# 3   Access to Information and Knowledge

**Kay Raseroka**

The World Summit on the Information Society (WSIS) Declaration of 2003 created a vision for the information society through representatives of the peoples of the world:

A people-centred, inclusive and development oriented Information Society, where everyone can create, access, utilise and share information and knowledge, enabling individuals, communities and peoples to achieve their full potential in promoting their sustainable development and improving their quality of life.

The declaration states an unqualified acceptance of the fundamental importance of human rights and cultural diversity. The key principles further commit the peoples of the world to building an inclusive information society through access to information and knowledge, for the purpose of generating personal well-being and economic wealth as a measure of development.

The initial proposals for the Declaration of Principles focused on the role of computer technology as the significant infrastructure for the realization of the information society. The declaration recognized in addition the equal importance of libraries as carriers of information content and as facilitators of access to information and its use in diverse ways by humanity. Libraries, in their various forms, permeate all levels of society throughout the world. Thus they form a basic information delivery infrastructure that may be enhanced by communication technologies and develop into a significant facilitator of the information society.

As repositories of information and knowledge, libraries provide access to information and ideas to people who can read. They facilitate intellectual engagement among human beings across time and space. This chapter seeks to address challenges that libraries need to overcome in order to capitalize on the niche they occupy in the process of realizing the ideals of the information society articulated in the WSIS Declaration of Principles. These challenges are orality, indigenous languages, and the culture of information exchange, as well as literacy and the reading culture as bases for building an inclusive information society. The chapter will address the challenges and opportunities offered by communication technologies to extend communication systems of nonreading cultures through the use of libraries in developing countries.

## Literacy and the Information Society

According to the United Nations, there are 799 million adult illiterates in the world. The majority of those people live in the developing world. The language in which printed sources of information are written is a significant factor for successful access to information stored in libraries. The world's printed information is predominantly in English and other principal languages, since the nations in which those languages are used are the most prolific producers of scientific and technological information that influences the accumulation of capital commodities (Zeleza 2002, 3). Considering the relatively small percentage of people in the developing world who have mastery of these languages, the number of people who cannot make meaning through reading information transmitted electronically has increased. Thus the vision of an inclusive information society is thwarted by the levels of literacy and the predominance of the principal world languages, such as English as the language of the Internet, which is the premier vehicle for global electronic transfer of information.

## Orality and Communication of Information

Orality is defined as a characteristic of communication systems that emphasize aural perception in contrast to communication systems with a visual bias, usually referred to as literacy (Houis 1980, 12). The term "literacy" has complex meanings that are linked to a measure of development; it has been observed that "literacy rates are factored into the growth rates of societies" (Dossou 1997, 282) and has been associated with analytical skills in interpretation of media content, including the Internet and legal systems. In this chapter reading literacy will be used to highlight differences between oral and print-based communication systems.

Through simply being human, people have the skills to communicate orally, exchange information, and share knowledge. They produce meaning through questioning, analysis of information, and clarification of issues. Interpretation and integration of received information facilitates its assimilation to individuals' own contexts and knowledge, which are embedded in the mother tongue, and thus affects their way of life and creation of new knowledge (Burton 2001, 222).

Nathan (2000) suggests that this form of generating perception through interactive communication, which underlies oral communication systems, does not transfer well into reading literacy because it tends to be perceived by indigenous oral communities as a "one way communication system quite discontinuous with indigenous forms of communication." It is suggested that this has caused the "historical indigenous alienation from the written word." Hence, oral communities do not develop a culture of reading literacy. The inability to make meaning through interaction with printed sources, which is currently the requirement for meaningful use of libraries as sources of information, excludes oral communities, at the very start, from participating in the envisaged information society.

The principle of freedom of access to information and ideas embodied in Article 19 of the Universal Declaration of Human Rights is thus not a reality to the majority of people in the developing world.

## Transformation of Libraries into Facilitators of People-Centered Information Services

The majority of people in the developing world rely on people-centered information networks and trusting relationships for exchange of information and sharing of knowledge (Burton 2001, 225). Trusting relationships and networks develop where individuals or communities have an opportunity to meet, to discuss issues of common interest or need, to solve problems and/or produce new information, or simply to exchange perspectives. Even when no solutions to shared problems are derived from communal exchanges, the stimulation may provide inputs for a chain of thought, observations on alternative approaches, or worldviews in relation to the identified needs or issues of common interest, thus facilitating learning. Interaction, rather than solitary intellectual engagement through printed media, is the communication framework for the oral society.

In the analysis of successful methods for providing information to predominantly oral, rural communities in developing countries, Leach (2001) has identified factors that contribute to exchange of information and sharing of knowledge:

- Convenient time and place
- Established relationship between the provider and those who seek information
- Absence of authoritative (top-down) communication between an institution/organization that owns information and the user who needs information and objectively seeks it
- Development of an interactive process of sharing based on interdependence in the exchange of news, information, and knowledge, thus creating a trusting relationship.

This approach to information has been best illustrated in community resource centers where "users and facilitators utilise resources . . . both of the centre and of the users and produce a two-way process of interaction" (Karelse 1991). This provides a participatory approach to information-sharing and creation of local content in addressing problems and information needs in a community.

Libraries are social instruments and thus take their shape and purpose from the society they serve (Shera 1973). Considering orality and the characteristics of the socially prescribed information exchange culture, libraries in the predominantly oral societies of the developing world need to acknowledge that existing information communication systems have served communities successfully over centuries. These systems should therefore recognize the threat to local heritage that arises as traditional paths for transmittal of information are eroded by changes in traditional learning methods and by intercultural influences. The role of librarians should become one of deep engagement with, and embeddedness in, communities as a basis for development of trusting relationships between libraries and the communities they serve. The establishment of oral communication circles that evolve out of self-selected, trusted information networks has the potential of contributing to the emergence of an information society on terms that support interactive information-sharing.

Human development indicators, which have been developed internationally as a measure of advancement within a given society, provide a useful framework for libraries in pursuing inclusive information services needed for support of the interactive information society. The indicators are identified in the Human Development Index (HDI) as life expectancy and health, education and literacy rates, gender equality, and the opportunity to participate in government structures.

However, this pragmatic approach to creating libraries that fulfill the role of a social instrument demands a vision of the library as a people-centered service, presented by Mchombu (2004, 19) as

- Access to information for all groups in the population (including women, youth, and rural and urban poor)
- Access to information as a process for building self-reliance, empowerment, civil society participation, and gender equality
- High status for indigenous or traditional knowledge and locally generated information
- Respect for traditional channels of communication rather than regarding them as a barrier to development.

The use of this frame as a basis for library service moves the library from a focus on documents to a focus on people. In order for library personnel to effectively meet these diverse life issues, library information service has to be informed by the communities in which the libraries operate, and information needs to be based on regular assessment processes.

The library as a space utilized in this way will support and validate an oral culture. It can become a place where the practice of orality predominates. The assistive and nurturing role of librarians in the emergence of community valuing of indigenous knowledge is one of the most challenging and significant roles that needs to be developed through professional training for librarians who work with oral societies. Indigenous knowledge is the core of local content, which needs to be collected, organized, and preserved sufficiently to maintain its integrity over time and across generations.

Repackaging the products of orality (both manuscript and print) in appropriate media, such as video, digital photos, and tapes, in a collaborative and ethical manner based on the professional contributions of librarians is the next assistive stage. However, repackaging needs to be based on the understanding of the communities to whom the service is being provided, in order to decide which communication systems are to be used. These may be indigenous systems (ICS), defined as the "information sharing channels that bind society together, changing a group of people living in the same place or sharing the same interests, into a group that shares identity and purpose," or the exotic communication system (ECS), "which seeks to give information and obtain response regardless of social structure" (Rosenberg 1987, 13). The successful introduction and continuation of these roles is dependent on the continuing nurture and maintenance of trusting relationships with the oral communities served. The products should aim to provide primarily locally needed information that contributes to the development of the local community, so that benefits are an engine which sustains the relevance of locally created resources and also spurs local creativity and innovation. Success at this stage lays the base for future inputs into the global arena, according to principles understood and agreed upon by the community and also safeguards intellectual property, thus validating the library as a steward of heritage innovation and facilitation of a knowledge society that is inclusive. This is an essential transformative partnership role for libraries in predominantly oral communities.

## New Frontiers for Empowerment of Populations, Communities, and Individuals

The WSIS Declaration of Principles indicates the resoluteness in the

quest to ensure that everyone can benefit from the opportunities that ICTs can offer ... to meet these challenges, all stakeholders should work together to: improve access to information and communication infrastructure and technologies as well as information and knowledge ... create an enabling environment at all levels. (WSIS Declaration of Principles, Article 19)

This recognition of the potential for information and communication technologies (ICTs) to serve as a tool to enable people "to produce, record, process and disseminate information without any constraints in terms of time, distance and or volume" (Samassékou 2003, 5) should not be taken in isolation from the existing conditions and influences that have created the information divide caused by orality, reading literacy, and language issues discussed above. This issue is well summarized by Menou (2002, 4) when he observes: "ICT infrastructures more than any other ones are useless if they cannot be served by skilled operators and meet a public with the skills required to serve them." ICT is a set of tools that necessitate, at the individual level, the acquisition of skills for their productive use.

The integration of orality to the audio and visual communication of information, made possible by information and communication technologies, closely matches the communication system in oral cultures. It may remove the barriers of alienation encountered in the solitary engagement with print, referred to by Nathan (2000). This provides a unique opportunity for transformation of the library (book storage and silence) space into an information and communication (discussing, listening) space that focuses on community interaction and partnership. Herein lies the opportunity for empowerment of communities to share and contribute their stories and for librarians to facilitate the capture, preservation, and dissemination of local information through various communication technologies, subject to applicable intellectual property rights. Important principles for the new library space are thus

- Knowledgeability about capabilities of various communication technologies and, thus, the ability to select what is most appropriate to enhance access to information through various formats
- Good training in the social aspects of information service
- Partnership with community development agents for collaborative approaches to information needs analysis and to development of interactive information environments.

In the disadvantageous environment occupied by the majority of people who live in developing countries, and the urban poor in developed countries, the lack of access to ICT is the first hurdle. Where it is accessible, the cost of use and the skills needed for ICT use are barriers. The introduction of ICTs in this environment therefore has a potential to amplify existing inequalities.

- Its novelty requires changes in ways people think about information, work with it, and use it in the management of their social patterns of life.
- The effective use of the majority ICTs depends on a battery of literacies that include functional reading literacy, computer literacy, and specific language literacy.
- ICTs may not be widely available and/or affordable.

If one or a combination of these is not realigned to provide a supportive base on which to use ICTs as a tool for developing skills and confidence for populations to utilize information, the information society will not be realized. The need for extensive support of these communities is well articulated in DOT Force (2001, 15–16) proposals for action, one of which is "Give special attention to disenfranchised and illiterate people (particularly youth and women), through innovative partnerships to disseminate knowledge and skills using ICT."

Libraries are a well-established part of the social infrastructure with a well-organized administrative environment that may be used to introduce information and communication technologies for use by the public to access information at minimal cost, for governments that pay for ICT installation, and for communities that use them to access government information, locally created content, and globally available information.

Library instructional programs (LIPs) can play a crucial role by extending the building of skills within the traditional library to include development of community-based skills, which empowers communities to

- Develop attitudes that value local and national information resources
- Create their own information products and services
- Communicate their own stories through the Internet in the native language
- Build social and cultural capital as well as the intangible capital of the world's global economy.

Examples of the use of the ICTs as invaluable carriers of content in disadvantaged communities are emerging as part of the telecenter concept in Latin America, Asia, and Africa. According to Shadrach and Raj (2004, 52), telecenters may be privately or publicly owned, part of a private enterprise or provided by international donors. Their services range from phone shops to cybercafés, cottage telecenters for telework or telecommuting, and specially constructed multipurpose community telecenters (MCTs), some of which offer advanced services such as medical diagnosis and telemedicine. Although this type of information resource developed independently of libraries, efforts are under way whereby telecenter information managers (TIMs) and LIPs are investigating ways of partnering in order to extend the reach of information services, as at the 70th IFLA Conference Workshop (Buenos Aires, August 2004). The objective is to help individuals develop necessary skills for mastering the technologies as well as to facilitate the necessary attitudes and behaviors toward information so they are empowered to be part of the knowledge society. Since libraries are supported by public funds, partnership with telecenters has the potential for long-term sustainability.

LIPSs need to facilitate interactive information and communication systems based on orality and the inherent patterns of information knowledge, and to integrate these with those facilitated by ICTs. This approach will support the conventional pedagogic principles stressing that learning advances best when new information is related to existing knowledge. In this way the process of learning will help communities to use their own understanding and local knowledge as a basis for taking advantage of ICTs—primarily to satisfy their intrinsic information needs and to resolve day-to-day problems, through the use of accessible information, be it from within the community or derived from interaction with external sources of information. The product will be authentic information based on accepted tenets of information literacy skills, defined as "an understanding and a set of abilities enabling individuals to recognise when information is needed, and have the capacity to locate, evaluate and use effectively the needed information" (Council of Australian University Libraries 2001). This approach will transform book-focused services so as to address information needs through a variety of sources, mediated by means of the information and community embeddedness of librarians.

An example of a telecenter's role in repackaging of information to meet the needs of local communities is well demonstrated by the M.S. Swaminathan Research Foundation.

## Linkage Efforts: Orality, Information, and Technology

Education has traditionally been marketed, as a tool for accessing economic assets for personal and national development. The WSIS declaration focuses in a similar fashion on the "promotion of sustainable development and improving . . . quality of life." The linkage between information-sharing, analysis, and integration to existing cultures as a basis for learning has been downplayed, if not ignored, in education. The information society development framework seems to follow similar approaches, as far as it applies to the developing world communities. The concept of information and how it is used for learning and functioning within the culture of a society must be the base for building a successful information society of the future.

The fundamental challenge in developing an information society in a generalized African culture is that there is already an information society model of hierarchy, age, and gender prescription that is opposed to the principles of human rights on freedom of access to information and freedom of expression. Unless this fundamental approach to information access and communication within traditional developing societies is addressed, the envisaged information society will be a mirage for millions who cling to traditions and indigenous cultures of information-sharing within prescribed systems.

**Case Study**

The case study presented below was prompted by the vision of an educated, informed nation (Botswana 1997) as an approach to piloting the development of change toward information access and freedom of expression, and to facilitating the emergence of an information society for future generations.

It is a case study of a multipronged project. Its aim is to nurture local content creation through the breakdown of cultural barriers to intergenerational information expression/access. It seeks to encourage elders to be open to answering children's questions and to nurture children's understanding that they are permitted to ask questions and to develop their rights and duties of asking questions, within the cultural norms. It is also seen as an opening into the development of attitudes and behaviors that facilitate incremental development of language and information literacy skills through the storytelling process.

The project involves elders in sharing local culture stories with rural primary school children in their mother tongue. Children are encouraged to ask questions about the stories as well as other issues during their retelling the story as a follow-up to the session with the elders. The approach capitalizes on the tradition of grounded friendship relations between grandparents and grandchildren. The stories are taped to preserve the heritage and are also intended to be used for learning purposes.

The primary school library is the focal point for these activities, through the support of head teachers. Parent–teacher committees are partners in infusing the traditional and cultural information sources embedded in artifacts, idiomatic expressions, songs, and the storytelling process. The various permutations of partnerships empower each group to engage in sharing information through sharing their own knowledge and being validated by being listened to by "others." It thus breaks communication barriers by facilitating exchange of the culture between

- The Western-educated teachers and the traditional learning tutors, by providing a platform for information-sharing in support of children's learning
- Elders and children, by breaking intergenerational silence on issues regarded as important by children, and accepting the right of children to ask questions, an entry to the ethos of freedom of expression for children, of elders.

Children retell the stories received from elders to their teacher, who helps them create their own storybooks. This process is facilitated through a pedagogical method referred to as "breakthrough to literacy." With the help of the teacher, the words that are understood and used by the children in telling their own stories, are written, linked phonetically to develop the "whole word recognition" and "learning to read and write" systems in the context of storytelling. Books thus created are owned by the children, and may be shared among themselves.

A significant part of the project is the provision of computers and appropriate software, in partnership with UNICEF. It is envisaged that the ICTs will help the children learn to word process their stories while learning to use the keyboard as a tool for writing. In addition, UNICEF provides child- and culture-friendly information on HIV/AIDS. This information is made available through appropriate books and CD-ROMs. These materials are located in the library space, which has print materials and artifacts of local culture contributed by elders as part of the illustration and learning that occurs in the storytelling process.

The project is multipronged at another level. It was conceived by an NGO, the Children's Information Trust (CIT), which consists of LIPs and teachers and parent–teacher associations. One of the other partners is the nation's Vision Council, which has a mandate to raise awareness of the population of Botswana to recognize (among other values) the values and strategic actions required by the populace in order to be an educated, informed nation by 2016. The CIT has consulted widely with both citizens and various government ministries, significant stakeholders in the development of the information society in the country that control

- Primary school infrastructure in rural areas
- Policies for development of curricula, teaching, and resource-based learning in primary schools throughout the nation
- Library services, including youth and cultural issues
- National ICT policies and infrastructure development.

There are efforts to engage the private sector through acknowledgment of its social responsibility, as well as a long-term investment in human resource development of the country. The strategic action is to convince the private sector that it is in its interest to contribute to the development of youth who understand the emerging role of information and who develop critical analytical skills that make them competent to access and use all types of information and to enjoy creation of local information and its integration into global information resources.

Although this project is at its early stages, it has demonstrated to the LIPs, which are part of the project, the challenges, opportunities, and rewards of holistic engagement with communities served by libraries in their new role in the emerging information society. The experience, so far, has confirmed that community partnerships demand patience, persistence, and politics.

In this case the politics include working with four government ministries, each with its own approach. However, they share the same vision of an educated, informed nation by 2016.

## Conclusion

Information and communication technologies are a tool that may provide opportunities for building a fair and just society, provided that

- The principles of the Universal Declaration of Human Rights are reaffirmed by all representatives of the peoples of the world and, in particular, by governments, while also being addressed meaningfully through recognition of cultural pluralism, especially in developing countries.

- All populations have access to affordable ICT information content (libraries) and to the infrastructure.
- All people are empowered to communicate in their own voice and language, and to generate local content for their own use and exchange.
- All populations can afford to access each other's information sources on the basis of fair rights of exchange of information resources, mutually agreed between equals.
- LIPs and NGOs have forged partnerships based on similar core values and shared understanding of the requirements for an authentic information society that is based on holistic approaches to empowerment of populations, communities, and individuals, in line with Paulo Freire's (1970, 57) problem-posing, transformational philosophy of education and development.

If, however, there is a failure to construct holistic approaches to empowering communities to create an information environment, the intended information society will be owned and manipulated by technologically advanced and economically powerful nations of the world. Future areas for potential contestation seem to be based on benefits obtained through unequal relations in the control of the Internet.

## References

Bundy, Alan ed. *Australian and New Zealand Information Literacy Framework: Principles, Standards and Practice*, 2nd edition. Adelaide: Australian and New Zealand Institute for Information Literacy, 2004.

Burton, Simon. "Development communication: Towards a social action perspective." In Christine Stilwell, Athol Leach and Simon Burton, *Knowledge, Information and Development: An African Perspective*, 215–228. Ed. Pietermaritzburg: School of Human and Social Studies, 2001.

Botswana Presidential Task Group for a Long-term Vision for Botswana. *Long-term Vision for Botswana: Towards Prosperity for All*. Gaborone: The Task Group, 1997.

Digital Opportunity Task Force. "Digital Opportunities for All: Meeting the Challenge. Enhance Human Capacity Development, Knowledge Creation and Sharing," 15–16. Report of the Digital Opportunity Task Force including a proposal for a Genoa Plan of Action, May 11, 2001.

Dossou, François. "Writing and Oral Tradition in the Transmission of Knowledge." In *Endogenous Knowledge: Research Trails*, 281–308. Ed. Paulin Hountondji. Dakar, Senegal: CODESRIA, 1997.

Freire, Paulo. *Pedagogy of the Oppressed*. New York: Herder and Herder, 1970.

Hope, Anne, and Sally Timmel. *Training for Transformation: A Handbook for Community Workers*. 3 vols. Gweru: Zimbabwe: Mambo Press, 1994.

Houis, Maurice. "Oralité et scripturalité." Cited by Dossou, Francois (1997), "Writing and Oral Tradition in Transmission of Knowledge." In *Endogenous Knowledge: Research Trails*, 283. Ed. Hountondji, Paulin. Oxford: CODESRIA, 1997.

Kaniki, Andrew. "A Community Profiling and Needs Assessment." In *Knowledge, Information and Development: An African Perspective*, 187–198. By Christine Stilwell et al. Pietermaritzburg: School of Human and Social Studies, University of Natal, 2001.

Karelse, C-M. (1991) "The Role of Resource Centres in Building a Democratic Non-racial and United South Africa." *Innovation* 3: 3–8. Cited in Stilwell et al. 2001: 181.

Leach, Athol. "'The best thing is communicating verbally': NGO information provision in rural KwaZulu-Natal and some observations relating to library and information services." In Christine Stilwell, Athol Leach and Simon Burton, eds., 2001.

Mchombu, Kingo J. *Sharing Knowledge for Community Development and Transformation*. Ed. Gwynneth Evans. Ottawa: Oxfam Canada, 2004.

Menou, Michel. "Information Literacy in National Information and Communication Technology (ICT) Policies: The Missed Dimension, Information Culture." White paper prepared for the Information Literacy Meeting of Experts, Prague, Czech Republic, July, 2002. Available at http://www.nclis.gov/libinter/infolitconf8meet/papers/menou-fullpaper.pdf: Now may be accessed through: http://www.infolit.org/International_conference/Prague Papers.Subject.htm (view under author's name)

M. S. Swaminathan Research Foundation Web site. Available at http://mssrf.org. (Accessed Nov. 15, 2004.)

Nakata, M. "Indigenous Knowledge and the Cultural Interface: Underlying Issues at the Intersection of Knowledge and Information Systems." In *Disrupting Preconceptions: Postcolonialism and Education*, 19–38. Ed. Anne Hickling-Hudson et al. Flaxton, Australia: Post Pressed, 2004.

Nathan, D. "Plugging in Indigenous Knowledge: Connections and Innovations." *Journal of Aboriginal Studies* 2 (2000): 39–47.

Rosenberg, Diana. "Repackaging Scientific and Technical Information for Illiterate and Semi-literate Users: A Case Study of the Southern Sudan." In *Standing Conference of Eastern, Central and Southern African Librarians: Libraries and Literacy. Proceedings*, 8–22. Gaborone: Botswana Library Association, 1987.

Samassékou, Adama. "World Summit on the Information Society: The First Step Toward a Genuine Shared Knowledge society." *IFLA Journal* 30 (1) (2004): 5–13.

Shadrach, Basheerhamad B., and Raj Nikhil. "Empowering People Through ICT Enabled Lifelong Learning. Role of Libraries and NGOs in South Asia." In *Libraries for Lifelong Literacy*, 39–58. IFLA/FAIRE Theme Report. Copenhagen: IFLA/FAIFE, 2004.

Shera, J. H. "The Aims and Content of Graduate Library Education." In *Targets for Research in Library Education*, 9–13. Ed. Harold Borko. Chicago: American Library Association, 1973.

Stilwell, Christine, et al., eds. *Knowledge, Information and Development: An African Perspective*. Pietermaritzburg: School of Human and Social Studies, University of Natal, 2001.

World Summit on the Information Society (WSIS). Declaration of Principles, paras. 1, 19. Available at http/www.itu.int/wsis/documents/doc_single-en-1161.asp.

Zeleza, Paul Tiyambe. "The Dynamics of Book and Library Development in Anglophone Africa." In *The Book Chain in Anglophone Africa: A Survey and Directory*. Ed. Roger Stringer. Oxford: International Network for the Availability of Scientific Publications, 2002.

# 4 Intellectual Property Rights and the Information Commons

Robin Gross

As we enter an information age, the rules governing the use and dissemination of information become increasingly important. Clashes between fundamental freedom of expression guarantees and intellectual property rights are upsetting the traditional balance struck between creators and the public. The ease of copying and redistributing of digital information concerns industries dependent on traditional publishing models. These companies have successfully petitioned for changes in the copyright laws at the national and international levels. But these recent increases in copyright holders' rights have come at the expense of the public's rights to use media and communicate freely. This chapter discusses the threat to traditional civil liberties posed by expanding copyrights and recommends some principles for creating communication rights in a digital world.

## Dispelling the "Intellectual Property" Myths

One of the most common misunderstandings regarding intellectual property rights, particularly copyright, is that the actual creators are the main beneficiaries of the grant. In reality, it is the large companies that employ creators and then strip them of their copyright through contracts who actually benefit from the grant that society intended as a reward for authors. This important misunderstanding is no accident. Misleading "romantic notions of authorship" are systematically spun by the companies who stand in the shoes of creators to justify the generous monopoly right rewarded to them.

Another major myth regarding "intellectual property" protection is that it is the same as more traditional forms of property, such as personal property or real estate. But this conflation of intellectual property is grossly misleading and harmful. Copying another's intellectual creation does not end the owner's right to make use of the original. Intellectual property rights are created only as a means to encourage further creativity for the ultimate benefit of all society, while more traditional forms of property rights are designed to protect the personal and private interests of their owners. This crucial distinction can be seen when considering that one's house is not intended to pass into the public domain at some time; nor does anyone have a fair-use right to borrow another's car. Intellectual property is intended to have ownership "holes," to be imperfect in its control, while real or personal property is more absolute in its grants to owners.

Equating these very different forms of property rights leads to the inevitable restriction of the public's rights, giving way to more absolute property rights for large entertainment companies. Those wishing to maximize copyrights often merge the differing types of property, appealing to society's natural affection for traditional property rights in an effort to confuse and extend that affection to a different concept.

Many in the entertainment industry erroneously claim that all unauthorized copying is the equivalent of "theft." But in actuality, most ordinary copying is not infringement. For example, copying for personal use, education, research, commentary, criticism, parody, or other socially important uses is generally lawful under copyright law. And anything created before 1923 unequivocally belongs in the public domain and may be freely copied by anyone for any purpose, including commercial purposes. So claims that all unauthorized copying is the same social horror as theft hits far from the mark of legal accuracy.

Another significant myth often promoted by the copyright extremists is that without copyright protection, creativity would cease. This claim ignores history. The concept of copyright was created only within the last few centuries. Many of the greatest works ever created were inspired outside of the business model of copyright's pay-per-copy system. Mozart, Shakespeare, and Sun Tzu all created without economic incentive from this particular business model. The Internet, the human genome project, and free and open source software development are modern examples that have been created outside this one particular business model. So it is a simple fact that much can be, and has been, created without the goal of securing a copyright, and we should not be too wedded to the idea that copyright is the only, or even the best, way of encouraging innovation and further creativity.

## Expanding Copyrights Threaten Traditional Rights

Among the greatest threats to civil liberties in an information age are ever-expanding copyrights that curtail individuals' freedom of expression rights. Certainly governments have an added incentive to give rights holders greater rights, because it provides governments with more power to control the use and flow of information.

In response to the invention of the printing press, a state monopoly copyright was developed. Copyright originated in England with a "stationer's copyright" granted by the king to particular publishers, thereby allowing the king to regulate precisely which ideas could spread. Thus copyright was first created as a tool of censorship. It was not until 1710 that the United Kingdom's Statute of Anne was passed, altering the nature of copyright to further encourage the dissemination of knowledge. But in recent years, copyright's power has expanded to such an extreme degree that it has returned to its roots as a tool for restricting the flow of information.

The very nature of digital technology makes copyright law "king" in an information society. Every time one accesses or uses a piece of music, video, literature, or software, a copy must be made, and copyright law rules are triggered. This key "accident" of technology turns what was once an obscure field, relevant only to publishers, into a major consideration in consumers' everyday lives. Many of the recent expansions in copyright holders' rights unhinge the delicate historical balance struck between creators, consumers, and distributors of creative works.

## Anti-Circumvention Laws to Enforce Technical Restrictions

Newly created laws against the circumvention of technological restrictions controlling copyrighted works dangerously impede freedom of expression, innovation, and competition. Digital Rights Management (DRM) schemes prevent many lawful uses of electronic media. An increasing number of musical CDs are sold that will not play on personal computers, car stereos, and other devices deemed "untrustworthy" by major record companies. These restrictions have the effect of controlling the personal experience with that medium, something outside the scope of copyright protection.

DVDs are designed to play only on DVD players licensed by the major Hollywood movie studios. Through licenses, the studios forbid innovative functions on DVD players, including any digital copying, and often disable the ability to fast-forward through commercials. Both of these restrictions, enforced by a combination of technology and law, exceed the rights granted to copyright holders and control an individual's personal experience of information.

Anti-circumvention laws against bypassing such "digital locks" also have the effect of outlawing "reverse-engineering"—taking technology apart, figuring out how it works, improving upon it, or altering it to make it compatible with one's own system. Reverse engineering has traditionally been ruled a lawful fair use because it is necessary to gain access to the uncopyrightable ideas in software in order to make use of them. But since the enactment of laws forbidding the circumvention of technological restrictions have come into place, most notably the controversial 1998 U.S. Digital Millennium Copyright Act (DMCA) and the 1996 WIPO (World Intellectual Property Organization) Copyright Treaty, the ability to reverse engineer technology has been outlawed. In 2001 the European Union passed a copyright directive with similarly broad anti-circumvention laws that is currently being included in national legislation throughout Europe.

These anti-circumvention laws prevent interoperability between incompatible systems, giving copyright holders powerful new rights to control the devices on which media can be enjoyed. This new power impedes competition and creates a monopoly for existing industry players at the expense of innovative competitors. Anyone who wants to build adjacent or compatible devices must secure permission from the copyright holder of the medium, a radical new concept for copyright. Imagine if Sony could decide who may make record players because Sony makes records. Yet this is the brave new world we are creating under DMCA-style anti-circumvention laws. Sony has the right to decide who can build DVD players because Sony makes DVD movies.

Anti-circumvention laws forbid tools capable of circumventing these digital locks, including software and even information that could help someone to bypass them. Since the enforcement of the DMCA in the United States, anti-circumvention laws have been used against scientists conducting research on the quality of technology, thereby preventing scientific papers and technical presentations that describe a technology's flaws. As a result, scientific and academic research, and freedom of information regarding computer security, have been chilled. Because the legal liability is too great (criminal penalties for publications or conferences that charge fees), crucial academic and scientific research has been stifled.

Laws that forbid bypassing digital locks or distributing tools capable of bypassing these locks also have the effect of preventing media from effectively passing into the public domain. Knowledge and culture remain locked up forever, inaccessible to the very public which granted the limited monopoly right in exchange for a promise that the knowledge and culture would eventually become freely accessible to all in the public domain.

## Shrinking Private Copying Rights

The elimination of the public's private copying rights is another casualty of misguided laws to prevent the circumvention of technological restrictions. In most countries, consumers enjoy private copying rights, such as fair use in the United States and fair dealing in the United Kingdom, Canada, and Australia. The legal doctrine of fair use grants consumers the right to make copies of works, even when the copyright holder does not wish to allow such copying. Fair use permits copying in many socially beneficially situations, such as education, research, commentary, criticism, news reporting, and personal use. The U.S. Supreme Court has ruled that fair use provides the breathing space which is required under the U.S. Constitution for copyright to avoid conflict with fundamental freedom of expression guarantees.

But when technological restrictions or DRM schemes disable the public's ability to engage in these lawful uses, private copying and other fair use rights are effectively eliminated. These restrictions can control, or prevent altogether, a person's ability to make personal use copies. Anti-circumvention laws forbid a person from bypassing these digital locks, and deny the legal means to engage in personal use copying rights. The entertainment industry argues that "digital is different," and the public cannot be expected to have the same rights in a digital world that have existed in an analog world.

## Liability of Innocent Third Parties

Another casualty in Hollywood's war on digital technology is the makers of tools and services capable of infringing copyrights who become subjected to increased liability for the uses of their tools. Under broad anti-circumvention laws, technology companies must receive approval from Hollywood lawyers before engineering or building devices that are compatible with the entertainment industry's CDs, DVDs, e-books, and other digital media products. Software tools that are necessary to engage in lawful fair uses are also outlawed by overbroad anti-circumvention laws.

Makers of archiving and librarying tools can be held liable, and thus prevented from distributing such tools because they might be used for infringing purposes. 321 Studios, an innovative software company that made DVD backup software, was sued out of existence by the Hollywood movie studios for contributory infringement. In the United States, Napster, maker of Peer-2-Peer (P2P) software, was found secondarily liable for the infringing activities of its users because the court believed the P2P company could have prevented the infringing activity.

Internet service providers (ISPs) in the United States also face increasing legal risk for the allegedly infringing activities of their customers. ISPs are being forced to police and control their systems to prevent any infringement and to hand over personal information on their customers to law enforcement or Hollywood attorneys if they suspect infringing activity on their systems. While it creates an incentive to police for infringement, increasing the legal liability for innocent third parties produces a chilling effect on freedom of expression and stifles innovation and technological development. The collateral damage in Hollywood's war on technology is too great a cost without showing any effectiveness.

## Database Rights: Exclusive Ownership of Facts and Information

With its 1996 database directive, the EU created new database rights that give companies the right to the exclusive control and ownership of facts, scientific data, and other information they collect or compile. Although some forms of data rights had existed in Europe, database rights have been flatly rejected by the U.S. Supreme Court as unconstitutional because they lack the creativity and originality necessary to receive copyright protection. In *Feist v. Rural Telephone Service*, the Supreme Court rejected a claim of copyright protection over the information in telephone books. Under the court's ruling, a company can copyright only the selection and arrangement of facts, but not the facts themselves. Despite its rejection by the U.S. Supreme Court in 1991, a proposed clause in the Free Trade Area of the Americas (FTAA) Treaty would require every nation in the Americas to adopt a World Intellectual Property Organization database treaty that has not even been written yet.

### Severe Enforcement of Intellectual Property Laws

Another international trend is the increasing severity of the legal penalties and enforcement mechanisms available against alleged infringers. One example of this trend is a move to lower the standard for application of criminal penalties against infringement. Under Article 61 of the WTO's Trade Related Aspects of Intellectual Property Rights Agreement (TRIPS), a person can be sent to prison for engaging in commercial infringement. Noncommercial infringements are civil matters, for which injunctions and financial penalties are available. But there is a growing international trend to send noncommercial infringers to prison in addition to enforcing the financial and civil penalties available against them. For example, in 1997, the U.S. Congress adopted the No Electronic Theft Act (NETA), which permits federal prosecutors to send consumers to jail for sharing a single infringing MP3 song with a buddy over the Internet. The FTAA Treaty also proposes to send noncommercial infringers to jail, going existing TRIPS legal obligations. And the EU is also discussing legislation to send people to prison for infringement that is neither commercially motivated nor produces any financial benefit.

Lawmakers also have granted rightsholders new subpoena powers to obtain personal information about people they suspect of infringing. Under the U.S. DMCA and the EU Intellectual Property Rights Enforcement Directive (IPRED), for example, there is no requirement that a judge be given evidence of infringement before a subpoena is issued to turn over personal information. Under these laws, a court clerk may simply "rubber stamp" a subpoena request based on a mere allegation of infringement, without any finding of infringement by a judge. Traditional personal privacy and due process rights are brushed aside by these broad new copyright subpoena powers. The EU IPRED also granted new powers to destroy the property and equipment of innocent third parties, such as ISPs, without a hearing on the matter.

## Copyright Term Extensions

Another growing threat to freedom of expression and creativity is the increasing term of copyright. While the duration of exclusive copyright protection was originally fourteen years in the United States, it has been consistently extended to a term of (generally) seventy years after the death of the author. In fact, since the 1960s, the U.S. Congress has increased the term of protection on eleven separate occasions. The European Union also has imposed a copyright term of seventy years after the author's death. Industry and performance rights last for fifty years in the EU, and database rights have a term of fifteen years.

The current international standard for the term of copyright under the GATT/TRIPS Agreement is fifty years after the death of the author, but the United States and Europe aggressively pressure other countries to adopt the new seventy-year term of exclusive rights. For example, there is a proposal in the FTAA Treaty that would require every other country in the Americas (except Cuba) to adopt the TRIPS-plus seventy years after the author's death.

No attempt has been made to show that a longer term benefits the public or stimulates further creativity. Because of these extensions to the copyright's term, 99% of creativity remains locked up and unavailable to the public, simply because in today's market it is not commercially attractive to exploit those older works. So music, literature, and other culture remains out of the hands of the public and unexploited by the rights holders, benefiting absolutely no one.

## New Broadcasters' Rights

The U.N. agency charged with standardizing intellectual property laws among member states, the World Intellectual Property Organization

(WIPO), has proposed a new treaty that would grant broadcasting companies powerful new transmission rights over the signals carrying programming that pass through their wires and over their satellites. Although WIPO claims this new treaty is meant only as an update of the "outdated" 1960 Rome Convention on Broadcasting, it in fact goes much further and creates a broad range of new rights for broadcasting companies. WIPO's proposal would create a fifty-year exclusive right to these broadcasts, even when the material is in the public domain. This right would be granted to broadcasters who neither have created nor own the programming being transmitted. And the United States has proposed to extend this new transmission right to all Internet distributions of audiovisual programming, a giant leap beyond any existing international treaties or national laws. This proposal would give today's broadcasting giants a competitive advantage on the Internet and shut out tomorrow's innovators. Many other nations, however, oppose including Web programming in the WIPO broadcasting treaty.

### "Maximalist" U.S. Agenda Exported Overseas

Only very recently did the United States become "religious" about expanding and enforcing copyrights. And through WIPO, TRIPS, and regional and bilateral trade deals, the United States is imposing this extremist view of copyright on the rest of the world.

Ironically, the United States became strong largely because it was historically a "pirate nation" that refused to respect the copyrights granted in other countries.

Today, the vast majority of countries are intellectual property importers that are being forced to adopt the policies of an intellectual property exporter, despite the wide differences in economic and social needs between countries. Developing countries are not allowed to set a shorter term of protection for textbooks, despite a compelling need to provide educational materials to the public at affordable prices. The consequence of imposing the "maximalist" U.S. agenda overseas is a massive transfer of wealth from the countries of the South to those of the North, and a one-way flow of ideas from the North to the South—a form of information age colonialism.

## Communication Rights for an Information Age

### Nations Must Retain Sovereignty over Their Domestic Information Policies

The growing "digital divide" warns that countries should tailor their information policies in accordance with their economic and social needs. Developing countries, in particular, should be free to set their intellectual property rules according to their own needs, traditions, and cultures.

There is no justification for the TRIPS's requirement that developing countries adopt the policies of an intellectual property exporter in order to be allowed to participate in world trade. The TRIPS agreement should be removed from the WTO, where trade sanctions are imposed for non-compliance with these rules, giving countries no choice but to adopt harmful intellectual property policies at home. This practice should be corrected to allow developing countries to retain their sovereignty so they can adequately address the needs of their people without fear of being cut off from international trade.

### Protection for the "Intellectual Commons"

Proper recognition for the value of the public domain in enriching society would be an important step to take in an information age. The public domain is a valuable resource that all share together. Musicians are free to perform Mozart in Central Park, actors practice with royalty-free plays written by Shakespeare, the Internet is largely run on free software, schools teach Beethoven without the need for expensive licenses—all because these works are freely available in the public domain. All of today's intellectual creations are based partly upon preexisting works. The public enjoys the benefit of knowledge developed centuries, even millennia, ago. Artists and future creators are harmed the most by the elimination of the public domain.

Governments should enable public access to scientific information that is acquired at public expense. Unfortunately, the present trend is for the public to pay for the research directly the first time, and then to pay again when the publicly funded information has been commercialized.

### Intellectual Property Rules Should Promote, Not Inhibit, Creativity

Too much "protection" of intellectual property hampers creativity and innovation. A delicate balance must be maintained between enough protection to provide an incentive to creativity and excessive protection that chokes innovation and further creativity. Creators must remain free to build upon the works of those who came before in order for society to advance. Existing intellectual property regimes should be reevaluated in light of the goals of promoting creativity and innovation.

**Promote Free and Open Source Software Development Models**
The spread of free and open source software development has created enormous social value and an increased shared wealth in recent years. Innovative new licensing systems, such as the Creative Commons licenses that permit consumer copying, are opening up entirely new models of content distribution. But existing intellectual property rules are often designed around one specific business model, such as copyright's "pay per copy" model.

A growing number of governments in developing countries, including Brazil, are choosing to use and promote free and open source software instead of proprietary software. By choosing free or open source software use, governments are able to spend their nation's scarce resources on more immediate needs, such as food and pure drinking water, instead of Microsoft licenses. In addition to being customizable to individual needs and operable with different systems, nonproprietary software provides more robust personal security than proprietary systems. The city government of Florence, Italy, passed a motion in 2001 stating that extensive use of proprietary software was creating the "computer science subjection of the Italian state to Microsoft." And laws against the circumvention of "digital locks" controlling copyright-covered works also endanger free and open source software developers. Although they are currently under threat, alternative business models and nonproprietary systems of development must remain lawful in a healthy information society.

**Intellectual Property Rules Should Shrink, Not Increase, the Knowledge Gap**
The ability of countries to adequately educate their people is directly impacted by intellectual property rules such as the term for copyright or the extent of fair use privileges. New laws with expanding rights and increased penalties are making it too risky for libraries and archives to continue functioning.

It is somewhat ironic that technology moves us closer to a "pay per use" society, where one's level of education depends upon parents' income, at exactly the time when it costs virtually nothing to disseminate information. The Internet and other communication technologies can be revolutionary tools for education, but only if the technology is not crippled by efforts to destroy its most promising features—the ease and low cost of disseminating knowledge.

### Protect Private Copying Rights

Most reproductions of copyrighted works that people make every day are not infringements. The type of ordinary copying that individuals do in the course of their normal enjoyment of their music or video collection is lawful under private copying rights or fair use rights. Lawful activities such as "time-shifting," to view a recorded program at a more convenient time, or "space-shifting," to copy one's music onto an MP3 player or computer hard drive, put limits on a copyright holder's right to control the individual experience of the media. Private copying rights ensure a level of personal autonomy and enjoyment in the media experience. And consumers must have access to the tools that are necessary to engage in private copying if the rights are to have any meaning in a digital world.

The lessons of history are particularly relevant. Every time a new technology has been invented that made consumer copying easier, the entertainment industry fought to outlaw the new technology (including the invention of piano rolls, radio, VCRs, and MP3 players). But in the past, the U.S. courts and Congress have not allowed the industry to kill the technology, and as a result, the industry learned how to profit from it. Although the entertainment industry fought hard to outlaw VCRs in the 1980s, today video rental and sales is the number one revenue-generating segment of the movie industry. Consumers having the ability to make private copies does not harm an artist; quite the contrary, it increases the value of the work to the consumer.

### Protection for Intellectual Freedom

Protection for intellectual freedom should be of highest priority in an information age. Freedom of thought and freedom of expression are fundamental human rights that require access to ideas and information in order to develop fully.

The common practice of "reverse engineering,"—taking a technology apart, learning how it works, and figuring out how to improve upon it— is part of a heritage that values intellectual freedom. This "right to tinker" can be thought of simply as being the right to open up the hood of one's automobile and make whatever adjustments are necessary to suit the owner's individual needs. But today's overbroad copyright laws can be used to prevent a car owner from "tinkering" with its engine. Technology gives us greater opportunities to learn, particularly to teach ourselves; we must preserve our legal tradition of protecting individual intellectual freedom.

## Conclusion: Communication Rights Are Human Rights in an Information Society

The impact of expanding copyrights reaches a spectrum of existing fundamental legal rights: freedom of expression, freedom of the press, freedom of thought, intellectual freedom, and more are all harmed by such a dramatic shift in the traditional balance of rights.

Historically, when society was primarily agricultural economy, the key ingredient to wealth and development was ownership and use of land. When society moved into an industrial era, the key to wealth and development shifted to ownership and use of capital. Now, as we move into an information society, access to knowledge is the key factor for continued development and wealth on a personal and national level.

Just as human bodies require food and medicine for good health, so our minds require knowledge to function and develop. Technology promises the unprecedented opportunity to disseminate information and foster collaboration that will dramatically expand human knowledge and social development—but only if we do not allow the technology to be crippled by an overreaction of industries rooted in the past.

The free speech guarantee in the Universal Declaration of Human Rights, although adopted by the U.N. General Assembly in 1948, speaks directly to the Internet age: Article 19 guarantees that "Everyone has the right to freedom of opinion and expression; this right includes freedom to hold opinions without interference and to seek, receive, and impart information and ideas through any media and regardless of frontiers."

This universal guarantee of freedom of expression is not limited to speech in analog media, but rather, explicitly, "... *in any media and regardless of frontiers.*" While proponents of limiting freedom of expression guarantees argue that "digital is different," and traditional rights must be sacrificed to protect private property rights, the Universal Declaration of Human Rights has already answered that digital is no different, and that our traditional rights are meant to continue with us into a digital environment.

Now "we the people" must hold our governments accountable to this standard.

# 5 Privacy as Freedom

Gus Hosein

Everyone who works in a specific issue area tends to believe that what he or she works on is essential to humanity's future and/or sense of dignity. Environmentalists argue that the future of our global commons is at stake. Those who struggle against the arms trade contend that we cannot be a civil world united in peace so long as we continue to make trade in the artifacts of destruction. Gun lobby groups contend that the possession of firearms is a key constitutional right in some countries, or key to survival in others. Antiabortionists are struggling for the lives of the unborn and the morality of the future. Those who focus on development and aid believe that they are helping to heal the inequalities of the world. Through participation in political processes, without regard to differing political persuasions and methods, all these people work for change and for the attention of the silent majority.

Privacy advocates are no different, for the most part. You will rarely find privacy advocates protesting outside of buildings or summit locations, though. They do not often warn of Armageddon, although warnings of dystopias of Orwellian proportions are hardly different. Privacy advocates also contend that there are legal, sociological, and historical foundations to privacy. Most important, privacy advocates are well aware that they are in a struggle for the hearts and minds of the general public.

Yet privacy never has the same primacy in public discourse as those other issues. When I am asked, "What do you do for a living?," I describe myself as a privacy advocate. People then look at me, confused.[1] This probably never happens with antiabortionists or environmentalists. All the while, free speech advocates are given even higher regard because they seem to be calling for the right of the others to advocate their points. This relegation to the back of the queue of "popular causes for which we must advocate" is inappropriate. As a right, privacy provides an inherently valuable service to society. As a subject of study, understanding privacy complements our understanding of politics. Privacy and freedom are tightly linked, and opening up this relationship opens our eyes to political trends. The politics of privacy is analogous to the politics of the World Summit on the Information Society (WSIS) process. The attempts to minimize or relegate privacy within the WSIS process are attempts to tamper with freedom itself. Privacy advocates by nature shudder at claims by government officials of striving for the "common good," or industry representatives' calls for minimal regulations, because we understand the agendas and objectives behind these statements.

This chapter will seek to acquaint readers with these agendas and objectives, and the political playground of civil liberties in the information society. After an attempt to define privacy, the chapter will present the dissenting views on privacy. A discussion of the legal and regulatory landscape will follow, and this will be contrasted with the threats to privacy and the politics of surveillance. The chapter will conclude by laying out privacy as a necessary foundation of an open information society, because it is a key component to freedom.

### Privacy and Freedom

One of the best definitions of privacy that I have ever heard is in fact quite vague and nonrational. In response to the proposed ID card in the United Kingdom, Lord Philips of Sudbury said that while there are many logical reasons to oppose the policy, most prominent in his mind was that it just "felt wrong":

> I instinctively and quite deeply reject [the proposed policy]. I can't quite find the language to rationalise the depth of my feeling about this.[2]

Such a feeling is perhaps the most helpful delineation between when an incursion into the private life of an individual is reasonable and when it is not. As Philips indicates, we often enshroud our arguments behind more "rational" language, but I would like to emphasize that it starts with a core belief. Everything else is a cover for this gut instinct. We do not like being watched unless it is under circumstances of our own choosing, and it is possible also to say that when we surveil others, there is also a gut instinct which tells us we are up to no good.

There are many other ways of defining privacy, in more formal and eloquent terms. In an early form, as we moved toward modern democratic systems of governance, privacy was considered a protection from invasion, a protection from the king. According to William Pitt in 1763, "The poorest man may in his cottage bid defiance to all the force of the Crown. It may be frail; its roof may shake; the wind may blow through it; the storms may enter; the rain may enter—but the King of England cannot enter; all his forces dare not cross the threshold of the ruined tenement." This thinking emerges from the notion that "every man's home is his castle." Shortly thereafter, in 1765 Lord Camden, a noted judge, commented that the police had overreached their authority by searching someone's home in order to seize papers: "We can safely say there is no law in this country to justify the [police] in what they have done; if there was, it would destroy all the comforts of society, for papers are often the dearest property any man can have."

From the time of these noble Englishmen to the twentieth century, privacy was embedded in leading constitutional documents, including the French Rights of Man and the American Bill of Rights.

Privacy reemerged as a key issue of modern times in the late 1800s. Building on definitions and the work of other legal minds of their time, Louis Brandeis and Samuel Warren wrote in 1890 that privacy is the "right to be let alone." This seminal article, published in the *Harvard Law Review*, was a reaction to technological and market developments of the time. Warren, a wealthy member of "high society," had his family's privacy intruded upon by the tabloid press. The article warned of the growing media frenzy and the threats posed by cameras: "Recent inventions and business methods call attention to the next step which must be taken for the protection of the person."[3]

In contrast to cameras of the late 1800s, with the advent of modern computing, concerns increased dramatically. With the threat of potential data processing and the storage of personal information in databases, we sought a more developed definition of the constitution of privacy. Responding to this threat, in the late 1960s Alan Westin defined informational self-determination. Privacy, he said, is "the claim of individuals, groups, or institutions to determine for themselves when, how, and to what extent information about them is communicated to others. . . . [It is] the desire of people to choose freely under what circumstances and to what extent they will expose themselves, their attitude and their behaviour to others."[4] That is, individuals must be allowed to choose what information is made available about them, and under what circumstances. This is tightly bound with the notion of human dignity. According to Robert Ellis Smith, privacy is "the desire by each of us for physical space where we can be free of interruption, intrusion, embarrassment, or accountability and the attempt to control the time and manner of disclosures of personal information about ourselves."[5] Similarly, Rhoda Howard and Jack Donnelly argue that, as enshrined in the Universal Declaration of Human Rights, "The right to privacy (Article 12) even more explicitly aims to guarantee the capacity to realize personal visions of a life worthy of a human being."[6]

While other definitions abound, most contemporary definitions draw links between self-determination, autonomy, dignity, surveillance, power, and technology.

In an information society, where almost all attributes of an individual can be known, all interactions mapped, and all intentions assumed on the basis of records, our "instincts" have led us to worry. Since the advent of the modern computer, or even as the possibilities of computers entered our minds, and since we saw what we have been capable of when our guardians were given too much control over our personal information and our lives, we have endeavored as a society to protect privacy. Modern privacy law, after all, emerges from these lessons, struggles, innovations, and developments. The legal definitions, however, still come after the "feeling" and "instinct" of privacy. The point to understanding privacy as a core feeling, something inexplicable, is that it is tightly intertwined with our sense of right and wrong, our moralities. Even beyond morality, beyond the debates of relativism and absolutism of norms and morals, there is something about human dignity. When we peer into the life of any individual to a large degree, we are peering into an area that we know it is wrong to investigate. In a civilized society we limit such gazes because we understand that there is something undignified about knowing so much about an individual.

A regard for privacy is a belief that we must maintain human dignity, and that this is the core objective of human rights. Invading human dignity not only produces embarrassment, however. It redefines our sense of individuality and our conduct as humans. As such, privacy can be seen as a core protection of individual autonomy and human agency. Knowing everything about someone reduces that person to a set of known facts, controllable and manipulatable. As long as a zone of autonomy exists around each and every individual, the opportunities for abuse and oppression are lessened.

Knowing everything about the activities of all people greatly enhances the powers of a ruler. And in a deliberative and open society, privacy provides a core precondition to participation, a most basic civil liberty. Knowing the actions and intentions of your political opponents reduces their ability to oppose your rule and arguments. Privacy is thus a fundamental component of freedom. As Alan Westin noted at a time that may have been the dawn of the information age:

No society with a reputation for providing liberty in its own time failed to provide limits on the surveillance power of authorities. In this sense, American society in the 1970s faces the task of keeping this tradition meaningful when technological change promises to give public and private authorities the physical power to do what a combination of physical and socio-legal restraints had denied to them as part of our basic social system. (22)

Privacy protection is intertwined with liberty. In modern society we need to protect privacy even more than previously, since technology and modernity influence our conduct. Yet everywhere, privacy rights are burdened.

## Privacy as a Threat

Not everyone agrees on the primacy of privacy. Through benign or malignant intentions, indirect or directed attacks, exogenous forces or forces from within, privacy is under constant threat. Since it is a core principle of autonomy and human dignity, and its reduction enables control, manipulation, oppression, and increased power, this should come as no surprise.

Although it is often claimed that privacy rights around the world changed in September 2001, they were threatened long before. Looking at the 1990s alone, we can see significant changes in law. Even though laws on data protection were introduced by a number of countries throughout the 1990s, as well as laws on freedom of information, encroachments abounded. In France silly regulations restricting the use of technologies to secure communications continued unabated despite technological revolutions. In the United States, laws were passed to allow for interception of communications regardless of technological innovation. In the United Kingdom, any number of policies emerged, ranging from closed-circuit television cameras that now pollute the cityscapes to policies that give any arm of government significant access to your personal life. Similar policies were implemented elsewhere.

The threats to privacy, at their most intellectual foundations, arise from a number of sources, including communitarians, classical feminists, and those seeking well-functioning markets. Finally, there is a school of thought which contends that privacy is not as important as other, more valuable "civil liberties," such as free expression.[7]

### Communitarian Reduction

The communitarians argue that while privacy is a noble value, there are other noble values that we must consider. Amitai Etzioni, a leading proponent of the reduction of privacy in the public sphere, argues that we need to renegotiate our privacy rights, for the common good.

Although we cherish privacy in a free society, we also value other goods. . . . To begin a new dialogue about privacy, I [ask] if you would like to know whether the person entrusted with your child care is a convicted child molester. I further ask: Would you want to know whether the staff of a nursing home in which your mother now lives has criminal records that include abusing the elderly? Should the FBI be in a position to crack the encryption messages employed by terrorists before they use them to orchestrate the next Oklahoma City bombing? Addressing such concerns raises the question of if and when we are justified in implementing measures that diminish privacy in the service of the common good."[8]

Etzioni and the communitarians contend that we do not have an absolute right to privacy. Rather, privacy must be balanced with other rights. According to Etzioni, there is a set of criteria for this balancing act.

- The purpose for invading privacy must be for a known threat to the common good. For example, we don't need to demand full medical records to make sure someone wasn't lying about being too sick to go to work.
- Privacy can be invaded once we have exhausted alternative means of countering danger. Can we instead find out that the person was playing soccer/football with his friends by asking friends?
- When privacy is to be invaded, it must be minimally intrusive. Continuing the above example, we should get only the part of the medical record

that says he visited the doctor on the day he claimed to be sick, rather than the full record containing all his treatments since birth.

• Once privacy is invaded, measures must be taken to minimize and treat undesirable side effects. Try to get only his medical record, and not the listing of all people who visited the doctor that day, or do not ask any questions about the type of doctor (was it a sexually transmitted disease clinic?).

There are two key flaws in the communitarian approach to privacy. First, the mere threat of this information being made available has a chilling effect on its collection in the first place. That is, even under the most stringent balancing tests, if I know that my health information may be disclosed to my employer, I may be less likely to disclose this information to my doctor in the first place. This has a dangerous effect on the relationship between my doctor and me, and an even more disastrous effect on health care generally. If I don't disclose information to my doctor, this will lead to misdiagnosis or worse yet, a lack of treatment.

Second, the communitarians see power in a very benign way. To them, all initiatives to invade privacy are restricted to reasonable conduct by agents of the state, and have minimal impacts. They fail to acknowledge the way that politics rears its ugly head and expands any power, even the most benign. Early cases of communications surveillance in the United States involved society's struggle against drug dealers and alcohol bootleggers. The reasons quickly grew. Access to information relating to whom you've called or e-mailed, and servers to which you have connected from an Internet service provider in the United Kingdom was at first limited to the police. Subsequently, all government departments could access this information for any purpose, resulting in a dramatic increase in state power. Fingerprinting was once a measure to identify criminals; now it is used to permit people to work or cross borders. What starts small always ends with an avalanche of personal information. Powers, once created, are rarely regulated and minimized.

## Feminist Critique

The classical feminists contend that privacy is merely a right which is abused by men. The right of privacy, they argue, is based on Anglo-American common law, providing that a husband is master of his household; thus neither the state nor anyone else may enter to intervene in family matters. As a result, a man could subject his wife to beatings so long as he was within his home. The feminist critique goes on to say that the right of privacy is used to enforce and preserve such authority relations between man and wife. As Reva Siegel argues:

It seems just as likely that legal elites devised the story linking "privacy" and "domestic harmony" to wife beating. . . . This right of privacy is a right of men "to be let alone" to oppress women one at a time.[9]

Privacy, according to this line of argument, is used to protect men and the home, not women. And, this logic continues, privacy is used to conceal wrongful activity, to reduce and not to protect human dignity. This view is supported through historical precedents. In 1852, in the state of North Carolina, the courts held wives incompetent to testify against husbands in all cases of assault and battery, except where permanent injury or great bodily harm was inflicted. The final court decision stated:

We know that a slap on the cheek, let it be as light as it may, indeed any touching of the person of another in a rude or angry manner—is in law an assault and battery. In the nature of things it cannot apply to persons in the marriage state, it would break down the great principle of mutual confidence and dependence; throw open the bedroom to the gaze of the public; and spread discord and misery, contention, and strife; where peace and concord ought to reign.[10]

More recent discussions on feminism and privacy, however, contend that privacy no longer is used against women as it once was. Women (and more accurately, victims generally) may now be shielded in rape cases so that their names are not disclosed to the public. Women who were previously subjected to spousal abuse may now seek a zone of autonomy through delisting their telephone numbers and concealing their contact details as they try to start new lives. And even the controversial issue of abortion in the United States is sustained by privacy rights.

### Economic Argument

Informational self-determination, the ability to control information about oneself and how it is used, can be exploited in dishonest ways. In his economic analysis of the dissemination and withholding of information, Richard Posner contends that an individual's control over information dissemination leads to misrepresentation.

It is no answer that . . . individuals have the "right to be let alone." Very few people want to be let alone. They want to manipulate the world around them by selective disclosure of facts about themselves.[11]

According to Posner, at some point nondisclosure becomes fraud and the motive for concealment is to mislead others. He goes on to argue that it is more efficient to have organizational privacy (e.g., trade secrets) than to have personal privacy. Even within this economic approach, however, Posner notes that privacy in communications is valuable. The smaller the crowd of people we are speaking to, the more likely we are to speak privately, with informality and brevity. "Allowing eavesdropping would undermine this valuable economy of communication." He does note that the more we value the privacy of communications, the more likely that communications surveillance will be of value to the police, which is also advantageous.

Posner is not anti-privacy. "Ostentatious surveillance" does pose problems even to Posner. This is a form of surveillance that involves "following someone about everywhere." Such a form of surveillance is legally problematic when it exceeds what was reasonably necessary to uncover private information "and becomes a method of intimidation, embarrassment, or distraction." In this sense, there are limits as to what is reasonable, although Posner does not help anyone in defining what is "reasonably necessary," since his points approach the communitarian perspective quite quickly. And within the information society, "ostentatious surveillance" occurs with every move we make. It is fair to say that Posner's view of how society works best is . . . well . . . different. The economic view does acknowledge that privacy is a useful thing, particularly for communications and organizations. Posner just believes that in the conduct of business and economic affairs, personal privacy is often used for dishonesty. The weakness in his argument is that he holds "economic rationality" above all, viewing the world as filled with autonomous slaves.[12] In doing so, he avoids complexity,[13] and focuses too much on informational self-determination rather than on the larger picture of privacy as a whole. He intentionally avoids discussing privacy as a safeguard against political oppression.[14] Finally, according to Richard Epstein, in his response to Posner:

The nineteenth century arguments about the abolition of slavery did not in the slightest depend upon the relationship of slavery to material output. The abolitionist of that or any other era regards it as immaterial that the liberation of the slaves might reduce transaction costs or increase the gross national product. The gut position about slavery was, and is, that it is simply wrong for any person to own another person.[15]

Epstein's point is that legal theory does not depend on economic analysis. A "gut feeling" and an "instinctive reaction" may again be the point from which we start, and the laws follow afterward.

## Secondary to Other Rights

Those in the field of "traditional" human rights and civil liberties may criticize the notion of privacy as a human right, because they do not believe it is a right in itself. I intentionally use the conditional "may" in the previous sentence because often these traditional human rights experts ignore privacy altogether. They contend that there are more primary rights, such as the right to liberty, to be free from torture, and to free expression. Countless nongovernmental organizations, and even more lawyers and experts, exist in these other fields, and they hardly notice privacy. Many argue that privacy can be respected so long as it comes second to free speech, for example. Journalists and free speech advocates who deal with libel and defamation cases believe that the public's need to know takes priority over the individual's secondary right to privacy. Following this line of reasoning, they and others contend that privacy is not a direct constitutional right, but rather an interpretation of other rights, such as the protection from arbitrary search and seizure, and self-incrimination. This is an almost reasonable interpretation of constitutional law, at least in the United States, where the Constitution does not once mention the word "privacy." It took many years for privacy to be regarded as a proper right within the United States, and much of the hard work was laid out by Louis Brandeis, following his work on the right to be let alone.

Privacy is now seen as a right in itself by the law. And the reason for this development is that legal minds realized that privacy actually enables the other, more traditional rights. Free expression is enabled by privacy; freedom from torture also can involve freedom from obtrusive surveillance; and even more "social rights," such as the right to health and welfare, are enabled only when privacy is respected, reducing the chilling effect of surveillance. The communitarians, the feminists, the economists, and the traditionalists all have interesting perspectives on privacy, freedom, and society. These approaches are not very helpful in understanding what is truly at stake within the information society, nor are they fair reflections of the current state of affairs.

## Privacy as Law and Regulation

Privacy is generally protected in two forms of law. The first is constitutional and international human rights rules and laws, where privacy is protected as a core individual right, thus affecting all of a government's other activities. The second form of privacy law focuses on the specifics of information privacy, and the fair treatment of information by both governments and industry. This is what we call data protection law, which I will discuss in a more limited manner here.

### Privacy as an Individual's and Citizen's Right

One of the earliest constitutional statements on privacy emerged from the French Revolution. The Declaration of the Rights of Man and the Citizen of 1789 declared: "Since property is an inviolable and sacred right, no one shall be deprived thereof except where public necessity, legally determined, shall clearly demand it." Admittedly, this was not a clear declaration of the right to privacy, but when linked with the idea that "a man's home is his castle," this placed a limit on the reach of government. And if a man's zone of privacy/property was violated, there *must be* clear reasons for this.

The U.S. Bill of Rights was a bit clearer on this idea of privacy and property. The Fourth Amendment, to the Constitution of the United States says:

The right of the people to be secure in their persons, houses, papers, and effects, against unreasonable searches and seizures, shall not be violated, and no warrants shall issue, but upon probable cause, supported by oath or affirmation, and particularly describing the place to be searched, and the persons or things to be seized.

Here the violation of an individual's person, home, and effects is given greater protection and clearer grounds to question an intervention (including a warrant, under "probable cause," etc.).

Neither of these rights, however, is a clear articulation of a legal privacy right. In neither of those historic documents does the word "privacy" actually appear. Privacy does appear in other human rights documents, however. Article 12 of the Universal Declaration of Human Rights states:

No one should be subjected to arbitrary interference with his privacy, family, home or correspondence, nor to attacks on his honour or reputation. Everyone has the right to the protection of the law against such interferences or attacks.

In creating the Universal Declaration of Human Rights, its writers knew that privacy is a foundation of human dignity, but also of political participation, particularly after the atrocities of the 1930s and 1940s. Also, the authors of this document were not just Western legal theorists; countries from around the world collaborated on it, reaffirming the importance of privacy as a universal right and value. This document, however, is nonbinding legally; states can only be shamed into complying with the UDHR, and there is no court that judges compliance. But as a universal statement of values, it is strong and clear.

The International Covenant on Civil and Political Rights is slightly more binding upon nations. Article 17 states:

1. No one shall be subject to arbitrary or unlawful interference with his privacy, family, home or correspondence, nor to unlawful attacks on his honour and reputation.
2. Everyone has the right to the protection of the law against such interference or attacks.

This document not only calls on states not to interfere arbitrarily in the private life of individuals; the state also has a positive obligation to implement laws to protect this right. But there are no legally binding mechanisms for individuals to enforce their rights under the covenant since, again, there is no court to which individuals may appeal, although individuals can raise the case within their own country's legal system. The European Convention for the Protection of Human Rights and Fundamental Freedoms (ECHR) of 1950 was the first binding treaty on human rights. It created the European Court of Human Rights, where individuals can bring cases against their governments, once national resources have been exhausted.

Article 8 of the ECHR establishes the right to privacy within states that have ratified it.

(1) Everyone has the right to respect for his private and family life, his home and his correspondence.
(2) There shall be no interference by a public authority with the exercise of this right except as in accordance with the law and is necessary in a democratic society in the interests of national security, public safety or the economic well-being of the country, for the prevention of disorder or crime, for the protection of health or morals, or for the protection of the rights and freedoms of others.

Again, not only do states have to abstain from interference, but they have a positive obligation to protect these rights. Within this definition in the ECHR we see the contemporary challenges of European public policy. The protection of the right to privacy is paramount and is protected by the ECHR, Article 8(1). If only it were so simple, the regulatory landscape would be clean and clear. Under Article 8(2) national laws may be created to interfere with this right, in the name of many causes. The landscape becomes, in a word, complex.

The ECHR remains remarkable for two developments that are privacy-enhancing for the most part. First, the European Court of Human Rights has a rich history of reviewing laws and imposing sanctions on countries for failing to protect privacy. In interpreting Article 8(2) the Court has decided that any initiative to interfere with an individual's right to privacy must be in accordance with law and necessary in a democratic society. "In accordance with law" means that there must be a law which states the conditions for invasion, but it also must be "foreseeable," in that an individual should be able to change her actions to avoid such an invasion (i.e., if you don't commit a crime, you will not have your home searched). "Necessary in a democratic society" means that there must be a pressing social need and that the action must be proportionate to the legitimate aim pursued (i.e., you can't read someone's e-mail if you suspect them of having lied about being sick and taken a day off work. The Court has also expanded the protections of Article 8 beyond government actions to those of private persons (i.e., the private sector, where it appears that the government should have acted to prohibit certain conduct).

## Informational Privacy

The positive obligation to protect privacy and personal information has taken the form of "data protection," and is often used to protect individual privacy against abuse from both public agencies and private companies. The first modern data protection law was enacted in the state of Hesse in Germany in 1970. This was followed by national laws in Sweden (1973), Germany (1977), and France (1978). These laws eventually led to a harmonizing European Union directive of 1995, the EU Data Protection Directive (95/46/EU).

Data protection rules hinge on the fair information practices. These were developed in the late 1960s in response to the threat of secret databases holding vast amounts of information on individuals. In simple terms the fair information practices place requirements on "controllers" (collectors of personal information):

- Personal data should be collected only for specified, explicit, and legitimate purposes.
- The persons concerned should be informed about such purposes and the identity of the controller revealed.
- Any person concerned should have a right of access to his/her data and the opportunity to change or delete data that are incorrect.
- If something goes wrong, appropriate remedies should be available to put things right, including compensation for damages through the competent national courts.

In essence, data should be collected with informed consent of the individual; processed fairly and lawfully, for limited purposes and limited use; and retained for a limited period of time. Data must be kept secure and accurate, and not transferred to countries without adequate protection.

In full, the fair information practices are required within a number of international legal documents and standards, such as the EU 1995 Directive, the OECD Guidelines of 1980, and the Council of Europe Convention of 1981. These standards require that

- Data must be processed fairly and lawfully.
- Data must be collected for explicit and legitimate purposes, and used accordingly.
- Data must be relevant and not excessive in relation to the purpose for which they are processed.
- Data must be accurate and, where necessary, kept up to date.
- Data controllers must provide reasonable measures for data subjects to rectify, erase, or block incorrect data about themselves.
- Data that identify individuals must not be kept longer than necessary.

Tighter regulations tend to apply to "sensitive data." In the EU Directive of 1995, this type of information is defined as

data relating to racial or ethnic origin, political opinions, religious or philosophical beliefs, trade union membership, data concerning health or sexual preference. In principle, such data cannot be processed. Derogation is tolerated under very specific circumstances. These circumstances include the data subject's explicit consent to process sensitive data, the processing of data mandated by employment law, [situations] where it may be impossible for the data subject to consent (e.g. blood test to the victim of a road accident), processing of data has been publicly announced by the data subject or processing of data about members by trade unions, political parties or churches.[16]

Member states may provide for additional exceptions for reasons of substantial public interest.

Such exceptions are permitted if, among other things, it is necessary on grounds of national security, defence, crime detection, enforcement of criminal law, or to protect data subjects or the rights and freedom of others.[17]

These are consistent with the exemptions listed under the ECHR.

## Key Threats to Privacy in the Information Society

Now that you have an understanding of privacy as a human right, and privacy as a legal right, you may better appreciate the threats to privacy. It is important to remember that many of the intellectual revolutions in privacy were influenced, if not spurred, by technology. Warren and Brandeis were reacting to the use of cameras by the tabloid press. Communications privacy laws arose in response to technological innovations such as the telegraph, radio, and telephone. And data protection and modern privacy law arose in response to the prevalence of database and data-processing technologies.

Now we are well beyond those days. Personal information is everywhere, to be collected and used and stored. The difficulties and costs of performing surveillance have decreased dramatically, just in time for all of this information to be in the form of bits and communicated across wires and in the air, for all to access. There are currently a number of policy initiatives to increase surveillance powers even more.

### Surveillance of Communications

In the old days, communications "traffic data" consisted of information found on your telephone bill: whom you called, when you called, and how long you spoke. Now, things are different. According to a committee of European privacy commissioners:

A feature of telecommunications networks and of the Internet in particular is their potential to generate a huge quantity of transactional data (the data generated in order to ensure the correct connections). The possibilities for interactive use of the networks (a defining characteristic of many Internet services) increases the amount of transactional data yet further. When consulting an on-line newspaper, the user "interacts" by choosing the pages he wishes to read. These choices create a "click stream" of transactional data. By contrast more traditional news and information services are consumed much more passively (television for example), with interactivity being limited to the off-line world of newspaper shops and libraries. Although transactional data may in some jurisdictions receive a degree of protection under rules protecting the confidentiality of correspondence, the massive growth in the amount of such data is nevertheless a cause of legitimate concern.[18]

As communications media are increasingly interlinked (e.g., using your computer on a wireless network, connecting to the Internet over your mobile phone), this information becomes more and more detailed. It is not just about what you read; now your mobile phone company knows where you were, your wireless LAN provider can point to other people who were in the same area as you, and your Internet service provider can pinpoint whatever you did while you were online months ago. All human conduct in the information society makes use of electronic systems, and this information is now waiting to be linked together.

Considering all of the discussion above regarding privacy rules and laws, one would think that this information was deemed sensitive. However, privacy laws have been rewritten in order to enable surveillance. Laws in the United States that protected information about what we watch were modified by the USA-PATRIOT Act so that the police could gain access to the Web sites we visit with minimal restraints. Across Europe laws were introduced that transformed prior privacy laws. Previously, European Internet service providers, telephone companies, and mobile phone companies had to delete "traffic data" when it was no longer required for business purposes. Since September 11, 2001, a number of European countries have introduced laws requiring these communications service providers to keep this information for between one and ten years, just in case one day your Internet usage information may be of interest to the police or other government authorities.

New policies have also been introduced to allow for the interception of communications and for real-time monitoring of traffic data. The Communications Assistance for Law Enforcement Act in the United States requires that all new communications systems be designed so as to enable surveillance. The United Kingdom's Regulation of Investigatory Powers Act requires communications service providers to ready their networks for surveillance in the event that a warrant is issued. These "modern" laws are very different from the old days of intercepting your post and telegraphic messages. Real-time monitoring of communications involves tracking all of your movements while you are online, whom you talk with, what you talk about, what you seek and what you find, and what you read and what you say. These new policies are being implemented to increase surveillance while reducing the constraints upon authorities. The new laws being devised not only guarantee access to this data, they also increase the purposes for which governments may access this information. Previously, warrants were issued only for specific, serious criminal activity, and public oversight was thorough and detailed. Now information that was once considered "sensitive" can be accessed without probable cause, without a clear articulation of suspicion, and for any crime.

Much of the momentum behind these policies arises from two sources. First, governments argue that they are compelled to act because of the changing technological environment and the increased risks associated with this environment. They argue that we must adapt old laws to deal with these new technologies. This is despite the fact that these new technologies already tend to amplify and transform government power.[19] The second source of momentum behind these policies is multilateralism. After a number of failed national policy initiatives dealing with the Internet in the 1990s, governments began to work at the international level to establish an international policy. Through such organizations as the Council of Europe and the Group of 8 industrialized economies, governments established international treaties and agreements on surveillance, so as to bring these rules home under the guise of harmonization and international obligations.[20] These international initiatives are fraught with problems, however, including a deficit of democracy and a lack of adequate protections for civil liberties.

The surveillance of communications is not limited to government, however. Private firms are increasingly monitoring our interactions online. In the early days of electronic commerce, this constituted the monitoring of movements through the use of "cookies," in order to create profiles for marketing purposes. New forms of revenue generation have since arisen, with new forms of tracking computer users while online. Even the sanctity of communications content is regularly breached, with employers monitoring the conduct of employees as they surf the Web and reading e-mails, to Web-mail service providers scanning e-mail contents in order to provide "improved" advertising.[21]

## Surveillance of All Activity

Surveillance in an information society is not limited to communications. Increasingly we are breaking fundamental rules of data protection by using information collected for one purpose for a number of other purposes. And we are joining these sources of information together in order to surveil with even more authority and power.

The U.S. government considered developing the Total Information Awareness program (TIA), an advanced collection of personal information for mining and analysis. TIA was developed within the Pentagon Information Awareness Office, and its purpose was to

Imagine, develop, apply, integrate, demonstrate and transition information technologies, components, and prototype closed-loop information systems that will counter asymmetric threats by achieving total information awareness useful for preemption, national security warning, and national security decision making.[22]

After much controversy, this system was abandoned, even while other systems are arising. Now the United States is intending to profile airline passengers under its Secure Flight regime[23] that brings together airline and reservation databases with government databases to assess the risk of each traveler and to see whether she should be prevented from traveling. This sharing of information between industry and government also involves the sharing of information across borders. U.S. laws require that any airline which flies into the United States must provide the U.S. Department of Homeland Security with access to its "passenger name record" information to combat terrorism and enhance airplane security. This initiative is not limited to the United States, however. While it was originally a U.S. idea, when the United States required foreign carriers to submit this information to the U.S. government, a number of other countries decided to adopt similar practices. The European Union is already moving toward a similar data-sharing agreement between airlines and governments for general law enforcement purposes. Australia has a similar initiative, and Canada is requiring access even to domestic travel information.

Policy initiatives are also emerging that aim to increase the collection of information. We have already seen the United States start fingerprinting and face-scanning all visitors under the U.S. Visitor & Immigration Status Indication Technology System (US VISIT).[24] These *biometrics* are taken from the up to 30,000 visitors each day and are then stored in U.S. government databases for 75 to 100 years; then they are combined with other information regarding these visitors and aliens.[25] Similar systems are being called for elsewhere. In response to the terrorist attacks on a Russian school, the Russian government stated its intention to fingerprint all foreigners at its borders. Japan is considering such a system as well. The United Kingdom is planning a similar system as part of its larger biometric identity card regime. The European Union has announced its intention to create a similar regime that will also involve the fingerprinting of all EU citizens. The EU is proposing that all EU passports include fingerprints, and that all 450 million EU residents' and citizens' fingerprints be kept in a central database.[26] Finally, the United Nations is playing an active role in establishing standards for biometric passports; which would effectively globalize the American practice.

These surveillance initiatives again are not limited to government. More and more companies are requiring the collection of fingerprints from their employees, and are conducting background checks of prospective employees. One interesting example of corporate surveillance is the controversial privately run profiling system MATRIX (Multistate Anti-TerRrorism Information eXchange). This system combines information from government databases and private companies. According to its promotional material, "When enough seemingly insignificant data is analyzed against billions of data elements, the invisible becomes visible." The system was developed by the Florida-based company Seisint, and was used extensively in the months following the attacks on the World Trade Center and the Pentagon. The system identified 120,000 people who showed a statistical likelihood of being terrorists. This "high-terrorism factor" was used to conduct investigations and make arrests after the information was submitted to state police, the Immigration and Naturalization Service, the FBI, and the Secret Service.

All of the systems and policies outlined above are merely the starting point for more invasive practices. Centralized biometric databases are not as interesting as a listing of all the times someone has been verified. For example, a biometric identity card system will generate transactional data whenever someone is scanned as they visit their doctor, cross a border, and are stopped on the street. The same is true for all of the policies for communications surveillance. The listing of all of these transactions will provide private and public entities with a great deal of information regarding our daily practices and our private lives. These are the inevitable challenges of the information society. But the outcome need not be disastrous.

## Privacy as Freedom

Privacy is often regarded as a less important right. First, it is regarded as secondary to other, more important rights, and possibly as derivative from them. Second, it is seen as the first impediment to combating crime, terrorism, and other social ills. Here I want to destroy this notion and show how privacy is essential to freedom.

Even within the United States, where there is no comprehensive data protection law, privacy is left with an awkward constitutional status. As mentioned above, the word "privacy" does not appear in the U.S. Constitution. However, there are other rights that, when combined, may be interpreted as "privacy rights." To provide Americans with a constitutional right to privacy, the U.S. Supreme Court has relied upon combining the right to free speech and the right to assemble peacefully in the First Amendment to the Constitution with the Fourth Amendment, which protects against illegal search and seizure, and with the Fifth Amendment, which protects against self-incrimination. Since the 1960s these have been interpreted so as to allow individuals to speak and assemble freely without prior identification, to protect the privacy of places and people, and to limit the ability of government to compel information disclosure.

The Supreme Court argued that privacy is within the "shadows" of the Constitution.[27] A number of interesting Supreme Court decisions followed from this constitutional grounding for privacy, leading perhaps to a foregrounding of privacy and its emergence from the shadows. Privacy can be seen as the enabler of all these constitutional rights. In the 1950s, for example, the government of Alabama tried to compel the National Association for the Advancement of Colored People to disclose its membership list, in an attempt to intimidate the members. The Supreme Court sided with the NAACP in this case. In *Talley v. California* the Supreme Court upheld the right to distribute written material without identification.

Anonymous pamphlets, leaflets, brochures and even books have played an important role in the progress of mankind. Persecuted groups and sects from time to
time throughout history have been able to criticize oppressive practices and laws
anonymously.

The press licensing law of England was due in part to the knowledge that
exposure of the names of printers, writers, and distributors would lessen
the circulation of literature critical of the government. The old seditious
libel cases in England show the lengths to which government had to go
to find out who was responsible for books that were obnoxious to the
rulers. John Lilburne was whipped, pilloried, and fined for refusing to
answer questions designed to get evidence to convict him or someone else
for the secret distribution of books in England.[28]

The Court argued that the right to speak anonymously is firmly rooted
in the history of the country, but also in the roots of political participation. More recently, in 1995 the U.S. Supreme Court argued that
anonymity is an enabling component of the marketplace of ideas, and
essential to free expression.

The interest in having anonymous works enter the marketplace of ideas unques-
tionably outweighs any public interest in requiring disclosure as a condition of
entry. Accordingly, an author's decision to remain anonymous, like other decisions
concerning omissions or additions to the content of a publication, is an aspect of
the freedom of speech protected by the First Amendment.[29]

The most recent Supreme Court decision upheld the view that requiring
an individual to gain a permit on which one's name appears in order to
engage in door-to-door advocacy of a political cause was unconstitutional.
"Anonymity is a shield from the tyranny of the majority. . . . It thus exem-
plifies the purpose behind the Bill of Rights, and of the First Amendment
in particular: to protect unpopular individuals from retaliation—and their
ideas from suppression—at the hand of an intolerant society.[30]

Drawing from the argument that anonymity is a shield from oppression,
privacy emerges from the shadows of other rights. Privacy is not just derivative from these other rights, nor is it secondary. Privacy is at the core of
public participation, and as such is essential to freedom. Without privacy,
freedom is weakened because individuals are without protection from retaliation. Without privacy, the individual is reduced to judgment by all-seeing
observers, both public and private. Without privacy, people will never be

able to organize peaceful assembly in opposition to government without government's prior knowledge, and with its increased ability to intimidate.

If a government had the ability to perfectly observe its opposition, the consequence would be either that the opposition would go underground or that it would be the last such opposition. Antiabortionists would not be able to protest, environmentalists would not be able to organize, gun lobbyists would be registered and watched, those who lobby against the arms trade would be marked. Privacy is thus essential to an open and participatory democracy.

## Privacy in an Open Information Society

It is not enough, however, for me to claim privacy as a constitutional right, as essential to democracy, and to leave it at that, hoping that no further incursions will arise. No constitutional right, nor any moral right for that matter, is absolute.

When the U.S. Supreme Court ruled that individuals have a constitutional right to privacy, it issued the following condition: the individual who claims that his constitutional right to privacy was invaded must have had a *reasonable expectation* of privacy. Similarly, within the European Convention on Human Rights, the right to privacy is balanced against many other considerations, on the following condition developed by the European Court of Human Rights: incursions on privacy must be in accordance with law and necessary in a democratic society. Thus our autonomy, dignity, and freedom are at the mercy of social trends. The "reasonable expectation" is actually a two-pronged test. First, the person must act as though he expected privacy. He should not post copies of his e-mails on his Web site, for example. Second, society must be prepared to recognize that expectation as reasonable. To extend the above example, that individual had a reasonable expectation of privacy not only because he kept his e-mails private, but also because society deems e-mail privacy to be reasonable. Similarly, according to the European Court of Human Rights, "in accordance with law" means that there must be a law which states the conditions for invasion and prevents arbitrary interference. While this test is easy, the second test is more challenging. "Necessary in a democratic society" means that any intervention into the private life of an individual must not be overly broad in application. There must be a pressing social need, and the action must be *proportionate* to the legitimate aim pursued.

The constitution of "proportionate" and "reasonable" is unclear. There was a time when we thought that capital and corporal punishment were reasonable and proportionate when the crimes were severe enough or when the public wanted vengeance, retribution, and entertainment. Generally, this is no longer the case. But there was also a time when we believed that national databases were problematic, that mass surveillance of communications was disproportionate and unreasonable. Yet within the information society, we see these systems and practices spreading.

Social trends are the barometer of the right to privacy. I began this chapter contending that privacy is a "gut instinct," something that, when invaded, we feel something is "wrong." Realizing all the critics who are out there, I quickly tried to ground this notion in legalistic terms, as constitutional rights and statutory rights under data protection. This granted privacy a primacy in the domain of human rights and civil liberties, particularly, as I said, because it is key to public participation and the functioning of an open and participatory democracy. But now we are back where we began, with privacy being subject to fuzzy concepts such as "proportionate" and "reasonable" that are up for human judgment and interpretation. Our human judgments and interpretations are in flux. Technological change is a component of this flux. Our attitudes toward privacy change in the face of technology, as they have changed since the advent of cameras, the tabloid press, the telegraph, databases, and the Internet. We now have the capacities to store millions of fingerprints in a single database to verify travelers to the United States. As these visitors grow accustomed to submitting their fingerprints in the United States, they are less likely to be offended when their home governments require their fingerprints for more general purposes.

The fear of terrorism is another component of the flux of human attitudes regarding privacy and human dignity. Previously we collected fingerprints of criminals, or collected information on suspects. Now society seems less concerned with due process, and many argue that they are willing to forgo liberty in the name of security. The "information society," when combined with the equally vague notion of the "war on terror," may produce a frightening state of affairs. Personal information will be the new currency of access and privilege, traded without our consent and possibly even without our knowledge. Technology and fear are determining much of what we do, and this must somehow be turned around.

Two news stories within two days are cases in point. On November 9, 2004, the New Zealand Press Association reported a story of an employee who was fired because he refused to allow himself to be fingerprinted. His company told the Employment Relations Authority that it needed to use fingerprinting technology to combat false time claims by employees. The fired employee claimed:

Your employer used to be able to make demands on your time only when you were at work, but now they can hold biometric information on you 24 hours a day—we are no longer employees and employers, but slaves and masters.31

He was fired for refusing a "lawful and reasonable request," and this dismissal was upheld by the Employment Relations Authority. According to the story, the Authority made its decision on the grounds that the national privacy commissioner argued that "finger-scanning technology did not breach privacy principles as it merely stored mathematical data rather than actual prints." This did not prevent it from infringing upon this man's sense of dignity, however.

The second case involved two press articles on a new security system at London's Heathrow Airport. Both described the testing of an X-ray device that peers through passengers' clothes before they board a plane. A *London Times* article[32] noted that the graphic nature of the results shocked the passengers. Although the system was very effective at identifying hidden devices on the body, the article quoted two "subjects" of the test who commented on how shocked, alarmed, and embarrassed they were. A CNN report[33] noted, instead, the passengers who claimed they didn't mind the invasiveness, so long as they were safe in the sky. The report also quoted a spokesperson for the airport, saying that 98 percent of participants gave positive feedback. The diversity in the reporting shows the diversity in social norms. Both articles noted, however, that the U.S. government had decided against adopting this technology because it was so invasive.

Morality and dignity may be the only forces left to fight against this continuing shift downstream. Many of our understandings of human rights and civil liberties hinge upon a sense of morality and dignity. We do not permit torture not only because it is against the law but also because it offends us. We regulate many activities not only because they are illegal but also because we feel that they are wrong, and unnecessary in the type of society within which we choose to live. The initiatives discussed in this chapter introduce new norms to an unsuspecting society, and risk changing our senses of morality and dignity along with our legal rights. Changing norms will change our regard for what are proportionate and necessary measures in a democratic society. Once it becomes accepted that all information which is derived from our interactions in modern society is collected by default in the eventuality that we do wrong to someone or to the state, there is little ground for us to feel offended by forced collection of DNA from all newborns, or the default fingerprinting of all individuals. After all, the logic goes, "Unless you have something to hide/fear, this data will never be used against you."

We should all be working to maintain a sense of liberty and freedom, not working even harder to ensure that every single source of information regarding one's life is subject to surveillance by default, and indiscriminately so. Five years ago we would never have pursued many of these policies and systems. I now worry most about what will happen five years from now, looking back and looking forward: What will we think is reasonable, proportionate, and necessary in a democratic society when all activities and intentions are recordable, accessible, and required?

Without an adequate grounding in the politics of privacy, information society politics as they manifest themselves in WSIS and other forums, may result in grave errors that may take years to reverse. Of course policies and laws can be changed, international statements and agreements modified; but once we have changed society's "gut instincts," and then introduced the technological foundations for a new form of society, this new path for our new world may be irreversible.

**Notes**

1. Although this may not be because of my answer.

2. Mistaken Identity Public Conference, London School of Economics, May 19, 2004.

3. Samuel Warren and Louis Brandeis, "The Right to Privacy," 4 *Harvard Law Review* 193 (1890).

4. Alan F. Westin, *Privacy and Freedom* (New York: Atheneum, 1967).

5. Robert Ellis Smith, *Ben Franklin's Website*, G. Providence, RI: Privacy Journal (2000).

6. Rhoda Howard and Jack Donnelly, "Liberalism and Human Rights: A Necessary Connection," 268–276. In *The Human Rights Reader: Major Political Writings, Essays, Speeches, and Documents from the Bible to the Present,* ed. Micheline Ishay (New York: Routledge, 1997).

7. This classification of criticisms is from Daniel, Solove, and Marc Rotenberg, *Information Privacy Law* (New York: Aspen, 2003).

8. Amitai, Etzioni: *The Limits of Privacy* (New York: Basic Books, 1999).

9. Reva B., Siegel, "The Rule of Love: Wife Beating as Prerogative and Privacy," 105 *Yale Law Journal* 2117 (1996).

10. *(North Carolina) State v. Hussey,* 44 N.C. (Busb.) 123, 126–27 (1852).

11. Richard Posner, "The Right to Privacy," 12 *Georgia Law Review* 393–422, 400 (1977–1978).

12. Charles Fried, "Privacy: Economics and Ethics. A Comment on Posner," 12 *Georgia Law Review* 428 (1977–1978).

13. Edward J. Bloustein, "Privacy Is Dear at Any Price: A Response to Professor Posner's Economic Theory," 12 *Georgia Law Review* 430 (1977–1978).

14. Ibid., 437.

15. Richard A. Epstein, "Privacy, Property Rights, and Misrepresentations," 12 *Georgia Law Review* 457 (1977–1978).

16. European Commission, "Data Protection in the European Union," available at http://europa.eu.int/comm/internal_market/en/dataprot/guide/guide_en.pdf.

17. Ibid.

18. Article 29 Working Party, "Recommendation 3/97: Anonymity on the Internet" (Brussels: European Commission, 1997).

19. Alberto, Escudero-Pascuale, and Ian Hosein, "Questioning Lawful Access to Traffic Data," *Communications of the ACM* 47, no. 3 (2004): 77–82.

20. Ian. Hosein, "The Sources of Laws: Policy Dynamics in a Digital and Terrorized World," *The Information Society* 20, no. 3 (2004): 187–199.

21. Cf. Electronic Privacy Information Center and Privacy International, "Privacy and Human Rights 2005," available at http://www.privacyinternational.org/phr.

22. Report to Congress regarding the Terrorism Information Awareness Program, May 20, 2003.

23. This system followed the demise of the Computer Assisted Passenger Prescreening System (I and II).

24. There is currently an exception for Canada and Mexico.

25. Privacy International, "The Enhanced US Border Surveillance System: An Assessment of the Implications of US-VISIT," Sept. 28 2004.

26. Privacy International, "PI Advises the European Parliament to Stop Biometric Passports," Oct. 25, 2004.

27. Solove and Rotenberg, *Information Privacy Law*.

28. U.S. Supreme Court, *Talley v. California*, 362 US 60 (1960).

29. U.S. Supreme Court, *McIntyre v. Ohio Elections Commission*, 514 US 334 (1995).

30. U.S. Supreme Court, *Watchtower Bible and Tract Society of New York, Inc., et al., Petitioners v. Village of Stratton et al.* 240 F.3d 553 (2002).

31. "Man Sacked for Refusing to Give Employer His Fingerprints," Nov. 9, 2004.

32. Dipesh Gadher, "Plane Passengers Shocked by Their X-ray Scans," Nov. 7, 2004.

33. "Airport X-ray Sees Through Clothes," Nov. 9, 2004, posted 10:43 A.M. EST (1543 GMT).

## II  Freedom of Association, Participation, and Procedural Protections

# 6 The Right of Assembly and Freedom of Association in the Information Age

Charley Lewis

(1) Everyone has the right to freedom of peaceful assembly and association.
(2) No one may be compelled to belong to an association.
—Universal Declaration of Human Rights, Article 20

It is perhaps a truism to state that the information and communications technology (ICT) revolution of the 1980s has dramatically reshaped the way in which individuals and groups live, work, and play. Despite the exclusions of the digital divide, the personal computer and the mobile phone are commonplace features of everyday life. E-mail, the Internet, and ubiquitous telephony permeate the fabric of social interaction.

It is therefore hardly surprising that these new technologies have been adopted and adapted by civil society groups around the world as innovative platforms that open up new possibilities, and allow individuals and groups to exercise their fundamental human rights in exciting new ways. Conversely, ICTs have evoked a range of responses from authorities seeking to limit or abrogate the exercise of fundamental human freedoms.

This chapter examines the rights of assembly and freedom of association in the context of the ICT revolution, both the nature of these two rights and the opportunities that the new ICT tools provide for their exercise. I argue that e-mail and the Internet provide powerful new platforms for individuals and groups to assemble and associate, and give a range of examples, from the opposition in Zimbabwe to the union movement. Conversely, the same tools provide new means—as well as new manifestations of some traditional repressive tactics—for the state and others in authority to monitor and crack down on the exercise of these rights.

## Zimbabwe, 2003

In early June 2003 hundreds of thousands of supporters of Zimbabwe's Movement for Democratic Change (MDC) sought to exercise their right to freedom of assembly and association by embarking on a nationwide stay-away. Faced with media almost exclusively under government control, together with a heavy presence of police and soldiers on the streets to forestall demonstrations and marches, they were forced to resort to ICT-enabled tools to exercise their right of assembly and freedom of association. The use of mobile phone text messaging (see box) was supplemented by a plethora of Web sites that carried information and news about the unfolding protests.[2]

It is tempting to speculate on, but impossible to quantify, the impact of these online tools for information, association, mobilization, and assembly on the week's events. Certainly the week's actions fell short of being the "final push" that the opposition MDC had called for. In part this was due to the massive show of government force, which included the deployment of police and troops in trucks and jeeps, supported by water cannons, helicopters, police on horseback, even (reportedly) army tanks. The widespread use of mobile phone text messaging, alongside more traditional newspaper advertisements and leaflets, was widely reported,[3] and was a key component of the campaign.

Opposition activists in Zimbabwe were not the first to use mobile phone text messages in support of their right of assembly—the 1999 anti-

---

June 2003. The streets of Harare, capital city of Robert Mugabe's Zimbabwe, are eerily quiet. It is the second day of an opposition-led pro-democracy stay-away. Bands of armed thugs and soldiers roam industrial areas, their boots loud in the empty streets, beating on doors, trying to force businesses to open. Across town, opposition councillor Sydney Mazaranhanga is assaulted and abducted. In the city center thousands of copies of the country's only independent daily, *The Daily News*, are seized and burned.

As night falls, in homes around the city and across the country, mobile phones beep quietly. A text message passes from phone to phone, home to home: "Business 99% closed, June 3. Stay closed on Wednesday. Together we can do more. Pass on to others."[1]

globalization protesters in Seattle may well be considered to hold the pioneering honors.[4] The opposition in Zimbabwe has, however, used ICTs in several innovative ways to exercise the right to assembly and freedom of association in the face of ongoing government repression.

With television, radio, and press almost exclusively state-controlled, and the draconian Public Order and Safety Act forbidding almost all forms of gathering that can vaguely be construed as political, Zimbabwe's opposition activists have had little option but to explore ICTs as a means to assemble, organize, and mobilize. The sole independent daily newspaper suffered continual government harassment, was regularly confiscated and burned, and had its offices firebombed before finally being forced to close down under provisions of the misnamed 2002 Access to Information and Protection of Privacy Act.

As the channels and spaces to assemble and associate were progressively closed, opposition activists had to turn to innovative, often ICT-enabled, means. An early example can be drawn from the campaign preceding the June 2000 parliamentary elections. The largely urban opposition movements took "advantage of the growing number of Internet and e-mail users and exploited the urban–rural travel habits of Zimbabwean people."[5] Election materials were made available for printing on the Internet or via e-mail, so that they could be taken for distribution in rural areas on weekends. Out of this grew Kubatana, an NGO whose database-driven portal Web site[6] "encourages Zimbabweans to get involved in using electronic communication to advocate for change."[7] In a similar vein, the Zimbabwe Congress of Trade Unions circulates newsletters to its shop stewards and structures by e-mail for posting on factory notice boards.

### Association and Assembly in the Information Age

The Zimbabwean experience illustrates graphically how the development and spread of ICTs—in particular e-mail and the Internet—have since the mid-1990s fundamentally altered both the spaces and the channels through which individuals and organizations interact and mobilize, assemble and associate. In many contexts, as this chapter will argue, the organizational Web site has now become a primary node of assembly, and the e-mail message, a key channel of association.

This poses a range of challenges for organizations, with implications for structures, communications, and skills. It also opens new avenues for those seeking to undermine or abrogate these fundamental rights as they spread into cyberspace. In the pages that follow, we will examine the rights of assembly and freedom of association, looking at selected examples of how organizations have sought to exploit e-mail and the Internet in the exercise of these rights, and exploring the dimensions of their repression, before concluding with a brief discussion of the issues and challenges that emerge.

### The Freedom of Assembly and Association

What is meant by the freedom of assembly and association? At the minimum, the freedom of association encompasses the right to form and join an association of individuals, whether a political party, trade union, NGO, religious body, interest group, or society, or to form a grouping or alliance of such entities. The freedom of assembly goes somewhat further, implying the right of individuals or associations to meet, assemble, or congregate for whatever purposes they deem fit, whether in protest or merely to discuss their issues or affairs. The two rights are also clearly congruent: an association that has no right to assemble is clearly fundamentally hamstrung; likewise, it is unlikely that the right to assemble can properly be exercised except through the formation of associations, except on rare and intermittent spontaneous occasions.

Together with Articles 19 and 21, the right to freedom of association and assembly forms a cluster of overtly political rights in the Universal Declaration of Human Rights. It is hard to see how citizens can freely participate in elections or how the "will of the people"[8] can be expressed in democratic governance, without the right to associate freely in political organizations of their choice and to assemble in political meetings. Likewise, the protections inherent in the right to freedom of assembly and association may be a necessary guarantee, but on their own they are by no means a sufficient condition for the full and unfettered exercise of these two rights. Like many other rights, the ability to effectively exercise the freedom of association and assembly depends in large measure on the protections afforded by other rights. Without the right to privacy,[9] association cannot be free. Unless there is freedom of movement,[10] assembly is curtailed. Without freedom of thought, conscience, and religion,[11] the right of association is undermined. Freedom of opinion and expression[12] is essential if the right to associate is to be undertaken freely, and the right of assembly is to be exercised. The close interdependence of both the overtly political rights and the others required for their exercise necessarily means that the discussion in this chapter will closely relate to, and to some extent overlap with, both preceding and subsequent chapters.

It is often these other rights that have been the focus of attention for human rights activists, leading to the freedom of association and assembly being dubbed by Human Rights First the "neglected right."[13] This is in part because governments or authorities seeking to roll back or limit the rights of association and assembly often do so by restricting rights in other areas, such as freedom of expression or privacy, that are required to exercise freedom of association and assembly. Such attacks are frequently exercised not only through limitations placed on associated rights, but also by a range of other measures designed to undermine the ability to associate or assemble. This is all the more the case where individuals or groups have sought to take into the virtual realm of cyberspace the right to associate and assemble—which may be circumscribed or undermined in the physical world of meetings and demonstrations.

Human Rights First supports this view, noting that "the right to 'form and join' an organisation may not be sufficient to enable an individual to fully realize his or her right to freedom of association," and identifying a range of interventions through which "governments could restrict the ability of groups to operate freely."[14] These include restricting or imposing unreasonable conditions on the ability of associations to register or acquire status as legal persons, blocking or hampering free access by groups to sources of funding, and interfering in or imposing restrictions on the governance arrangements of organizations, including their right of international affiliation. A case in point in this regard is the recent furor over Zimbabwe's Non-Governmental Organisations Bill, which has been widely seen as a sustained indirect attack on the freedom of association and assembly, and has been criticized for placing unreasonable restrictions on the registration, funding, and governance of NGOs.[15] And where organizations and individuals have sought to exploit e-mail and the Internet as platforms from which to exercise their right to associate and assemble, governments have frequently responded by curtailing access to those platforms, as we shall see below.

The U.N. Universal Declaration of Human Rights, quoted at the head of this chapter, sets two limitations on the rights of association and assembly, one intrinsic and the other a corollary. The intrinsic qualifier stipulates that the right to assembly and association must be exercised in a "peaceful" manner, thus excluding violent associations (such as "terrorist," insurrectionary, or criminal groupings) and nonpeaceful assembly (including riot or armed conflict) from the protections of the right. The corollary is perhaps not so immediately obvious, but is, on reflection, fundamental to the freedom of choice inherent in the right of association: it stipulates the right *not* to associate, the right to exercise choice in a *negative* manner by *not* belonging to an organization, thus protecting individuals against coercion into membership in any organization, such as enforced membership in a political party or trade union.

### Legal Status

What is the legal status of the right of assembly and association? It has been noted by Irish and Simon that the Universal Declaration of Human Rights is not a formal international treaty,[16] and hence does not have legal force and weight, although it exerts a powerful global moral influence. Convention 87 of the International Labour Organisation, "Freedom of Association and the Right to Organise," adopted earlier in the same year, refers more specifically to the right of employers and workers to associate in employer bodies and trade unions. But it likewise, although ratified by many countries around the globe, lacks the force of law. Of more legal authority are international treaties within which the rights of freedom of association and assembly are enshrined, such as the 1953 European Convention on the Protection of Human Rights and Fundamental Freedoms (ECPHRFF), with over forty signatories in Europe, and the 1976 International Covenant on Civil and Political Rights (ICCPR),[17] with over 140 signatories worldwide. Interestingly, neither overtly protects individuals from compulsory association, although they add a specific rider to the Universal Declaration of Human Rights in the "right to form and join trade unions."[18] The 1961 European Social Charter and the 1996 International Covenant on Economic, Social and Cultural Rights (ICESCR) explicitly extend and protect freedom of association for workers. Articles 5 and 6 of the former protect the rights to organize, to bargain collectively, and to strike, and Article 8 of the latter protects the rights to organize and to strike.

In both cases these are applications of the rights to associate and assemble in forms specifically appropriate to workers and trade unions.

Many conventions and treaties provide for specific, usually tightly constrained, exceptions or derogations of the rights they seek to guard. Both the ECPHRFF and the ICCPR (the 1976 covenant was closely modeled on the 1953 convention) also recognize the rights of governments to prescribe in law "restrictions" that are "necessary in a democratic society in the interest of national security or public safety, public order [ordre publique], the protection of public health or morals or the protection of the rights and freedoms of others."[19] This limitation, as the detailed analysis of international human rights case law by Irish and Simon makes clear, cannot be construed as endorsing the kinds of interference with registration, funding, and governance described earlier; rather, it amplifies the rather vague "peaceful" qualifier of the Universal Declaration of Human Rights. Similar, limited derogations of workers' rights are permitted under the European Social Charter and the ICESCR.

The freedom of association and assembly is widely, and with far greater legal weight, enshrined in national constitutions that function as the supreme law in countries around the world. These rights are, for example, to be found in the constitution of the Republic of South Africa, within its Bill of Rights, Clauses 17 and 18 of which respectively provide for the right of "assembly, demonstration, picket and petition" and the "freedom of association."[20]

## The Impact of ICTs

We have seen what is traditionally and historically encompassed by the rights of assembly and association. How, then, do the advent of the information age, and the consequent pervasiveness of cheap and readily available tools offered by ICTs, impact on the choices open to individuals and organizations in the exercise of these rights?

Quantitatively, the information revolution has seen an exponential increase in the computing power available to individuals and organizations, coupled with a dramatic decrease in the cost of that computing power (known as Moore's Law).[21] This in turn has fueled an orders-of-magnitude spread in the availability and pervasiveness of computing technology. Qualitatively, it has been the development of e-mail, toward the end of the 1980s, and of the Internet as we now know it, from about 1993.

Together, the impact of this technological revolution has been to bring about what Manuel Castells and others have theorized as the "information age." The new technologies have facilitated the much-hyped "death of distance," sometimes conceptualized as the compression of space and time. In essence this allows association, communication, and assembly to take place beyond the boundaries of geography and across the constraints of time—asynchronously and not co-located.

One consequence of this has been the mushrooming of organizational Web sites worldwide. Notwithstanding the digital divide (itself arguably merely the manifestation, in the sphere of ICTs, of the yawning global gap in development between nations, communities, and individuals), which still sees swaths of our planet with little connectivity or capacity, in connected areas of the globe almost every commercial company, political party, NGO, or trade union of any substance has its own Web site. This is not to overlook the immense barriers faced by individuals and organizations in poor communities and regions, afflicted by poverty, illiteracy, and skewed ICT network development, in seeking to exploit the new technologies to associate, organize, and assemble. Those struggles are properly the subject of another book chapter, but while the digital divide hampers the ability of marginalized communities to exploit the possibilities of ICT, the initiatives and examples discussed here clearly point the way forward.

I have already suggested that the organizational Web site is in the process of becoming the locus of association and assembly. This is possible because of the possibilities that Web sites offer, possibilities not always exploited by organizations. At the most basic level, a Web site functions merely as a billboard in cyberspace, a display of static content relating to the organization, setting out its mission, goals, personnel, and contact details, but little more.

Properly utilized, an organizational Web site provides, in cyberspace, a nodal point for the organization, its members, supporters, associates, and friends. It may do this by providing restricted-access content for members (if the organization is membership-based); up-to-date information about the organization, its policies, programs and campaigns; and facilities such as guest books, blogs,[22] and chat rooms for members and others to interact with the organization. A number of such Web sites include facilities that allow interested parties to apply for membership, donate to the organization, or sign up to receive newsletters or similar material from the organization.

E-mail, which may be used on its own, or is often used to supplement and extend a presence on the Web, provides an effective channel for virtual association between individuals. Perhaps the best example of this form of association is the use of e-mail mailing lists, where individuals join or subscribe to a mailing list, and any e-mail message is automatically distributed to all subscribers or members. The technology provides an ideal vehicle for discussion and debate, whether structured under the control of a moderator or facilitator, or open-ended, unstructured, and free-flowing. Such mailing lists also provide an ideal channel through which organizations can distribute newsletters, press statements, or messages of various types. The very vocabulary associated with mailing lists suggests their role as a channel of association: "subscribe," "join," "member." It is therefore no accident that a number of organizational Web sites offer visitors the opportunity to associate with them by subscribing to one or more of their mailing lists.

This close integration of the ICT technologies of assembly, association, and communication is reflected in a recent U.N. human rights declaration, Article 5 of which brings together the rights to "meet or assemble"; "form, join and participate" in organizations; and "communicate" with other organizations.[23]

The point can be extended further. E-mail and the Internet are not merely additional channels or spaces extending the boundaries of freedom of association and assembly into cyberspace. They allow forms of association and assembly that were previously not possible, going beyond mere virtual equivalents of physical association and assembly to a new integration of information, communication, expression, association, and assembly, enabled by ICTs, that are sometimes referred to as "online communities."

An e-mail message crosses the world in the space of a few seconds. Web content can be copied and distributed with a few mouse clicks. The rapidity and ease of reach of e-mail and the Internet, together with the replicability of content, promotes networked forms of organization that are relatively less hierarchical and far more amorphous than traditional organizations. This allows individuals the freedom of different levels of association with an organization (as member, supporter, associate, or friend) and shifting levels of engagement with its activities.

Some have conceptualized the use of ICT tools and platforms to associate, assemble, and engage in activities to promote social change as "cyberactivism," which can be thought of as the integration of offline activism with online activities, including "web sites, e-mail, listservs, interactive databases and other Internet tools [giving] advocacy groups today . . . much greater reach than they had previously."[24] The more ideologically loaded term "netwar," coined by policy analysts John Arquilla and David Ronfeldt,[25] perhaps comes closer to capturing the dynamic of integration and interaction between the ICT tools themselves and the organizational forms through which advocacy and activism are exercised. They conceive of "netwar" as "the use of network forms of organization, doctrine, strategy, and technology attuned to the information age."[26]

### Che Guevara Meets the Internet

Although certainly not the first to exploit the possibilities of e-mail and the Internet to exercise the right to associate and assemble, the Zapatistas are widely, perhaps romantically, considered to have marked a turning point in the use of cyber tools in support of activism.[27] The iconic status accorded the Zapatistas may in part stem from their being seen as Robin Hood crusaders for economic and social justice, but also surely derives from their ability to turn the nascent Internet into a newsworthy platform for their cause.

In early 1994, the Zapatista National Liberation Army (EZLN) launched a social justice insurgency in the Mexican state of Chiapas. It might have been just another quickly forgotten guerrilla war but for its extensive links with NGOs based in Mexico and beyond, and for its talented spokesperson, Subcomandante Marcos. The ability of the NGOs to utilize the new ICT communications tools—e-mail, the Internet, even the fax—gave Subcomandante Marcos an almost instant channel for a series of EZLN communiqués publicizing the plight of the people of Chiapas and popularizing the demands of the Zapatistas, which began to appear on mailing lists and Web sites around the world.

It is this ICT-enabled wave of global publicity that was to splash the Zapatista cause around the world's media and, perhaps more important, to enable the Zapatistas to forge a broad, loose global network of support within the NGO community. This in turn placed the issues they had raised squarely on the table, and was one of the factors making a purely military solution untenable for the Mexican government. As Wray notes, the "rapid, widespread dispersal of these communiqués and other information, and the subsequent establishment of intercontinental networks of solidarity and resistance, accounts for part of the reason why the Zapatistas survive."[28]

The Zapatistas can thus be considered among the first groups worldwide to exploit the possibilities to extend association and assembly through the new forms enabled by ICTs. E-mail became for them a means of forming and joining a global network of organizations supportive of their cause. The Web sites emblazoned with their message became worldwide rallying points around which that support could be assembled. It is these features that led Castells to describe them as the "first informational guerrilla movement."[29]

### Seattle and the "Infosphere"

The 1999 anti–WTO and anti-globalization protests in Seattle, Washington, may in many respects be considered a direct descendant, of the Zapatista program—albeit with a metropolitan locale, with far greater levels of connectivity and ICT resources, and, given the passage of five years, with access to a far more sophisticated e-mail and Internet environment. The Seattle protests were similarly characterized by a loose, nonhierarchical networked alliance of NGOs with differing, but overlapping and congruent, agendas. They were also characterized by extensive use of ICT tools, not only to generate publicity but also to serve as the backbone of command and control structures, in what de Armond has poetically described as a "pulsing infosphere of enormous bandwidth."[30] De Armond's account of the unfolding protests catalogs an extensive use of ICTs: mobile phones were widely used for communication between the various groups and structures of the protest, giving them enormous flexibility and the ability to respond rapidly to the changing disposition on the ground; portable and handheld computers with wireless modems allowed Web sites to be updated dynamically with on-the-ground news and situation reports as events unfolded; digital cameras and digital video enabled live images and footage to be reported and flashed around the world; some groups even used police scanners to eavesdrop on the police.

It is interesting to note that one of the entities at the center of this ferment of informational activities continues to exist as the global and multilingual Independent Media Centre.[31] It describes its role in Seattle as "[acting] as a clearinghouse of information for journalists, and [providing] up-to-the-minute reports, photos, audio and video footage through its website." It also "produced a series of five documentaries, uplinked every day to satellite . . . [as well as] its own newspaper, distributed throughout Seattle and to other cities via the internet, as well as hundreds of audio segments, transmitted through the web and Studio X, a 24-hour micro and internet radio station based in Seattle."[32]

The Seattle protests offer a clear example of the ways in which ICTs can be deployed in support of the freedom of association and the right to assemble. It was these ICT communications—e-mail, the Internet, mobile telephony—that became the tentacles of the network of association through which the various protest groupings coalesced. It was the same technological backbone that supported the various groups as they assembled to voice their protests. De Armond points to this when he notes that it "is the richer informational environment, which makes the organization of civil (and uncivil) society into networks easier, less costly, and more efficient."[33]

Extrapolating from this experience, a number of writers have gone on to investigate what are variously referred to as "mobile ad hoc social networks" or as "smart mobs,"[34] whose applications range from gaming syndicates to the January 2001 removal from power of President Joseph Estrada of the Philippines by over a million protesters mobilized by a short textmessage summoning them to assemble in Epfinaio de los Santos Avenue wearing black—"Go 2 EDSA. Wear Black," it read. Others have written of the "tectonic shifts"[35] through which the ICT revolution is transforming the nature of what some refer to as "cyberpolitik"[36] and others, as "netpolitik."[37] The terms may vary, but what is clear is that ICTs have opened an entire new dimension on how individuals and organizations exercise their rights to freedom of association and assembly.

## Unions Online

Less flamboyant, perhaps, but equally important as an example of the use of ICT tools for association and assembly, has been the exploration of the opportunities of cyberspace by trade unions. As noted earlier, the rights of trade unions to assemble and associate freely have been deemed deserving of explicit protection in human rights treaties.[38] These rights have been further taken up by the International Labour Organisation. The ILO's constitution makes explicit mention of the principle of freedom of association, and two of its eight fundamental conventions explicitly seek to extend and codify freedom of association as it applies to trade unions and the workplace.[39]

Of interest here is the degree to which ICTs have been used by unions and workers to exercise and extend the rights to associate, organize, and assemble. There is already a fairly extensive literature relating to unions and the Internet.[40] The discussion here will be rather more limited, seeking to illustrate the role that ICTs have played in strengthening the ability of unions to effect these rights, as well as in changing the ways in which unions act.

The Congress of South African Trade Unions (COSATU) may have far fewer resources than the unions of the north, but serves in many respects as a useful example of the deployment of ICT by unions.[41] COSATU also provides an example of a rather more prosaic application of ICT to support the right of freedom of association: the development of membership databases and systems. Membership, as an expression of the choice of individual workers to associate with the union of their choice, is of key importance for unions, as for other membership-based organizations. Financial bottom lines, as well as the ability to service and support members, depend on the quality and accuracy of membership information. Driven by the twin imperatives of the need to achieve post-apartheid financial self-sufficiency and a court decision that invalidated a strike ballot of one of its member unions because it was unable to produce a membership register, COSATU devoted considerable resources to developing a computerized membership system. Unfortunately, the federation's initial vision of a comprehensive, integrated database for each affiliate, providing individualized records for all members as a basis for training, communications, and benefits has remained unrealized, although almost all of its affiliates have some form of membership system.

Unions with more resources, such as the AFL–CIO affiliate Service Employees International Union (SEIU), have been rather more successful in this regard. Its highly successful and long-running "Justice for Janitors" campaign[42] made extensive use of targeted communications by means of faxes and e-mails to individual union members based on information drawn from the union's membership database. Through that database the union was able to translate membership, as an expression of association, into a campaign, arguably an expression of assembly. In a similar vein, the Internet commentator Eric Lee, who is affiliated with LabourStart, describes the online dimensions of the global campaign by both unions and NGOs against the giant U.S.-based retailer Wal-Mart, whose antiunions activities are the stuff of legend. Listing a number of anti-Wal-Mart sites, which include the use of blogs for people to vent their responses to Wal-Mart, as well as more traditional forms of support, such as getting on Wal-Mart mailing lists or joining unions trying to organize at Wal-Mart, he shows how the "battle over workers' rights at Wal-Mart is increasingly being fought in cyberspace"[43]—an online manifestation of association and assembly.

In contrast to those unions for which a presence on the Internet is considered more of a nuisance requirement—a kind of online business card—than an organizational opportunity, there are many others whose choice and arrangement of content suggests they see an Internet presence as a key locus of assembly for their members. The COSATU Web site (http://www.cosatu.org.za), for example, places a high premium on information of direct relevance to its membership and support base. Prominence is given to the informational output of the federation: speeches by union leadership, press statements, submissions to Parliament on legislation affecting workers, and other COSATU publications and documents in addition to basic information about the federation, its constitution, and its affiliates. In this the COSATU Web site is similar to many of the other excellent union Web sites around the world—in Canada, Australia, and elsewhere. Many, like the Trades Union Congress (TUC) in the United Kingdom, now provide restricted-access sections of their Web sites with specific content and functionality for active union members. Unusually, COSATU places most of the documentation relating to its highest decision-making structures, its congresses and central committee meetings, on the public section of its Web site.

Unions also use their Web sites as a vehicle for association. It is now common for union Web sites to provide online membership application forms, which are completed in cyberspace and processed electronically.

Like many other union structures, COSATU uses e-mail as a channel of communication and association, operating at least two substantial electronic mailing lists, one to distribute a daily e-mail digest of labor news stories relating to South Africa and the other to circulate the press statements it issues on matters of importance to the federation. Showing the integration and cross linkages between the various ICT tools, COSATU's Web site is used as a platform to encourage union members and supporters to sign up for these mailing lists. In a similar vein, the labor researcher and commentator Andrew Bibby has suggested the need for unions to exploit the possibilities of the new technologies to reach out to and to service members.[44]

ICTs not only have provided new opportunities and vehicles for unions; they also have extended the global integration and reach of the labor movement in an era of globalization. The international union umbrella bodies at the sectoral level, formerly (clumsily) called international trade secretariats (ITSs), now call themselves global union federations and place great emphasis on e-mail communication with their far-flung affiliates, as well as on their Web sites, which are readily accessible via a portal site (http://www.global-unions.org). When one of them, Union Network International, was launched on January 1, 2000, as the outcome of a merger of three smaller ITSs, bringing together some 1,000 unions in 150 countries representing 15 million members, its incoming general secretary, Philip Jennings, held a twelve-hour online press conference that spanned the globe.

The labor movement has also moved to exploit the capacity of ICTs to support the mobilization for and conduct of a range of campaigns. Sometimes this has taken the form of the online petition borrowed from NGO activism, either a Web page where individuals can register their names in support of a particular cause or issue or—far less effectively, and bordering on spam—an e-mail to which individuals add their name in similar fashion before forwarding (and proliferating—to both good and bad effect!) the message to their list of contacts. At other Web pages, as in the case of a Swaziland Federation of Trade Unions protest against state repression, people were asked to download, print, and sign a protest letter, and were given a list of government fax numbers at which to lodge their protest.

Far more effective have been cyber campaigns of the sort mounted by the global labor news portal LabourStart, whose Act Now! feature[45] showcases several union campaigns from around the world at any one time, from places such as the Democratic Republic of Congo, Thailand, Australia, Turkey, and the United States. Visitors to the facility are provided with information about the campaign and given a form letter that they can customize before adding their signature. An e-mail message is then generated and fired off at the target of the campaign, often the CEO of a company. The number of e-mails emanating from most of these campaigns runs into the thousands, and several clear victories have resulted—the recognition of a union, reinstatement of dismissed employees, the resolution of a strike.

Such campaigns are made more effective by the wide circulation of what are often called "action alerts"—the wide circulation of e-mail messages in support of the campaign and directing people to its Web page. Some of the earliest successful online campaigns were in fact conducted almost exclusively via such e-mailed "action alerts." LabourStart's Eric Lee cites as examples the international protests against the arrest of leaders of the Korean Confederation of Trade Unions in 1999, and mobilization for a shipping boycott in support of an acrimonious 1998 labor dispute involving Australian dock workers ("wharfies").[46] Lee also cites several examples of the use of e-mail to create and mount internal union campaigns against unpopular decisions by leadership, in support of his contention that the new technologies have the potential to alter profoundly the dynamics of unions: internationalizing, democratizing, and strengthening their operations and activities.[47] Steve Walker,[48] an academic, in chronicling a series of "cybercampaigns" conducted by the global union federation ICEM (International Federation of Chemical, Energy, Mine and General Workers Unions), explores their relationship and similarities to the "social netwars"[49] described earlier, in which networked forms of association and the primacy of information play central roles.

It is probably premature to speculate that the cybercampaign may be about to displace the more traditional strike and picket line, in which unions and their members assemble to confront their corporate adversaries. But ICTs certainly offer unions new and powerful ways to organize and act, associate and assemble. The possibilities of the new ICT tools are well summed up by Steve Davies, founder of the aptly named Cyber Picket Line[50] Web site:

For too long unions all over the world have been on the ropes. Now we're on the Net and it's already beginning to pay off. It's now possible for workers to communicate effectively with each other as never before. It is also possible for rank and file stewards and branch activists to have access to the sort of information resource and research capacity that was previously only available to senior full time officers. It is potentially one of the most powerful and democratic weapons at the disposal of the labour movement.[51]

## Online Rights Under Attack

Those who are the adversaries of the organizations using e-mail and the Internet to exercise their right to freedom of association and assembly, or those who have found themselves the targets of the various forms of cyber-campaign outlined above, be they governments or corporations, have not sat idly by in the face of the new ICT tools. They have actively sought by various means to limit the exploitation of the new technologies by their opponents, as well as to subvert the right to freedom of association through more traditional repressive methods.

The very nature of the new ICT technologies makes countering them extremely difficult. The ability of ICTs to break the boundaries of space and time, their digital ubiquity, is precisely what makes them so hard to repress: e-mail and the Internet are not constrained by time or space. A Web site can be hosted on any computer anywhere in the world, and can be copied or moved within seconds, and hence easily "mirrored" or replicated. An e-mail exists in the cyberspace of a chain of mail servers until downloaded, and it, too, is capable of almost instant replication and distribution. It often remains easier for the authorities to target the individuals and their organizations in the flesh, through more traditional means—such as detention of activists; proscription or banning of their organizations; prohibition of the right to meet, demonstrate, or picket—than to close down their activities in the elusive domain of cyberspace.

This is not to say that countermeasures against e-mail and the Internet and similar ICT tools have not been attempted. They most certainly have, as the following discussion will show. There has also been widespread surveillance of these technologies, which we will also discuss.

## Unweaving the Web

If an Internet Web site can act as either a locus for the assembly of activist groupings, or a source of information for them and their activities, the authorities seeking to restrict the rights to assembly or information for such groups would clearly be interested in preventing access to such sites. It is therefore unsurprising that the filtering of Web content and blocking of access to Web sites is widespread in jurisdictions less well known for their human rights records, including China, Myanmar, Saudi Arabia, Vietnam, and Zimbabwe.[52]

The blocking and filtering of the Internet ranges from explicit, structured control of the sort found in Saudi Arabia to the covert, sometimes chaotic, jamming that is frequently referred to as the "Great Firewall of China." Short of blocking public access to the Internet altogether, as has been done by North Korea, control of access to the borderless global domain of the World Wide Web is problematic, with the vast majority of targeted sites and content located on servers outside of national jurisdiction and ultimately identifiable only by numeric IP address.

Such censorship of the Web is thus made all the easier in an environment where Internet access is exclusively via a state-owned, government-controlled Internet service provider (ISP). Markets with a plethora of ISPs are much more difficult to control, because unwanted content has too many places through which it can leak. Saudi Arabia is an example. Although the country boasts some thirty ISPs, all are required to source their international connectivity via a national Internet Services Unit (ISU) that was set up in 1998 by the government's science institute, the King Abdulaziz City for Science & Technology (KACST).[53] The censorship of the Internet is conducted under terms of a 2001 Council of Ministers resolution that "prohibits users within the Kingdom of Saudi Arabia from publishing or accessing certain content on the Internet . . . [in order to preserve] 'our Islamic values, filtering the Internet content to prevent the materials that contradict . . . our beliefs or may influence our culture.' "[54]

The ISU's Web site is altogether more explicit and specific: "All sites that contain content in violation of Islamic tradition or national regulations shall be blocked."[55] It describes a twofold approach to blocking: the censorship of "pornographic sites", which is managed through KACST, partly on public request, and the blocking of other sites "upon direct requests from the security bodies within the government."[56] The filtering appears to be via a series of proxy servers and based on a list of banned Internet addresses. Jonathan Zittrain and Benjamin Edelman undertook an extensive survey of the Saudi government's Internet filtering practices and found over 2,000 blocked pages dealing with a wide range of subjects—content targeting women (including *Skirt!* magazine) and gays, as well as "pages perceived to be hostile to Saudi Arabia" (among them Amnesty International) and "pages about Middle Eastern politics, organizations, or groups"[57] (including Hezbollah and the Israeli Defense Force).

The challenge of government control of the Internet in China is vastly different in both scale and scope, in a country with over 26 million Internet users and more than 600 ISPs,[58] but with international connectivity channeled through a mere nine Internet access providers. Zittrain and Edelman undertook a similar empirical investigation of Internet censorship in China.[59] They found a system altogether vaster and more comprehensive, but whose very existence is officially denied. An interesting feature of Chinese censorship of the Internet is its inconsistency, both in reach and in scope—between 18,000 and 50,000 of the 200,000 sites Zittrain and Edelman tested were inaccessible at different times and from different points, with some unexpected sites (such as *Hustler* magazine) seemingly overlooked by the censors. The range of censored content is extensive, including a number of health, education, entertainment, religious, and government sites, as well as some more obvious candidates such as news (including the BBC) and a range of dissident, democracy, Falun Gong, Taiwanese, and Tibetan sites. They also note that a high proportion of the top Google sites returned on searches with keywords such as "tibet" or "democracy china" or even "equality" were blocked.[60]

In a similar vein the BBC reports that the search engines Google and Alta Vista were blocked in 2002,[61] the former presumably because its caching facility gives users access to content even if the originating site is blocked. Likewise, the OpenNet Initiative reports extensive keyword filtering and delisting of results by the popular Chinese search engines Yisou and Baidu—for example, a search on "free tibet" returns no results[62]—versus the 2,200,000 found by Google.[63] Zittrain and Edelman also noted that Internet filtering by the Chinese authorities was becoming increasingly sophisticated, moving from cruder IP address blocking or redirecting, to some keyword and search results blocking.[64]

Perhaps unsurprisingly, the Zimbabwe activist news portal ZimOnline has recently reported on the intention of the Zimbabwe government to acquire the technology from China to block access to "subversive" information and "independent" online media sites.[65]

Beyond restricting access to unwanted online content, governments are able to seek to monitor and control the access of individuals to the Internet. For example, Chinese citizens seeking to open accounts with ISPs are required to register with the Public Security Bureau. Zittrain and Edelman suggest that "The government might encourage Internet access through cybercafés rather than in private spaces so that customers' surfing can be physically monitored."[66] Restrictions on cybercafés, including enforced installation of monitoring software, and the compilation and retention of detailed records of those using their facilities, have been widely reported.[67] More details on such measures can be found in Amnesty International's damning catalog of state interventions to restrict access in China.[68] A powerful array of regulations and laws has been introduced since 1994 to limit and restrict the Internet rights of citizens. Penalties include the revocation of ISP licenses, and even the death penalty for placing "state secrets" on the Web. Amnesty International records thirty-three cases of Chinese citizens detained for offenses under these laws and regulations.

It is important to note that attempts to censor the Internet are not the prerogative of states alone. For example, in 1998 the water multinational Biwater attempted to take legal action against a global "Stop Biwater!" campaign, which came to a head when Biwater sought a court order to force a South African ISP to take down an allegedly defamatory press statement by the South African Municipal Workers Union. In the event, the company backed down,[69] but this and similar cases have led Privacy International and GreenNet to recognize this as part of a trend in the "growth of multinational corporate censors whose agendas are very different from those of governments" and to conclude that "it is arguable that in the first decade of the 21st century, corporations will rival governments in threatening Internet freedoms."[70]

The examples given above of measures taken to block access to the Internet by citizens, NGOs, and activist groupings represent but a few examples of a trend that is disturbingly widespread in certain jurisdictions. Behind them lies a clear recognition on the part of the authorities that the Internet provides an important space for individuals and groups to assemble and associate. Together they represent a concerted assault on the right to associate and assemble freely and peaceably.

Interestingly, perhaps naturally, the groups that have been the victims of this sort of censorship have sought means to wriggle through its tentacles. In the case of Biwater cited above, the company was persuaded to back down by the global proliferation of "mirror" sites, which had copied the press statement it sought to suppress, and against which it would individually have had to take costly legal action. The use of proxy servers to disguise the IP addresses of Web sites has been reported by Chinese dissidents, but these are easily blocked.[71] To counter this and to obviate the need for proxy routing, the Dutch Internet activist Felipe Rodriguez reports using a technique called "IP rotation" to continually alter the IP address of his own Web site.[72] There is also reportedly a range of software applications designed to counter Internet censorship, including Surfing Without Borders[73] and Dongtai,[74] as well as projects such as Peekabooty[75] and FreeNet,[76] which seek to provide tools to circumvent Internet censorship.[77]

### Tapping into e-Mail

Attacks on the use of ICT technologies to advance and enable the rights of assembly and association have not been directed solely at the Internet. It was earlier suggested that e-mail is a powerful means of strengthening and facilitating the freedom of association, and it, too, has been the subject of restriction, again by both governments and corporations. While the blocking of e-mail messages is certainly technically feasible, and is widely practiced in relation to suspected spam,[78] it has received far less attention than Internet blocking.[79]

While this may be due in part to the higher profile of the freedom of expression and access to information issues associated with the Internet, it is more likely that authorities prefer to monitor e-mails than to block them. This view is echoed by Privacy International and GreenNet. Their 2003 survey of Internet censorship agrees that "e-mail is monitored more often than it is openly censored,"[80] and notes an increase in e-mail monitoring subsequent to 9/11 because the attackers reportedly used e-mail as a key communication channel. Countries as far afield as India, New Zealand, Switzerland, the Philippines, and Zimbabwe have legislation enabling the surveillance of e-mail traffic under various conditions, often but not always related to cybercrime.

The existence of a highly sophisticated global system—code-named Echelon and allegedly involving the United States, the United Kingdom, Canada, Australia, and New Zealand—to monitor communications, including e-mail, has been widely reported on in the popular press for some years.[81] So much so that the European Parliament launched an official inquiry, whose findings, later endorsed in a formal resolution, were that the existence of such a system "is no longer in doubt,"[82] although its capacity and capabilities had been exaggerated. The use of widely available encryption techniques, such as freely downloadable pretty good privacy (PGP) programs,[83] limits the effect of such systems—hence the attempts by several governments to limit their use. Such encryption technology does, however, provide an important element of protection for human rights activists. The human rights lawyer Geoffrey Gordon notes the "advantages allowed by computer networks for human and civil rights work"[84] and the important role played by encryption technologies in "neutralizing [the] eavesdropping capabilities"[85] of repressive regimes.

There is no doubt that e-mail surveillance is widely undertaken, and that this constitutes an infringement on the right to freedom of association and communication. This trend is documented more fully in other chapters of this book. Suffice it to say here that any such surveillance needs to be carefully controlled in terms of specific laws that permit it: first, only under very tightly circumscribed circumstances in relation to prima facie criminal activity, and second, in accordance with precisely prescribed procedures.

The outright blocking of and deliberate interference with e-mail traffic are practiced in some jurisdictions, and is perhaps more disturbing in relation to the freedom of association and assembly, both of which it impacts directly. Once again China provides a useful, well-documented example of the possible means through which this may be done, although such measures are likely to be practiced in other countries as well.

China also illustrates the difficulties that authorities face in attempting to block e-mail traffic. Chase and Mulvenon's examination of the phenomenon reports widespread use of e-mail as a channel for association and assembly: "Mainland dissidents regularly use e-mail, as well as Internet chat rooms and bulletin boards, to communicate and coordinate with each other and with members of the exile dissident community."[86] They also report extensive use of political e-mail spam by Falun Gong and dissident

organizations, targeting e-mail users across China. Attempts by the authorities to block this flood of messages through filtering according to e-mail
addresses can be countered by techniques to change or disguise the origin
of such messages. Filtering according to keywords certainly is technically
feasible, but is thought to be impractical, given the high volumes of e-mail
traffic.[87] More common countermeasures include hacking into servers
known to be the source of such measures or disabling them through denial-
of-service attacks. In addition, disinformation e-mail messages are used to
confuse or disorganize these groups. Finally, known e-mail addresses of
opposition figures have been subjected to floods of counter-spam as a
technique of harassment.[88] This demonstrates both the widespread use of
e-mail as a vehicle for individuals and organizations in China as a means
of association, as well as the difficulties experienced by authorities seeking
to block the exercise of this right. Surveillance aside, countermeasures
are largely limited to the kind of guerrilla-style harassment Chairman Mao
would have applauded.

### Online Rights in the Workplace

The actual blocking of e-mail messages or the denial of access to e-mail
and the Internet is more common in the workplace and in relation to the
right of employees to associate with a trade union. Corporate blocking of
e-mail is relatively straightforward because such messages are received or
accessed via the corporate e-mail system. It is also widely practiced, with
the 1999 Ansett case in Australia being but the most notorious example.
In this case, the now-bankrupt airline Ansett fired a union official, Maria
Gencarelli, for circulating a union newsletter via the company's e-mail
system. In this case, Australia's Federal Court upheld Ms Gencarelli's right,[89]
but others haven't been so lucky. Also in Australia, the Australian Industrial Relations Commission in July 2003 ruled against the right of a trade
union to contact its members at Channel 7 via the company's e-mail
system. In a similar vein numerous accounts can be found in the press of
employees disciplined or dismissed for the circulation of "inappropriate"
e-mail messages.[90]

Paul Mobbs, a researcher writing about increased levels of monitoring
and surveillance of employees by employers, either on the justification of
security or to assess performance, cites an American Management Association study which found that in 1999 some 74 percent of U.S. companies

conducted some form of "active monitoring" of employees, with 38 percent monitoring employee e-mail. Mobbs describes such monitoring as a "form of intimidation."[91] In many countries, the surveillance of employees is now formalized through legislation or regulation. Mobbs gives the example of the United Kingdom's Regulation of Investigatory Powers Act of 2000, which "provides that the owner of a private telecommunications system may monitor that system lawfully, within certain limits."[92]

The right of workers to associate with a union of their choice, and to communicate with that union via the corporate communications network, is naturally a highly charged issue for unions, and has been taken up internationally by Union Network International (UNI),[93] the global umbrella body for many workers whose jobs involve the use of ICT, including e-mail. The "Online Rights for Online Workers"[94] section of UNI's Web site catalogs a series of infringements of employee rights, but also showcases a sample code of conduct[95] governing access to and use of ICT facilities by employees, which UNI recommends its affiliates seek to negotiate with employers. The code deals with the right of workers to utilize employer ICT communications facilities, as well as questions of surveillance and inappropriate online behavior. In a similar vein, the Congress of South African Trade Unions adopted in 1999 a landmark resolution that commits the affiliates of the federation to campaign actively to secure online workplace access rights for each and every shop steward to an employer-supplied computer with e-mail and Internet access.

## Conclusion

As we have seen, the rights of freedom of association and assembly have to a considerable extent been extended beyond their traditional domains as a growing range of individuals and organizations seeks to exploit the platforms and possibilities that the new ICT technologies provide for developing new forms of association and new spaces for assembly. The ability to access and use e-mail, the Internet, and the growing range of ICT technologies and tools has given new, twenty-first-century forms to association and assembly. From the action alert to the Web site to the blog, cyberactivism is on the move.

But those seeking to undermine or limit this use of cyberspace are also on the move, looking to block, limit, or monitor the use of the new ICT tools. Many of these attacks on the rights to associate freely and assemble peaceably in cyberspace are perpetrated by those regimes around the world whose track record of human rights violations in more traditional spheres is notably blemished.

Disturbingly, however, much of this intervention occurs in countries long considered bastions of democracy and freedom. It may be considerably different in scale and scope, but it is no less insidious. The prevalence and pervasiveness of the interference in respect of these rights has led the American Civil Liberties Union to coin the phrase "surveillance-industrial complex"[96] to describe the phenomenon.

The argument that the sinister nature of organized crime or "global terror" justifies such drastic countermeasures should be exposed for what it is: self-justification to interfere with the rights of individuals and organizations. Writing in the context of encryption, Geoffrey Gordon has noted how the undiscriminating nature of ICT technologies sets up the dilemma between the need to protect the freedom of association, and the freedom of speech that underpins it, and the duties and imperatives of law enforcement to combat criminals and "terrorists."[97] But such dilemmas are not new to ICTs: they are inherent in all human rights. Their very nature is to protect the guilty along with the innocent. And any limitation imposed on them needs to be sharply targeted and carefully framed. Gordon therefore concludes that it is "reasonable that human and civil rights activists claim an edge in the argument between anti-terrorism and pro-encryption."[98]

The undermining of the rights to freedom of association and assembly in the sphere of ICTs requires that human rights activists work to ensure that their protection is explicitly extended into cyberspace in a clear and codified way. This includes protecting the right of individuals to access the Internet, to send and receive e-mail, to participate in online blogs, and to make use of encryption technologies should they so choose. And we need to recognize how the right to freedom of association and assembly interfaces and interlinks with the other rights described and explored in this book. As one activist put it: "Freedom of speech plus freedom of assembly equals freedom of association."[99]

But we also need to recognize the interaction between online association and assembly and its manifestations in the flesh-and-blood world of the party meeting and the protest march. As the Mexican grassroots activist

Gustavo Esteva puts it: "E-mail is very useful as a means of contact between different groups. One of its main uses is to convene meetings. But then you meet."[100] The virtual exercise of freedom of association and assembly may be a new, ICT-enabled manifestation of those rights, but the struggle to protect them remains part of the long, proud, and integrated tradition of the protection of fundamental human rights worldwide. To return to the case described at the outset of this chapter, it is not enough to ensure that the mobile phones of Zimbabwe are able to beep loudly and openly, and that its e-mail messages and Web sites can carry the voices of opposition parties, NGOs, and trade unions. It is also imperative to ensure that its newspapers are unbanned, that rallies and meetings are no longer broken up by police whips and batons, that its citizens no longer reel from the brute force of bulldozer blades.

**Notes**

1. For a fuller report of events, see Zvakwana, "The Zimbabwe Situation," *Zvakwana Newsletter* no. 29 (June 3, 2003), available online at http://www.zimbabwesituation. com/jun4a_2003.html.

2. These included Zvakwana (Shona slang for "enough is enough," at http://www.zvakwana.org/), the NGO Network Alliance Project's Kubatana site (Shona for "working together," at http://www.kubatana.net), and Zimbabwe news portal ZWNews (at http://www.zwnews.com/).

3. See, for example: Crisis in Zimbabwe Coalition, *Defiance vs Repression: Critical Reflections on "the Final Push" June 2–6 2003* (Harare: Crisis in Zimbabwe Coalition, 2003), available online at http://zimbabwe.ms.dk/themes/zimupdate/ junemassactionreport.pdf.

4. See P. de Armond, "Netwar in the Emerald City: WTO Protest Strategy and Tactics," in *Networks and Netwars: The Future of Terror, Crime, and Militancy*, ed. by J. Arquilla and D. Ronfeldt (Santa Monica, CA: RAND, 2001), available online at http://www.rand.org/publications/MR/MR1382/MR1382.ch7.pdf.

5. APC, APC Betinho Communications Prize (San Francisco: Association for Progressive Communications, 2001), available online at http://www.apc.org/english/ betinho/2001/bet_app_full.shtml.

6. See http://www.kubatana.net.

7. Ibid.

8. Universal Declaration of Human Rights, Art. 21.

9. Ibid., Art. 12.

10. Ibid., Art. 13.

11. Ibid., Art. 18.

12. Ibid., Art. 19.

13. See Human Rights First, *The Neglected Right: Freedom of Association in International Human Rights Law* (New York: Human Rights First, 1997). Human Rights First was formerly the Lawyers Committee for Human Rights. See http://www. humanrightsfirst.org/pubs/descriptions/neglrt.htm.

14. Ibid.

15. See Human Rights Watch, *Zimbabwe's Non-Governmental Organizations Bill: Out of Sync with SADC Standards and a Threat to Civil Society Groups* (Human Rights Watch, 2004), available online at http://hrw.org/backgrounder/africa/zimbabwe/2004/12/ zimbabwe1204.pdf.

16. See L. Irish and K. Simon, "Freedom of Association: Recent Developments Regarding the 'Neglected Right,'" *International Journal of Not-for-Profit Law* 3, no. 2 (Dec. 2000).

17. See the International Covenant on Civil and Political Rights (1976); Article 21 recognizes the right of peaceful assembly, and Article 22 protects freedom of association.

18. European Convention on the Protection of Human Rights and Fundamental Freedoms (1953) and International Covenant on Civil and Political Rights (1976).

19. International Covenant on Civil and Political Rights (1976).

20. Constitution of the Republic of South Africa (1996).

21. See the definition in *Wikipedia*, which includes both the narrower, more historically accurate processing power formulation, as well as the broader and more recent pricing formulation, at http://en.wikipedia.org/wiki/Moore's_law.

22. "Blog" is a shortened form of "Weblog." Weblogs originally came to prominence in the late 1990s as an online, free-flowing, unstructured expression of individual thoughts and ideas, a "mixture in unique proportions of links, commentary, and personal thoughts and essays." R. Blood, *Weblogs: A History and Perspective* (2000). Available at: <http://www.rebeccablood.net/essays/weblog_history.html">. More recently a number of blogs have been devoted to debating and discussing a range of ideas, issues, and themes.

23. United Nations, Declaration on the Right and Responsibility of Individuals, Groups and Organs of Society to Promote and Protect Universally Recognized Human Rights and Fundamental Freedoms, General Assembly resolution 53/144

(1999), available online at http://www.unhchr.ch/huridocda/huridoca.nsf/(Symbol)/ A.RES.53.144.En?OpenDocument.

24. See, for example, T. Price, *Cyber Activism: Advocacy Groups and the Internet* (Washington, DC: Foundation for Public Affairs, 2000), available online at http://www.pac.org/pages/cyber_activism.pdf.

25. J. Arquilla and D. Ronfeldt, *The Advent of Netwar* (Santa Monica, CA: RAND, 1996).

26. J. Arquilla and D. Ronfeldt, "The Advent of Netwar (Revisited)," in Arquilla and Ronfeldt, *Networks and Netwars*, available online at http://www.rand.org/publications/MR/MR1382/MR1382.ch1.pdf.

27. See, for example, D. Conklin, "The Internet, Email, and Political Activism—The Case of Tiananmen Square," presentation to "Changing Media and Civil Society" workshop, European Consortium for Political Research, Edinburgh, Mar. 30, 2003, available online at http://www.essex.ac.uk/ECPR/events/jointsessions/paperarchive/edinburgh/ws20/David%20Conklin.pdf; and J. Arquilla and D. Ronfeldt, "Emergence and Influence of the Zapatista Social Netwar," in Arquilla and Ronfeldt, *Networks and Netwars*, available online at http://www.rand.org/publications/MR/MR1382/MR1382.ch6.pdf. Conklin notes that the Tiananmen Square case predates both the Zapatista movement and the Internet, and relied exclusively on e-mail.

28. S. Wray, *Transforming Luddite Resistance into Virtual Luddite Resistance: Weaving a World Wide Web of Electronic Civil Disobedience* (Free Range Activism, 1998), available online at http://www.fraw.org.uk/library/003/hacktivism/wray_resistance.html.

29. M. Castells, *The Information Age: Economy, Society and Culture*, vol. 2, *The Power of Identity* (Malden, MA: Blackwell, 1997).

30. De Armond, "Netwar in the Emerald City."

31. See its Web site at http://www.indymedia.org/.

32. Indymedia, "About Indymedia" (n.d.), http://www.indymedia.org/en/static/about.shtml.

33. De Armond, "Netwar in the Emerald City."

34. See, for example, H. Rheingold, *Smart Mobs: The Next Social Revolution* (Cambridge, MA: Perseus, 2002).

35. D. Rothkopf, "Cyberpolitik: The Changing Nature of Power in the Information Age," *Journal of International Affairs* 51, no. 2 (Spring 1998), available online at http://www.ciaonet.org/olj/jia/jia_98rothkopf.html.

36. Ibid.

37. D. Bollier, *The Rise of Netpolitik: How the Internet Is Changing International Politics and Diplomacy* (Washington, DC: Aspen Institute, 2003).

38. See European Convention on the Protection of Human Rights and Fundamental Freedoms (1953) and International Covenant on Civil and Political Rights (1976).

39. See ILO, "Freedom of Association and Protection of the Right to Organize," Convention no. 87 (Geneva: ILO, 1948), available online at http://www.ilo.org/ilolex/cgi-lex/convde.pl?C087; and ILO, "Right to Organize and Collective Bargaining," Convention no. 98 (Geneva: ILO, 1949), available online at http://www.ilo.org/ilolex/cgi-lex/convde.pl?C098. The ILO is not, despite the common misperception, a labor body, but rather a tripartite forum with labor, employer, and government representation. Its conventions are subject to ratification by individual member states, and need to be given effect through national legislation.

40. For two seminal works, see E. Lee, *The Labour Movement and the Internet: The New Internationalism* (London: Pluto Press, 1997); and A. Shostak, *cyberUnion: Empowering Labor Through Computer Technology* (Armonk, NY: M. E. Sharpe, 1999).

41. The author served from 1994 to 2001 as COSATU's head of IT. The account here is presented from a participant observer point of view. For a fuller, more historical account, see C. Lewis, *Unions and Cyber-activism in South Africa—Critical Perspectives on International Business* (Durham, UK: University of Durham, forthcoming).

42. SEIU, "Justice for Janitors" (Washington, DC: SEIU, n.d.), available online at http://www.seiu.org/building/janitors/.

43. See E. Lee, *Wal-Mart, Workers and the Web* (2005), available online at http://www.ericlee.me.uk/archive/000116.html.

44. See, for example, A. Bibby, *Organising in Financial Call Centres* (Geneva: Union Network International, 2002), and *Trade Unions and Telework: A Report for FIET* (1996), available online at http://www.eclipse.co.uk/pens/bibby/telework.html.

45. See http://www.labourstart.org/actnow.shtml. For a similar example, see UNI, "Standard Chartered Must Reinstate Sacked Zimbabwe Bank Staff" (2001), available online at http://www.union-network.org/uniindep.nsf/f0fa5a094742095ac1256800 00253538/c4861752f084d186c12569dd003674b9?OpenDocument.

46. E. Lee, *How the Internet Is Changing Unions* (London: LabourStart, 2000), http://www.labourstart.org/workingusa.shtml.

47. Ibid.

48. S. Walker, *To Picket Just Click It! Social Netwar and Industrial Conflict in a Global Economy* (Leeds, UK: School of Information Management, Leeds Metropolitan University, 2001).

49. See Arquilla and Ronfeldt, *The Advent of Netwar*, and *Networks and Netwars*.

50. The Cyber Picket Line is now located at http://www.cf.ac.uk/socsi/union/. Originally founded by Steve Davies in 1997, it no longer profiles union campaigns but still hosts an extremely valuable "World Trade Union Directory."

51. S. Davies, "Union Flying Pickets Head into Cyberspace," Press Release from Stephen Davies, DaviesSM3@cardiff.ac.uk, on International Workers Day, 1 May 1997, Cyber Picket Line, University of Cardiff. For other, more recent writing on cyberspace and its use by and impact on the labor movement, see A. Bibby, "International Trade Union Activity and Work of Works Councils on the Internet," report prepared for int.unity, United Services Union (ver.di), Stuttgart, available online at http://www.andrewbibby.com/socialpartners/intunity.pdf; W. Diamond and R. Freeman, "Will Unionism Prosper in Cyberspace? The Promise of the Internet for Employee Organisation," *British Journal of Industrial Relations* 40, no. 3 (Sept. 2002); R. Darlington, "The Creation of the e-Union, the Use of ICT by British Unions" (rev. July 2004), http://www.rogerdarlington.co.uk/E-union.html.

52. See, for example, Amnesty International, *People's Republic of China: State Control of the Internet in China* (London: Amnesty International, 2002), available online at http://web.amnesty.org/library/index/engasa170072002; Amnesty International, *Socialist Republic of Viet Nam: Freedom of Expression Under Threat in Cyberspace* (London: Amnesty International, 2003), available online at http://www.web. amnesty.org/library/index/engasa410372003; M. Chase and J. Mulvenon, *You've Got Dissent! Chinese Dissident Use of the Internet and Beijing's Counter-Strategies* (Santa Monica, CA: RAND, 2002), available online at http://www.rand.org/publications/ MR/MR1543/; Privacy International and GreenNet, "Silenced: Censorship and Control of the Internet," (London: Privacy International & GreenNet Educational Trust, 2003), available online at http://pi.gn.apc.org/survey/censorship/Silenced. pdf; F. Rodriquez, "Burning the Village to Roast the Pig: Censorship of Online Media," paper for the OSCE workshop "Freedom of the Media and the Internet," Nov. 30, 2002, http://www.xs4all.nl/%7Efelipe/OSCE_paper.pdf.

53. A. Al-Rasheed, "The Internet in Saudi Arabia," presentation to Communications Engineering Technical Exchange Meeting (CETEM), Apr. 30–May 2, 2001 (Al-Dhahran: ARAMCO, 2001), available online at http://www.isu.net.sa/library/ CETEM2001-AlRasheed.pdf. The ISU's Web site currently lists twenty-one ISPs in operation at http://www.isu.net.sa/saudi-internet/local-information/All-isps.htm.

54. J. Zittrain and B. Edelman, *Documentation of Internet Filtering in Saudi Arabia* (Cambridge, MA: Berkman Center for Internet and Society, Harvard Law School, (2002), available online at http://cyber.law.harvard.edu/filtering/saudiarabia/.

55. See ISU, "Local Content Filtering Policy" (Riyadh: Internet Services Unit, n.d.), http://www.isu.net.sa/saudi-internet/contenet-filtring/filtring-policy.htm.

56. Ibid.

57. Zittrain and Edelman, *Documentation of Internet Filtering in Saudi Arabia*.

58. Slightly dated (2001) figures from Human Rights Watch, *Freedom of Expression and the Internet in China: A Human Rights Watch Backgrounder* (New York: Human Rights Watch, n.d.), available online at http://www.hrw.org/backgrounder/asia/china-bck-0701.htm.

59. J. Zittrain and B. Edelman, *Empirical Analysis of Internet Filtering in China* (Cambridge, MA: Berkman Center for Internet & Society, Harvard Law School, 2002), available online at http://cyber.law.harvard.edu/filtering/china/.

60. Ibid. In each case they found all of the top ten results, and between 20% and 65% of the top 100, were blocked.

61. BBC, "China Blocks Second Search Website," Sept. 6, 2002, http://news.bbc.co.uk/1/hi/technology/2240493.stm.

62. OpenNet Initiative, "Probing Chinese Search Engine Filtering," Bulletin 005, Aug. 19, 2004, http://www.opennetinitiative.net/bulletins/005/.

63. Author's own search, performed on Jan. 18, 2005.

64. Zittrain and Edelman, *Empirical Analysis of Internet Filtering in China*.

65. Zim Online, "Zimbabwe Government Prepares to Bug Internet," *Zim Online*, July 30, 2004, http://www.zimonline.co.za/. "Internet Too Big for Zimbabwe to Control?," *Zim Online*, July 31, 2004, http://www.zimonline.co.za/. Both articles appear to have been deleted from Zim Online. A copy of the first can be found at http://www.zimbabwesituation.com/jul30_2004.html#link7 and a copy of the second appears at http://www.zimbabwesituation.com/jul31_2004.html#link2.

66. Zittrain and Edelman, *Empirical Analysis of Internet Filtering in China*.

67. See Amnesty International, *People's Republic of China;* and Tibetan Centre for Human Rights and Democracy, *Human Rights Updates* (Dharamsala: TCHRD, Apr. 2004), available online at http://www.tchrd.org/hrupdate/2004/hr200404.html.

68. Amnesty International, *People's Republic of China*.

69. See A. Weekes, "The State of Labour Media in South Africa in 1999" (1999), http://lmedia.nodong.net/1999/archive/e30.htm. The episode is also recorded in Privacy International and GreenNet, "Silenced."

70. Ibid.

71. Zim Online, "Internet Too Big for Zimbabwe to Control?" Zim Online, July 31, 2004, http://www.zimonline.co.za/. The article appears to have been deleted from ZimOnline. A copy appears at http://www.zimbabwesituation.com/jul31_2004.html#link2.

72. Rodriquez, "Burning the Village to Roast the Pig."

73. Available at http://www.ultrareach.com/company/technology.htm.

74. The author was unable to locate a download site for this widely reported product, allegedly by Dynaweb.

75. Reported on by Rodriquez, "Burning the Village to Roast the Pig." See also http://www.peek-a-booty.org.

76. See http://freenet.sourceforge.net/.

77. See also BBC, "Bypassing China's Net Firewall," Mar. 10, 2004, http://news.bbc.co.uk/1/hi/technology/3548035.stm.

78. See, for example, Z. Rodgers, "Study: URL-Based E-Mail Blocking on the Rise," *ClickZ News*, Sept. 27, 2004, http://www.clickz.com/news/article.php/3413501; Assurance Systems, "Fourth Quarter 2002 Email Blocking and Filtering Report," http://www.assurancesys.com/f/fourth-quarter-email-blocking-and-filtering-report.pdf. Both are e-mail direct marketers seeking to avoid having their e-mail blocked.

79. Many of the reports (such as the valuable work of Zittrain and Edelman) referred to in the previous section focus exclusively on Internet filtering. Others also touch on official interference with e-mail traffic.

80. Privacy International and GreenNet, *Silenced*.

81. See, for example, P. Poole, "Echelon: America's Secret Global Surveillance Network" (1999), http://fly.hiwaay.net/~pspoole/echelon.html. The Echelon Research Resources page on this Web site (http://fly.hiwaay.net/~pspoole/echres.html) contains links to several hundred news articles prior to 2001.

82. European Parliament, "Report on the Existence of a Global System for the Interception of Private and Commercial Communications (ECHELON Interception System)," 2001/2098(INI) (Brussels, EP, July 11, 2001), available online at http://www.fas.org/irp/program/process/rapport_echelon_en.pdf. The report's proposed resolution was adopted on Sept. 5, 2001, with minor wording changes (see http://www.statewatch.org/news/2001/sep/05echelonres.htm).

83. See http://www.pgpi.org and http://www.pgp.com.

84. G eoffrey Gordon, "Breaking the Code: What Encryption Means for the First Amendment and Human Rights," *Columbia Human Rights Law Review* 32 (2001): 477–515.

85. Ibid.

86. Chase and Mulvenon, *You've Got Dissent!*

87. Ibid.

88. Ibid.

89. See Australian Broadcasting Corporation, "Federal Court Makes Landmark e-Mail Ruling," Apr. 7, 2000, http://www.abc.net.au/news/2000/04/item20000407 124451_1.htm, copy archived on Asia Pacific Network Information centre mailing list, http://www.apnic.net/mailing-lists/apple/archive/2000/04/msg00006.html. "Union Claims Victory in e-Mail Case," Apr. 7, 2000, http://www.abc.net.au/pm/stories/s117056.htm.

90. See, for example, "Workers Sacked over e-Mail Porn Could Take Case to IRC," *Sydney Morning Herald*, Sept. 4, 2003, http://www.smh.com.au/articles/2003/09/04/1062548953378.html; and "Blogger Sacked for Sounding Off," *The Guardian*, Jan. 12, 2005, http://www.guardian.co.uk/uk_news/story/0,3604,1388249,00.html.

91. P. Mobbs, "Electronic Rights in the Workplace: Changes to Workers Rights and Employers Responsibilities in the New Information Economy," *GreenNet CSIR Toolkit Briefing* no. 10, http://www.internetrights.org.uk/.

92. Ibid.

93. See http://www.union-network.org/.

94. See http://www.union-network.org/UNIsite/Sectors/IBITS/ICT/online.htm.

95. UNI, "On-line Rights at Work: A UNI Code of Practice," http://www.union-network.org/UNIsite/Sectors/IBITS/ICT/documents/On-lineCodeE.pdf.

96. J. Stanley, *The Surveillance-Industrial Complex: How the American Government Is Conscripting Businesses and Individuals in the Construction of a Surveillance Society* (New York: American Civil Liberties Union, 2004), available online at http://www.aclu.org/Files/OpenFile.cfm?id=16225.

97. Gordon, "Breaking the Code."

98. Ibid.

99. P. Kellman, "Labor Organizing and Freedom of Association," *Rachel's Environment & Health News* no. 697 (May 18, 2000), available online at http://www.garynull.com/Documents/erf/LaborOrganizingFreedomAssociation.htm.

100. Gustavo Esteva, Mexican grassroots activist, interviewed by Sophie Style, *Z magazine* (May 2001), available online at http://www.zmag.org/zmag/may01style.htm.

# 7 The Right to Political Participation and the Information Society

Hans Klein

The right to political participation refers to citizens' right to seek to influence public affairs. Political participation can take many forms, the most notable of which is voting in elections, but also includes joining a political party, standing as a candidate in an election, joining a non-governmental advocacy group, or participating in a demonstration. The foundational legal articulation of this right can be found in the 1948 Universal Declaration of Human Rights, and it has been further formalized and elaborated in later treaties, most notably the 1976 International Covenant on Civil and Political Rights. As currently implemented by the United Nations, various operating entities assess signatory states' respect for this right and, when violations are determined to have occurred, may call on states to change their practices.

One aspect of the right to political participation merits special attention: its status as a *political* right. The right to political participation is restricted to *citizens*. Whereas the other rights recognized in the Covenant inhere in human beings on the basis of their status as human beings, the right to political participation is limited to people endowed with the status of citizen. Such a status does not exist in isolation. A person can be a citizen only in the context of a political community and, most significantly, a government, and thus the right to political participation presupposes the existence of a government.

With respect to the information society, this presupposition of a government raises a potentially thorny issue: Does the information society have a government? Are there citizens in the information society? If there is no government, then there may be no citizens, and if there are no citizens, then there may be no citizen rights. Thus the right to political participation in the information society hinges on whether that society has a government.

I consider two classes of institutions that might be considered governments of the information society. The first (and less interesting possibility) is that existing political institutions—national governments—constitute the government of the information society. In that case, citizenship and rights in the information society are no different from those in society generally.

The second, more novel possibility is that the information society is a society in its own right and has its own political institutions. In this second view, public affairs in the information society are conducted in political institutions separate from existing national governments. These new institutions constitute "governments," the people participating in those governments are "citizens," and the right of political participation applies to those citizens. I explore this line of thinking with respect to two candidate political institutions for the information society: the free and open source software movement (FOSS) and the Internet Corporation for Assigned Names and Numbers (ICANN).

In what follows, I first summarize the international legal instruments that define the right to political participation. Then I consider that right in relation to two conceptualizations of the information society, one as an information-rich society and the other as a distinct society. I conclude with some reflections on the need to define and enforce rights in the new institutions of governance and public affairs.

## Right to Political Participation

Two foundational instruments define the right to political participation: the 1948 Universal Declaration of Human Rights (Declaration) and the 1976 International Covenant on Civil and Political Rights (Covenant). The Declaration is a statement of general principles. Since it is not a treaty, the standards of behavior that it defines have only the status of nonbinding norms, but the document is nonetheless of enormous legal and political importance, for it provided the foundation not only for later, legally binding international treaties but also for many national governments' rights frameworks.

Ratified almost three decades years after the Declaration, the Covenant is similar to the earlier document in its content but enjoys the status of international law. As a binding treaty, the Covenant imposes obligations on signatory states and includes compliance mechanisms.

The right to participate is spelled out in similar language in the Declaration (Article 21) and the Covenant (Article 25). Article 25 of the Covenant states:

Every citizen shall have the right and the opportunity, without . . . unreasonable restrictions:

(a) To take part in the conduct of public affairs, directly or through freely chosen representatives;
(b) To vote and to be elected at genuine periodic elections which shall be by universal and equal suffrage and shall be held by secret ballot, guaranteeing the free expression of the will of the electors. (quoted in Steiner 1988)

This right has some distinguishing characteristics. As noted above, it is a political right that presupposes a political community with individual members (citizens) and with an organizational form (government). The Covenant and the Declaration refer to this political status differently, with the Covenant referring to "citizens" ("Every *citizen* shall have the right . . .") and the Declaration referring to "government" ("Everyone has the right to take part in the *government* of his country . . ."; emphases added.) With both formulations conditioning the right to participation on the existence of political institutions, it is clear that this right does not exist as a human right per se but only in the context of the political institutions of citizenship and government.

The Covenant refers to participation in both a general and a specific form. Participation in its general form is "to take part in the conduct of public affairs." Public affairs might include the activities of civic associations, neighborhood groups, social movements, and social clubs, as well as formal procedures of governments. Thus, although participants in public affairs must be citizens, the domain of action is not restricted to formal political institutions but includes social activities of a public nature. The second form of participation is more specific: elections. Elections are just one mode of public participation, but they are widely recognized and utilized. Whether a central element in a political system or just a limited one, whether open to all citizens or just some, most governments incorporate some kind of election in some part of their system. As the one mechanism specifically identified in this treaty, elections are assigned a special importance for participation.

The Covenant also suggests criteria for citizenship. Since different political systems have historically conditioned citizenship on various factors, such as wealth, gender, race, age, and mental capacity, the criteria of citizenship are always an important element of participation. The Covenant's language on elections refers to "universal and equal suffrage," which suggests that citizenship should also be universally and equally available. Who can enjoy citizenship and the concomitant right of political participation remains undefined, but the implication is for an inclusive definition.

Nearly 150 states have signed the Covenant, thereby agreeing to respect and implement the rights defined in the treaty. In operational terms, the treaty is implemented in a Human Rights Committee comprised of eighteen individual experts. Signatory states must periodically submit reports on their treaty compliance to the committee, which then holds additional public sessions in which nongovernmental organizations can participate. The committee makes a critical review of the reports and issues its own comments. Although its comments are not legally binding, they can bring public attention to states' practices. Ultimately, the Covenant does not benefit from strong enforcement mechanisms. The treaty did not create a Human Rights Court able to give an authoritative interpretation of the treaty's terms, and the Human Rights Committee has little real power (Nickel 2003).

In summary, the right to political participation is restricted to citizens but allows them to take part in all public affairs of their country, with special emphasis on participation in elections. Next I consider the relevance of political participation to the information society.

## Society in the Information Age

People increasingly live in information-rich societies. The creation, manipulation, and distribution of information have become some of the most important activities in today's world, be they in economics, culture, or politics. The importance and ubiquity of information are striking.

For our analysis of human rights, an important question is how to conceptualize this information-rich society. How novel is it? Is today's society fundamentally the same as it has always been? For example, for a resident of a U.S. city, is the society he or she lives in richer in information but still recognizably a U.S. society? Or are we experiencing something so novel that it constitutes a new kind of society, something we can call an "information society"? Does a U.S. resident now live in two societies—a U.S. society and an information society? Is the information society distinct?

The status of society is important for questions of political rights. Political rights exist in the context of governments, and governments exist in the context of societies. The modern state is defined not only by its territory but also by the society over which it rules. If today's information-rich society is coeval with existing society, then the existing government and the existing rights apply to that society. In this case, the right to political participation exists as we know it: it is a right established by international treaty and enforced by U.N. entities on national governments. The right to political participation in an information-rich society is not different from what it was in less information-rich times. For example, we already know that U.S. society is governed by the U.S. government, and we know (more or less) the status of political rights in the United States. As U.S. society adapts to the information age, questions of human rights in the contemporary (and information-rich) U.S. society are still questions about human rights. These are interesting questions, but they are also familiar.

Political participation might consist of seeking to take part in public affairs regarding information. Citizens might seek to influence tax policies for e-commerce, the regulation of online content, the definition of new forms of intellectual property, or the setting of privacy protections. Despite the novelty of the policies, the nature of public participation could be quite conventional. Citizens could vote (e.g., for candidates promising greater information security), they could sign petitions (e.g., against surveillance), they could demonstrate (e.g., against online pornography), and so forth. In so doing, they would be exercising their right to political participation. Should their government violate that right, the violation might be a candidate for review and possible comment by the U.N. entities that enforce the 1976 International Covenant on Civil and Political Rights.

It is worth noting that even if the status of a political right is not significantly changed, information systems may create more opportunities to exercise that right. An information-rich society offers powerful new means to exercise the right of political participation. For example, as the technology of voting changes, electronic voting systems offer benefits and risks for elections (Kohno et al. 2004). As the technology of public forums changes, e-mail lists facilitate the formation of citizen associations (Klein 1999). Election campaigns, too, are being transformed by the Internet (Bimber and Davis 2003). In the information society, the mode of participation changes as new technologies become available. Still, these new modes apply to participation in established institutions according to established rights.

The situation is considerably different if the information society exists in its own right. In that case, existing institutions no longer apply, and we need to reconsider our notions of society, government, citizenship, and right.

## The Information Society

The claim that there exists an information society in its own right is most strongly made with respect to cyberspace. A not insubstantial literature makes the claim that when we log on to the Internet, we leave physical space behind and enter a different dimension of existence with unique properties and unique social relationships. In cyberspace, personal identity is malleable (Turkle 1984). We are freed from our physical appearance: "no one knows you are a dog" (Steiner 1993). We enter an "electronic frontier" area where rules of social behavior are not firmly established and there are no lawmaking authorities (Rheingold 1993). We find an "Internet community" there that designs its own world through "rough consensus and running code" (Huizer 1996). This information society is an "unregulable" place of benevolent anarchy (Lessig 1999), where the sovereigns of the physical world have no power (Barlow n.d.). In cyberspace, people cooperate and produce information and knowledge in a manner that seems to contradict existing societies' laws of economics (Litman 2001). Space ceases to exist as people from around the world interact in immediate relations. Although there have been systems of global communication predating the Internet, cyberspace is unique in that it is a global *social* system where people immediately coexist and interact. In all these ways, cyberspace constitutes a distinct, separate, and autonomous "information society."

As opposed to the vision of an information-rich society described earlier, this information society is novel and distinct. No existing governments seem appropriate to exercise sovereignty over it. It presents fundamental puzzles about politics. What are the public affairs in this society, and where are they conducted? Does the information society have "information citizens" who conduct their public affairs in an "information government"? Increasingly, we can find answers to these questions. The information society does have its public affairs, and these public affairs are conducted in specific locations.

I consider two settings for public affairs in the information society. The first is the free software movement, and the second is ICANN.

In his book *Code and Other Laws of Cyberspace*, Lawrence Lessig (1999) argues that public decisions about the information society are made in processes of software development. Public policies for the information society are realized not by governmental decision but by technology design. For example, a technical standard may enhance or inhibit the anonymity of the user of a computer network, or copy-protection software may effectively define the fair-use rights of copyrighted materials. The properties of cyberspace are not fixed but can be designed (and redesigned) to embed values and governance capabilities in the system. In this way, the design of code is similar to the design of regulations. Code can make some behaviors impossible and others unavoidable, just as laws may make some behaviors legal and others illegal. Code is law.

There is an important difference between code and law, however. Law is produced in political institutions, whereas software is not. Citizens have a right to participate in legislative processes in political institutions; they can have a voice in the production of law-based regulations. In software development they have no such right. The design of software is not categorized as a political activity, and it does not occur in political institutions. It occurs in private forums, such as standards-setting committees, or within a single private company (Microsoft, for example). Although the decisions made in such places may have broad social impacts, access to the decision process may be forbidden. There is no right to participate in the internal processes of a private firm, even if that firm's software design decisions shape the information society.

Lessig finds a remedy to this situation in the free and open source software movement (FOSS). Software development processes in FOSS are open and participatory. This transparency makes it difficult for any entity to embed its interests or values into the software. The FOSS software development process ensures that any regulatory features are publicly vetted. In FOSS the characteristics of the process are well matched to the characteristics of the product: code that is law is developed through an open and transparent process which resembles good legislative procedure.

Indeed, public interest political groups have participated in code development. In the United States, the Center for Democracy and Technology (CDT) currently operates a project on Internet standards, technology, and policy in which it publicizes policy-relevant features of technical standards. The projects seek to "provide the public policy community with a . . . window into the Internet technical standards processes and the possible impact of new technical standards on issues of public concern" (CDT 2005). CDT has identified and publicized lawlike features of code in geolocational and telephone numbering (ENUM) standards.

FOSS processes allow for greater political participation, but they do define a formal right to participate. Software development activities are loosely structured, and there is no status of "citizen." Expertise rather than citizenship determines who can shape code. Openness and transparency serve to protect the public interest.

The second example of a governance institution in the information society is the Internet Corporation for Assigned Names and Numbers (ICANN). Created in 1998, ICANN is the global authority for allocating Internet identifiers (including Internet protocol addresses and domain names). It ensures that no two servers use the same identifier and that Internet addressing operates in a stable manner.

Although frequently described as a purely technical body, ICANN conducts public affairs. Its decisions have policy content. ICANN defines intellectual property rights in domain names (e.g., apple.com), it sets the base price for domain names, and it controls access to the domain name retail and wholesale markets (Klein 2002). Utility pricing, property rights definition, and market regulation are all classic public policy powers. The information society is regulated in important ways by ICANN.

Yet ICANN was incorporated as a nongovernmental corporation. Thus, with the public affairs of the information society conducted in a nongovernmental (private) institution, the right to political participation does not necessarily apply. (At the time of this writing, ICANN remains legally subordinate to the U.S. government, so its nongovernmental status was never fully realized. This is addressed below.)

As ICANN was originally designed, its corporate bylaws did take account of its political functions. Its designers recognized that they were creating a quasi-political institution, and they included mechanisms for popular sovereignty for the inhabitants of cyberspace. The bylaws reserved almost half of the positions on ICANN's board of directors for representatives of Internet users. The bylaws gave the people of the information society the right to participate in public affairs via representatives on the board.

ICANN subsequently elaborated a right to participate. It defined election rules to fill the user positions on its board through elections in which Internet users from around the globe could vote. Anyone over age sixteen who possessed an e-mail address and a physical mailing address had a right to vote for ICANN directors. These "citizens" (whose legal status was that of "at-large members" of a California-incorporated, nonprofit corporation) were thus allowed to participate in ICANN's public affairs. Although non-governmental, ICANN met a standard for public participation comparable with governments of other societies. The information society had citizens, a government, and elections.

Unfortunately, citizens' right to political participation in the information society was short-lived. In 2002, in what the U.S.-based Carter Center called a "palace coup," the industry representatives on ICANN's board eliminated user elections and representation. ICANN's board of directors radically modified its corporate bylaws, reducing citizen participation to an advisory committee whose members were appointed by the board of directors. Citizen participation in public affairs was rendered meaningless, and industry's control of public affairs was consolidated.

ICANN offers mixed lessons. As with FOSS, we can see that public affairs in the information society occur in novel institutional settings and are deeply intertwined with technical activities. Yet norms of participation did carry over to this new setting, where they were implemented in ICANN's bylaws. Unfortunately, political dynamics of interest and power that were already familiar in existing societies manifested themselves in the information society, and the information society's fledgling democracy was toppled within two years of its first election. Citizen participation in public affairs largely ceased.

## Conclusion

Our understanding of the right to participate depends on our conception of the information society. Conceived as the *information-rich* society, the information society is governed by the familiar institutions of national governments, in which citizens have a right to participate in the conduct of public affairs. The 1976 Covenant guarantees that right, and should states violate it, then its (weak) enforcement mechanisms can be brought to bear. On the other hand, if we conceive of the information society as a distinct society with distinct, emergent governance institutions that do not conform to the established definition of "political," then the notion of citizens' right to participate is more problematic. When public affairs are conducted in nongovernmental institutions, the right to participate is not guaranteed by laws binding upon governments.

Both FOSS and ICANN indicate the possibility of establishing a right to political participation in the information society. In FOSS, rights may be established through precedent and customary practice. As groups like CDT participate in software development processes, they raise awareness of the appropriateness and utility of such participation. Public awareness and established practice give substance to claims of right. Over time, participation in software development may come to be seen as right and natural, and in this way it may someday win formal recognition. This is an admittedly lengthy process. Also, it is relevant only if FOSS becomes a widely used mechanism for software development. FOSS offers us the *prospect* of a right to participation. Participation could also be formalized by articulating it in rules for participation on standards bodies.

ICANN offers a clearer lesson. If defined a right to participate, but that right suffered from too little legal protection. Expressed only in the bylaws of the corporation, it was eliminated by a majority vote of the board. Additional, less formal protections also failed: the national governments that oversaw ICANN in its early years probably could have used their influence to prevent the board's action. They failed to do so. Without sufficient protection, the right was eliminated, and meaningful public participation ceased. Yet the need for it did not decrease. ICANN remains in effect a global public utility and a global regulatory agency, and without user participation it suffers from a legitimacy deficit.

The right to participate could be reestablished in ICANN, but it would have to be in a more robust form. If the right were to be embedded in ICANN's corporate charter, it would be more robust, for charter revisions require a super-majority of the board. This would offer greater protection. A more strongly secured right to participation could be effective.

Such suggestions for securing rights in emergent governance institutions may be irrelevant, however. A different evolution of governance in the information society seems more likely. National governments are likely to chip away at the autonomy of the information society and to integrate its governance into existing institutions. The ICANN "coup" largely discredited the emergent political institutions of the information society. Following that event, movement toward ending U.S. oversight of ICANN slowed and may have ended. Simultaneously, the United Nations launched its World Summit on the Information Society (WSIS), at which national governments asserted their authority over ICANN and the information society generally. As traditional political institutions increasingly take over, the traditional rights of participation that inhere in national governments will serve as the legal framework for citizen participation.

The challenge of political participation in ICANN is increasingly the same as that for other global governance organizations (e.g., the World Trade Organization). It is less a challenge of a unique information society than of a functional system that crosses national boundaries. Global governance needs legitimate political authority, and currently that seems available only through intergovernmental organizations such as the United Nations. The right to political participation is formally guaranteed in such settings, because the national governments that are the building blocks of intergovernmental organizations recognize it. True, the right is even weaker and more attenuated here than in national governments, but nonetheless it exists. To the extent that mechanisms and rights of political participation develop, they will likely be in the traditional context of national and intergovernmental political institutions.

## References

Barlow, John Perry. "Cyberspace Independence Declaration." N.d. http://www.eff.org/~barlow.

Bimber, Bruce, and Richard Davis. *Campaigning Online: The Internet in U.S. Elections.* New York: Oxford University Press, 2003.

CDT (Center for Democracy and Technology). "Internet Standards, Technology and Policy Project." May 24, 2005. www.cdt.org/standards/bulletin/2.01.shtml.

Huizer, Eric. "RFC 2031- IETF-ISOC Relationship." Published by the Internet Engineering Task Force. 1996. http://www.ietf.org/rfc/rfc2031.txt?number=2031.

Klein, Hans. "Tocqueville in Cyberspace: Using the Internet for Citizen Associations." *The Information Society*, 15, no. 4 (1999): 213–220.

Klein, Hans. "The Feasibility of Global Democracy: Understanding ICANN's At Large Elections." *Info.* 3, no. 4 (2001): 333–345.

Klein, Hans. "ICANN and Internet Governance: Leveraging Technical Coordination to Make Global Public Policy." *The Information Society* 18, no. 3 (2002): 193–207.

Kohno, Tadayoshi, Adam Stubblefield, Aviel D. Rubin, and Dan S. Wallach. "Analysis of an Electronic Voting System." Presented at IEEE Symposium on Security and Privacy, May 9–12, 2004. http://avirubin.com/vote.pdf.

Lessig, Lawrence. *Code and Other Laws of Cyberspace*. New York: Basic Books, 1999.

Litman, Jessica. *Digital Copyright*. Amherst, NY: Prometheus Books, 2001.

Mueller, Milton. "ICANN and Internet Governance." *Info.* 1, no. 6 (1999): 477–500.

Nickel, James. "Human Rights." In Edward N. Zalta (ed.), "The Stanford Encyclopedia of Philosophy" (Summer 2003). http://plato.stanford.edu/archives/sum2003/entries/rights-human/.

Rheingold, Howard. *The Virtual Community: Homesteading on the Electronic Frontier*. Reading, MA: Addison-Wesley, 1993.

Steiner, Henry J. "Political Participation as a Human Right." *Harvard Human Rights Yearbook*, vol. 1, 77–134. Cambridge, MA: Harvard Law School 1988.

Steiner, Peter. "On the Internet, Nobody Knows You Are a Dog." *The New Yorker*, July 5, 1993, p. 5.

Turkle, Sherry. *The Second Self: Computers and the Human Spirit*. New York: Simon and Schuster, 1984.

# 8 The "Guarantee Rights" for Realizing the Rule of Law

Meryem Marzouki

When addressing the global issue of human rights in the information society, and how these rights may translate in such a context, one immediately thinks of civil and political rights that should be directly and naturally exercised through information and communication means, or protected against their misuse.

These obviously include the right to freedom of expression and to seek, receive, and impart information; the right to access public information and to take part in the conduct of public affairs; and the right to privacy.

Then, following a vision of an inclusive information society where all categories of individuals, social groups, minorities, and peoples have access to information and communication—where access means not only access to infrastructure but also appropriation and use of technology for empowerment and social justice—come issues related to non-discrimination, such as the right for men and women to enjoy all rights equally, rights for minorities to enjoy their own culture and to use their own language, the right to education and knowledge, the right to participate in the cultural life and to enjoy the benefits of scientific progress and its applications, the right to development, and the principle of non-discrimination itself.

Furthermore, in an extended understanding of the concepts of association, assembly, movement, and so on, the right to freedom of peaceful assembly and association emerges as an issue to be addressed in this context.

However, despite almost a decade of intense regulatory and legislative processes at the national, regional, and international levels, and despite many references to the rule of law in official outcomes of the first phase of the World Summit on the Information Society (WSIS) at Geneva in December 2003, fundamental human rights such as the right to a fair trial, the right to the presumption of innocence, the right to an effective remedy, the right to equality before the law, and the principle of no punishment without law are seldom if ever addressed in the context of information and communication.

This chapter will provide a rationale for the legitimate inclusion of these rights in the debate on human rights in the information society, showing how, as "guarantee rights," they are necessary conditions for the realization of the rule of law, and thus for the effective enjoyment of all other human rights; how they have been particularly challenged by regulatory and legislative processes that make procedural rather than substantive changes in the legislation; and, finally, how these rights may be upheld and effectively implemented in the information society.

### Historical and Legal Background

The origins of the "guarantee rights," protecting individuals against the arbitrary use of political power, date back to the Magna Carta, signed by King John of England on June 15, 1215. This historical document was a peaceful settlement between the monarchy and the nobility of England, which was tired of paying extra taxes for John's unsuccessful campaigns to regain lost territories in France. Among its sixty-three clauses, which mainly address the elimination of fines and punishments considered unfair by the nobility, and give power and privileges to the Catholic Church, to the feudality, and to the merchants, three of them (38, 39 and 40)[1] address what has been acknowledged as the right to the presumption of innocence and the right to a fair trial. The most famous of these clauses provides that "No free man shall be seized or imprisoned, or stripped of his rights or possessions . . . except by the lawful judgment of his peers." Although still limited in its scope ("free man," "peers"), the Magna Carta is now seen as the first guarantee provided by law to individuals against the arbitrary use of power—at that time by the monarchy and later by the state.

This concept was further developed, extended, and detailed during the seventeenth century, through legal acts imposed by the House of Commons on the monarchy (Lochak 2002): the Petition of Rights (1628) prohibited arbitrary arrest and imprisonment, and required a regular defense procedure; the Petition of Rights resulted mainly from the *Five Knights* case, in which a writ of habeas corpus had been brought.[2] Such a protection against abusive detention was formalized with the Habeas Corpus Act (1679), under Charles II. The habeas corpus (Latin, "you have the body") procedure still exists in most common law systems, and has a constitutional value in the United States. A writ of habeas corpus is brought to a court to have the legality of an imprisonment examined, and if the procedure is found illegal, the person is freed. Further, the English Bill of Rights (1689) required King William (of Orange) and Queen Mary, when they were crowned, to swear that they would obey the laws of Parliament.

As emphasized by Danièle Lochak, a common feature of these legal acts and documents is that they all aim at remedying precise abuses by defining concrete rules of procedure to guarantee the freedoms of English subjects (Lochak 2002). It took one more century to see the first declarations and bills of rights aiming at defining more abstract, and thus more universal, principles, with the mutual influence of French and British philosophers before and throughout the Enlightenment. In the United States, the American Declaration of Independence (1776), followed by the adoption of the Bill of Rights (ratification was completed in 1791), and in France, the Declaration of the Rights of Man and of the Citizen (1789), are the main results of this historical movement establishing or reaffirming not only the fundamental rights themselves but also their universal protection by law limiting the arbitrary use of power.

These "guarantee rights," so called because they provide procedural means to protect, defend, and recover the "substantive rights and freedoms" recognized by law, are nowadays affirmed in most existing declarations, charters, conventions, and treaties, so that they have, at least theoretically, acquired a universal status. Among the "guarantee rights," five[3] of them have caused debate or even controversy, and may be challenged in the context of the information society, although they all are recognized in the Universal Declaration of Human Rights (UDHR) and are protected by the International Covenant on Civil and Political Rights (ICCPR). In addition, these rights are protected by most of the binding regional instruments for human rights protection: the African Charter on Human and People's Rights, (ACHPR; adopted in 1981, entered into force in 1986); the American Convention on Human Rights (ACHR; adopted in 1969, entered into force in 1978); and the European Convention for the Protection of Human Rights and Fundamental Freedoms (ECHR, adopted in 1950, entered into force in 1953). These five "guarantee rights" are

The right to equality before the law   (Article 7, UDHR; Article 26, ICCPR; Article 3, ACHPR; Article 24, ACHR; Article 14 and Protocol 12,[4] ECHR), which implies that everyone, without any discrimination based on any ground, is entitled to equal protection by the law. This right is closely related to the general principle of non-discrimination.

The right to an effective remedy   (Article 8, UDHR; Article 2, §3, ICCPR; Article 10, ACHR; Article 13, ECHR), which allows everyone whose rights and freedoms have been violated to claim an effective remedy before the competent authority (judicial, administrative, or legislative, as provided by the national legal system) and to see this remedy recognized, granted, and enforced.

The right to a fair trial   (Article 10, UDHR; Article 14, ICCPR; Article 7, §1, ACHPR; Article 8, ACHR; Article 6, ECHR), which implies that everyone has the right to be publicly heard by an independent and impartial court where minimal guarantee of defense should be provided. This includes the right to be informed promptly, in a language one can understand, of the charges; to have legal assistance; and to have the right to a vigorous defense, both of the latter even if one cannot pay for legal assistance. In addition, no one should be forced to incriminate himself or herself or to confess guilt. Finally, the right to a fair trial also implies the right to be tried without undue delay and, if found guilty, to have the sentence reviewed by a higher court.

The right to the presumption of innocence   (Article 11, §1, UDHR; Article 14, §2, ICCPR; Article 7, §1(b), ACHPR; Article 8, §2, ACHR; Article 6, §2, ECHR), which states that everyone should be considered innocent until proved guilty after a fair trial. This implies, inter alia, that doubt should benefit the accused and that the burden of proof should rest on the prosecution.

The principle of no punishment without law   (Article 11, §2, UDHR; Article 15, ICCPR; Article 7, §2, ACHPR; Article 9, ACHR; Article 7, ECHR). It provides the guarantee that no one should be held guilty of a criminal offense which was not recognized as such by national or international law when the act was committed, or be subject to a more severe penalty than the one that was applicable at that time. Although this principle is mainly governed by time,[5] it can also be understood in a spatial context, as analyzed in a Council of Europe paper (Jakubowicz 2004). This applies especially in cyberspace, where an important and still unsolved problem relates to the competence of jurisdictions, due to the contradiction between the territo-rial definition of jurisdictions and the borderless characteristics of the Internet.

Moreover, specialized conventions and protocols and, in many cases, their implementation into national laws have detailed and reinforced the "guarantee rights." The Human Rights Defenders Office (HRDO) of the International Service for Human Rights (ISHR), based in Geneva, has com-piled a list of international standards sustaining the work of human rights defenders (ISHR 2002). Chapters 13 and 14 of this reference manual, for instance, deal with the right to a fair trial and the right to an effective remedy, respectively, as protected by international and regional instru-ments. Such a publication shows how universal the protection of these "guarantee rights" in international, regional, and national legislation has become.

### "Guarantee Rights" as Part of the Realization of the Rule of Law

Despite the diversity of legal cultures and systems,[6] as well as the histori-cal evolution of the theory of the rule of law,[7] this concept, or at least its main ideas, has progressed to the point that it has become "a true rheto-ric from which the sovereignty of States cannot escape any more in their relationship with the international community,"[8] as analyzed by Daniel Mockle (Mockle 2000).

It is, however, important to keep in mind the three main understand-ings of the principle of the rule of law (Chevallier 2004). It is instrumen-tal when understood as the legal means by which the state is acting. It is formal when it qualifies the state as subject to law, a vision that embeds the principle of the hierarchy of norms, as in the French system. It is sub-stantive when it identifies the state whose legislation shows intrinsic attrib-utes closest to the "British rule of law."

Yet Jacques Chevallier notes that it was only starting in the 1990s that the rule of law principle was put back on the political scene, in a some-what renewed view embedding at the same time the principle of the hier-archy of norms and the respect for fundamental rights, both by their recognition and by procedural means to guarantee them. According to Chevallier and Mockle, this evolution has led to a syncretic model of the rule of law, one more substantive than formal and that cannot be dissociated from human rights.

This trend has been formally acknowledged at the international level in binding documents. This first happened in 1990 with the Charter of Paris for a New Europe, adopted in Paris by thirty-four European and North American countries at the 1990 summit of the Conference for Security and Co-operation in Europe (CSCE).[9] This was extended in 1993 with the Vienna Declaration and Plan of Action, adopted in Vienna by the 171 states attending the United Nations World Conference on Human Rights.[10] The first document opens the statement of CSCE's vision of "a new era of Democracy, Peace and Unity" by linking "Human Rights, Democracy and the Rule of Law" as its three pillars. It declares that human rights and fundamental freedoms "are the birthright of all human beings, are inalienable and are guaranteed by law." It thus recognizes that "their protection and promotion is the first responsibility of government" and that "respect for them is an essential safeguard against an over-mighty State." Moreover, it acknowledges that respect for the human person and the rule of law is the foundation of democracy. The second document affirms all human rights as "universal, indivisible and interdependent and interrelated." It "strongly recommends that a comprehensive programme be established within the United Nations in order to help States in the task of building and strengthening adequate national structures which have a direct impact on the overall observance of human rights and the maintenance of the rule of law."

Even beyond the distance between the formal affirmation and the actual realization of human rights, democracy, and the rule of law, a counterpart of this internationalization movement is that the formal bases of the rule of law may become somewhat diluted in this transfer from only the legal scene to the social and political scenes as well. The risk is that of ending up in a "fuzzy" understanding of the rule of law. This has been highlighted by Chevallier: "The rule of law is affirmed as a value in itself, on which no compromise can be made: encompassing multiple and fairly contradictory understandings, it appears as a swing-wing fuzzy notion; finally, its inclusion in political discourse makes it the carrier of legitimating effects. The rule of law thus appears as a true myth, which scope is matched only by its inaccuracy."[11]

Guarantees are thus needed to avoid this risk, or at least to ensure some protection against it. For the realization of the rule of law, these guarantees should be both political, to protect the substance of democracy, and legal, to protect the substance of rights; and both need the definition and the respect of, at the same time and in interrelation, deliberative and legal procedures.[12]

## Challenges to "Guarantee Rights" in the Information Society

While "guarantee rights" are a necessary part of these procedures, as constitutive elements of the rule of law, it appears that they are particularly challenged in the information society, leading not only to possible violations of these rights themselves, but also to violation of a large range of substantive human rights and freedoms, of which they are a procedural protection. This is particularly highlighted in recent national, regional, and international regulations and legislation adopted or discussed in the information society sector, as shown with some examples in the following sections of this chapter.

The common nature of this legislative and regulatory trend has been to weaken the role of the judiciary power while extending the prerogatives both of the police and of private parties, mainly the technical intermediaries or Internet service providers (ISPs), though other private interests have been given important powers as well in some specific cases.

On the one hand, the police and other law enforcement authorities have progressively seen their investigative powers growing, particularly in terms of interception of communications, search and seizure of data, and international cooperation by exchange of data, without the need for any court order. On the other hand, a so-called self-regulation of Internet service providers is strongly promoted, when not made compulsory by the legislation, and even some penalties to third parties may now be applied (Internet users who subscribe to ISP services) through contractual means granted to ISPs and other private parties.

In both cases, these increased powers are breaching the rule of law by the violation of the "guarantee rights." However, they are being legitimized by a political discourse based on two kinds of considerations. This discourse first invokes human rights considerations, such as the fight against terrorism to protect the security of persons and goods, the protection of human integrity and dignity, and the protection of intellectual property. It is also based on technical and practical considerations, such as the technical difficulties of enforcing the law on the Internet, the need for immediate reaction—or even preventive action—where court trials are long processes, and so on.

### Extending the Prerogatives of Police Forces

The Council of Europe (CoE) Convention on cybercrime[13] is the first intergovernmental treaty dealing with international cooperation for investigating and prosecuting computer crimes. It is open for signature and ratification by the forty-six member states of the CoE, and by nonmember states, some of which have participated in its elaboration (Canada, Japan, South Africa, the United States). Currently, forty-two countries (including the four nonmember states) have signed the Convention, and ten of the thirty-eight member states that are signatories have ratified the treaty and are thus bound by its provisions. Other signatories have not yet ratified the treaty,[14] but have implemented some of its provisions in their national legislation. This is the case in France, for instance (PHR 2004, PI-GreenNet 2003). One treaty section (Chapter II, section 1) deals with substantive criminal law issues (computer-related fraud and violations of network security, child pornography, and infringements of copyright),[15] for the purpose of legislation approximation. Two other chapters, constituting the major part of the Convention, deal with procedural issues (Chapter II, section 2, "Procedural law," and Chapter III, "International cooperation").

According to Greg Taylor, the treaty has "attracted a storm of criticism from both civil liberties organizations as well as from computer industry organizations" since the first public draft was released in April 2000[16] (Taylor 2001).

Among the many provisions that have received strong criticisms, two of them were quite "innovative," since they created a breach of both the right against self-incrimination—thus in direct violation of the right to a fair trial—and the dual criminality requirement as a condition for mutual assistance between countries—thus violating the principle of no punishment without law. Article 19 of the Convention, dealing with search and seizure of stored computer data, aims at allowing "competent authorities" to force any person who has knowledge of data encryption keys to provide these keys or to decrypt encrypted files. Under such obligation, a computer user may be forced to provide evidence that could incriminate him. Article 34 of the Convention provides for mutual assistance of parties with respect to the interception of content data. This is allowed "to the extent permitted under their applicable treaties and domestic laws," although without demanding either that the related criminal offense allows for content data interception or that these content data are related to a criminal offense in both countries.

Moreover, though general "conditions and safeguards" have been added to Article 15 of the Convention after strong objections from civil liberties organizations to intermediate versions, these provisions have still been found "not adequate to address the significant demands and requirements for privacy-invasive techniques in the rest of the Convention."[17] This analysis was shared by the European privacy commissioners in their opinion of March 2001,[18] which notes that safeguards and conditions are not harmonized and are not required to be effectively in place. Moreover, this opinion highlights that the Convention is intended to be signed by non-Council of Europe countries as well. These countries are thus not bound by the European Convention on Human Rights ("granting the right to privacy and data protection, secrecy of correspondence, fair trial, no punishment without law, freedom of expression and imposing precise conditions in clear legal texts to lawfully limit those rights") and by other relevant European instruments. These countries would then be part of an international cooperation system requiring mutual assistance as provided by the Convention, without being subject to the safeguards applicable to Council of Europe countries. This is particularly true of the United States, one of the non–Council of Europe countries that has pushed hardest to have the Convention drafted and adopted. While the American Constitution indeed protects privacy in its Fourth Amendment, U.S. privacy laws offer far fewer guarantees to citizens than the European legislation (as, e.g., the negotiations of "safe harbor" agreements between the United States and the European Union has shown (Electronic Privacy and Information Center 2001).

The preparatory work leading to the Council of Europe Cybercrime Convention started as early as 1996, and the Convention was adopted and opened for signature some weeks after the September 11 attacks. Thus, the text doesn't contain provisions to deal specifically with the fight against terrorism, nor has it been legitimized—at least ex ante—by such an objective.

This is not the case with laws and regulations adopted in many countries and regions, specifically to address the fight against terrorism, that have led to important breaches in the rule of law, as controversies and strong criticism from civil liberties organizations have shown throughout the world.

Unsurprisingly, the first country that adopted such legislation was the United States, with the Patriot Act, passed in October 2001. As summarized by the American Civil Liberties Union (ACLU), "While its secret search, surveillance and investigative authorities are troubling in their own right, the Patriot Act has also become a rallying point for bipartisan concern about broad erosions of fundamental checks and balances against government abuse."[19] Since the Patriot Act was passed only a short time after September 11, and thus in an incredibly emotional context, about a tenth of its provisions are temporary, set to expire in 2005. The U.S. Congress has already passed bills to renew some provisions, making most of them permanent. Other very problematic provisions are already permanent.

Both kinds of sections violate most of the "guarantee rights" listed in this chapter. These include "government's ability to execute criminal search warrants (which need not involve terrorism) and seize property without telling the target for weeks or months" and "allowing the FBI to seize a vast array of sensitive personal information and belongings— including medical, library and business records—using secret intelligence tools that do not require individual criminal activity." Although the records can be seized only pursuant to a court order, judges are compelled to issue these orders, making such judicial review "nothing more than a rubber stamp." Other permitted activities are "seizing a wide variety of business and financial records and in certain instances accessing the membership lists of organizations that provide even very limited Internet services," "allowing the government to demand records and content from communications providers without consent, notice or judicial review in an emergency," and "interception of 'computer trespasser' communications without a judge's assent" (ACLU 2005).

As of early October 2005, the U.S. legislative process is not over yet, since the bills from both Houses of the U.S. Congress renewing Patriot Act temporary provisions still have to be reconciled. Obviously, one cannot foresee if the U.S. Congress will eventually renew all the provisions in their current form, or will adopt some of the safeguards adopted by the Senate in the bill it passed. However, at this step, the French case is not encouraging (Electronic Privacy Information Center 2004).

The first measure taken in France after the September 11 attacks was to add new antiterrorism provisions to a law being discussed at the time, the Daily Safety Law (Loi sur la Sécurité Quotidienne, or LSQ), enacted on November 15, 2001. It includes provisions on data retention and provides for government access to cryptography keys. While said to be a direct response to September 11, these provisions were extracted from the draft Law on the Information Society, introduced on June 13, 2001, by the government and purporting to implement the EU E-Commerce Directive (2000/31/EC). With the LSQ, Internet service providers (ISPs) are required to store log files on all their customers' activities for up to one year. Moreover, the government has access to private encryption keys, import and export of encryption software are restricted, and strict sanctions are imposed for using cryptographic techniques to commit a crime.

Many civil liberties groups opposed the LSQ because it heavily curtails human rights and was adopted hurriedly, in defiance of regular legislative procedure and under the pretense of the fight against terrorism. These so-called antiterrorism provisions of the LSQ initially were valid only until December 2003, and were supposed to be subject to revision by the French Parliament at that time. As a matter of fact, this limited duration has been one of the main arguments to justify the fact that the French Constitutional Council has not examined the compliance of this law with the French Constitution. Socialist Senator Michel Dreyfus-Schmitt even declared, "We may hope to be back to the legality of the Republic, to call a spade a spade, after December 31, 2003 or even before this deadline,"[20] de facto recognizing that these provisions were not even legal.

However, before this deadline was reached, the Internal Safety Law (Loi sur la Sécurité Intérieure, or LSI) was adopted on February 13, 2003, and made LSQ's so-called antiterrorism provisions permanent. At the same time, the LSI authorized the immediate access by law enforcement authorities to the computer data of telecommunications operators, including Internet access providers, as well as of almost any public or private institute, organization, or company. The second important measure in the LSI authorized the search without warrant of any information system, provided that the data are accessible through a network to which the computer being searched with a warrant is connected. If the data are stored in a computer located in a foreign country, access to them remains subject to applicable international agreements. The French Constitutional Council found these provisions valid, and the LSI was enacted on March 18, 2003.

The European Union itself has not escaped the "fight against terrorism" legitimating effect and the trend to adopt measures breaching the rule of law. It has even done this in a domain where the European Union has long had the most advanced legislation with respect to other countries. Such legislation includes the protection of privacy and anonymity through the confidentiality of communications provided, inter alia, by the EU Directive 97/66/EC of December 15, 1997, on the processing of personal data and the protection of privacy in the telecommunication sector.[21] In addition to the general obligation for telecommunication operators to erase traffic data or make it anonymous upon termination of a call, this directive imposed on member states the obligation to ensure by law the confidentiality of communications. The directive prohibits any kind of interception or surveillance of communications except when legally authorized: "when such restriction constitutes a necessary measure to safeguard national security, defense, public security, the prevention, investigation, detection and prosecution of criminal offences or of unauthorized use of the telecommunications system."

The revision of this directive, at first to extend its scope to any kind of electronic communication services and to implement EU internal market competition in the telecommunication sector, has led the European Union to abandon its established principle of forbidding any systematic surveillance of communications. Instead, it has authorized the systematic mandatory retention of data on all communications of EU citizens by member states, despite the opposition of civil liberties organizations[22] and of a mass movement of European citizens,[23] and even despite the opinion of the group of EU data protection commissioners. The commissioners found that the proposal "would undermine the fundamental rights to privacy, data protection, freedom of expression, liberty and presumption of innocence," thus causing a shift in the burden of the proof in criminal cases. (For a comprehensive account and analysis of this EU reversal and the role of European and non-European actors, see Marzouki 2002–2003).

Examples provided above are illustrate only some of the first steps in a movement that we are seeing in Europe and in the United States, as well as in the rest of the world. This movement undermines protection of due process through extended prerogatives given to police forces and weakens the role of the judicial power, if only by default of the requirement for a judge's assent to these kinds of police investigations. This trend is also worsened by the extension of prerogatives of private parties.

### Extending the Prerogatives of ISPs and Other Private Parties

Discussing how globalization may affect the law, Benoît Frydman identifies five main features of a new model of global governance: (1) a shift from institutional regulation to economic regulation; (2) a correlative shift from public regulators to private actors; (3) a shift from primary substantive rules to secondary procedural rules; (4) the increasing use of technical devices to implement regulations; and (5) a rhetorical emphasis put on basic human rights and fundamental liberties (Frydman 2004). This model, which Frydman applies to systems apparently as different as, on the one hand, global warming and tradable pollution permits and, on the other hand, Internet content coregulation, seems a perfect description of Internet governance regimes and mechanisms that can be observed in other domains as well, including privacy and personal data protection (Marzouki and Méadel 2004).

An increasing implementation of this model has been occurring since the 1990s—since Internet use has been growing in the general public, making public communications within almost anyone's reach—while practical problems are posed for civil or penal law enforcement, including exacerbated conflicts of rights and, obviously, conflicts of jurisdictions. This situation has led to new modalities of censorship (Marzouki "Nouvelles modalités," 2003), in which censorship is exercised either by private actors (especially Internet service providers) or by technical artifacts implemented by software, hardware, or even the Internet infrastructure itself (Lessig 1999). How this situation leads to violations of fundamental substantive rights, starting with the right to freedom of expression, has been extensively documented in the literature, and is also discussed in other chapters of this book. However, possible violations of the "guarantee rights" identified in this chapter are seldom addressed in this context, although many national and regional regulations include procedural measures that tend to affect these constitutive elements of the rule of law.

Prior to detailing these kinds of procedural measures and how they may violate "guarantee rights," it is necessary to discuss how the right to a fair trial applies in the context of civil rights and obligations. The extension of the prerogatives of ISPs and other private parties, examined in this section, mostly relates to situations falling within the scope of civil law issues. Recalling the most important jurisprudence[24] of the European Court of Human Rights in relation to the civil aspect of Article 6 of the European Convention on Human Rights, Susan Schiavetta highlights the right of access to the court as an integral part of the right to a fair trail. She concludes:

Seeing that the rule of law would be rendered superfluous if there was no actual access to the courts, it was thought that the ability to gain access had to be an intrinsic part of Article 6. The lack of explicit reference to the right of access was merely illustrative of the fact that such a right had been entrenched in society for so long that there was no need to guarantee it further. Indeed, the ability to submit a civil claim to court is internationally recognized as a fundamental principle of law, and as such the Convention does not just presuppose the existence of courts but also the existence of the right to access courts in civil matters as without this right no civil court could begin to operate. (Schiavetta 2004)

This breach of the right of access to a court is the main violation of the right to a fair trial that can be observed in the following three groups of procedural measures extending the prerogatives of ISPs and other private parties, particularly when this extension is enforced by law.

The first group of such procedural measures deals with the limitation of ISPs' liability for unlawful content they may be hosting, which is authored by one of their subscribers, provided that some conditions are respected. This is the case in the European Union, with the adoption in 2000 of the E-commerce Directive. One of its provisions states that an ISP may not be held liable if it either does not have actual knowledge of illegal activity or content it is hosting or, when having such knowledge, complies with the "notice and take-down" procedure by "acting expeditiously to remove or to disable access to the content." In the United States, a similar provision, though restricted to copyright infringements, applies through the Digital Millennium Copyright Act (DMCA), adopted in 1998.

Regarding other kinds of infringements, the U.S. Communication Decency Act, adopted in 1996, provides that ISPs are exempted from civil liability for content they host or give access to. However, "the Good Samaritan provision" allows ISPs to take voluntary actions "in good faith to restrict access to or availability of material that the provider . . . considers to be obscene, lewd, lascivious, filthy, excessively violent, harassing, or otherwise objectionable, whether or not such material is constitutionally protected" (Frydman and Rorive 2002).

In summary, the practical effect of these kinds of self-regulatory or coregulatory measures allows private sector actors to remove content they host, or block content they give access to, or breach the privacy of their subscribers, or violate the protection of their personal data, solely upon notification by third parties of controversial or allegedly illegal content or action. Since this is done without any court decision confirming that this content or action is indeed unlawful, if may cause indiscriminate private censorship, leading to freedom of expression and privacy infringements and resulting, in some cases, in a breach of the principle of no punishment without law. Moreover, except for the DMCA, according to which a "notice and put back procedure" can be issued by the author of the content to be removed, so that the case can be settled by the parties without any decision made by the ISP, the only solution remaining for the author of the removed content is to file a complaint. The burden of the proof then rests on him.

A second group of procedural measures relates to the use of contractual regulations either through an ISP's code of conduct or through specific subscription clauses. France provides one example of the first case. Three French ministers, representatives of the music industry, and major ISPs and telecom operators signed a charter in July 2004. This charter builds on the French implementation of the E-commerce Directive that implements the notice and take-down procedure, and the revised French privacy and data protection act that allows royalties collection societies, representing intellectual property right holders, to create files with telecommunication traffic data of supposed copyright infringers using peer-to-peer networks. By signing this charter, ISPs commit to terminate contracts of their subscribers whose IP addresses have been identified by representatives of property right holders. A judicial order is needed for contract termination following this charter. However, this order is not the result of a normal court case regarding a procedure in which each party is heard by a judge, but rather a simple ordinance signed by a judge upon presentation of a request. Consequently, there is a breach in the right to a fair trial and to an effective remedy as well (Marzouki 2005).

A third category of procedural measures limiting recourse to the courts is the increasing promotion of alternative dispute resolution (ADR) mechanisms, especially when implemented in online form (e-ADR). Susan Schiavetta provides an extensive discussion on the relationship between e-ADR and the right to a fair trial as provided by Article 6 of ECHR and in relation to the jurisprudence of the European Court of Human Rights (Schiavetta 2004). She analyzes, depending on the mandatory or voluntary character of the e-ADR mechanism, the requirements stated by the European Court in order for e-ADR to comply with the right to a fair trial. These requirements are not necessarily met when the substance of the dispute deals with Internet content or the designation of Internet content. Examples of such cases are provided by the global and mandatory Uniform Dispute Resolution Procedure (UDRP) set up by ICANN, the unique Internet domain names management organism, a private party registered in California. When a dispute over a domain name arises, the complainant—in most cases a trademark holder—may file a complaint according to the UDRP procedure, so that arbitration occurs. This process leads to a decision that the domain name is taken from the defendant and given back to the complainant, or to an enforcement procedure executed by the concerned registrar (an ISP whose role is to host the domain name). Mueller 2002 analyzes how this procedure leads to "arbitration forum shopping," which in many cases biases the result of the procedure to the benefit of the complainant. Moreover, it also results in the expansion of intellectual property rights (especially trademarks) to the detriment of other rights (e.g., freedom of expression). In the end this shows that the UDRP procedure is far from meeting the requirements for the respect of the right to a fair trial and the right to an effective remedy.

In addition to these three main categories of procedural measures extending the prerogatives of ISPs and other private parties, another major problem of law enforcement relates to competence of jurisdictions. As stated in Frydman (2004), "the classical rules of jurisdiction allow any State to interfere with any data posted on the Internet, as soon as these data can be accessed from a computer located in its territory." This obviously poses a central problem with respect to the borderlessness of the Internet and, at the same time, the fact that different countries have different substantive legislation. A court in one country may find a person guilty of a criminal offense, and require execution of the corresponding penalty in this person's country, while the legislation of this person's country recognizes the act as perfectly legal. A well-known and overly documented example of such a problem is the French Yahoo case (Frydman and Rorive 2002). A nonbinding document of the Council of Europe has, for the first time ever, tried to address the problem while respecting the principle of no punishment without law. This is done by recommending that member states "consider whether there is a need to develop further international legal frameworks on jurisdiction to ensure that the right to no punishment without law is respected in a digital environment."[25] However, it will be a long time before such a political statement becomes binding international law.

## Conclusion

As tentatively shown in this chapter, we are facing a strong trend toward weakening the role of the judiciary while extending the prerogatives both of the police and of private parties. Being based solely on procedural modifications of the law, the impact of this movement on the substance of fundamental rights may not immediately be obvious. Provided that the substantive rights themselves are not directly modified, these changes may still seem acceptable to many observers. However, since the "guarantee rights" are procedural means to protect, defend, and recover the "substantive rights," human rights defenders should understand that as soon as the "guarantee rights" are challenged, "substantive rights" are de facto endangered.

This tendency is the result of a globalized world, more and more ruled by economic regulation and market forces, and where states are increasingly leaving their sovereign prerogatives in the hands of private parties, promoting so-called self-regulation and coregulation procedures in the name of efficiency. These contractual procedures, mainly involving private actors (and also sometimes public actors), apply to a subject who is not even a party to the contract: the citizen. This is particularly shown by the "notice and take-down" procedure. At the same time, states are increasing their surveillance and monitoring powers over citizens: in the name of a war against terrorism, and with the pretension of increasing our security, human rights, the rule of law, and democracy are being violated, thus best realizing the objectives of the enemies of democracy.

In his analysis of how globalization affects the law, Benoît Frydman identifies two traditional ways to tackle legal issues involving international aspects: "the first one are [sic] the rules of jurisdiction . . . , the second one is for the international community . . . to agree on common rules and standards" (Frydman 2004: 228–229). Although some cases, such as the French Yahoo case, have shown that the first way has not yet been completely abandoned, explorations of the second way have already started.

Legislation approximation has been occurring at the European Union level, and this chapter has shown how, when dealing with the information society, this process is challenging the "guarantee rights" in many aspects. However, the European Union case is special in that it constitutes a coherent, regional union of states with its own institutional system, rules, and legal order.

The first real attempt at an international agreement between sovereign states is thus the Council of Europe Convention on Cybercrime. In this case, too, we have shown that the "guarantee rights" have been challenged.

The second attempt is the World Summit on the Information Society (WSIS). Human rights defenders have seen WSIS as "an important opportunity to carry the human rights agenda forward," as declared by the WSIS Civil Society Human Rights Caucus at the Geneva phase of the summit.[26] Though aiming "to actually translate human rights principles to the context of the information society," the Caucus task has, rather, "become defending the formal commitment to previously reached international consensus, that is, preventing complete backtracking on human rights." After completion of WSIS's second phase, the challenge of bringing forward the actual implementation of human rights standards has clearly not been accomplished. As numerous cases show, the main human rights problems today do not relate to lack of formal commitment, but rather to lack of effective implementation of human rights. The first international attempt to translate human rights into the context of the information society has thus been squandered (Marzouki and Joergensen 2004).

Any future attempt to tackle globalization and its impact on information society legislation will face the same failure, unless it starts by recognizing that procedural means to protect universally recognized human rights and fundamental freedoms, known as the "guarantee rights," do have their precise translation in the information society, and should be protected as such. The first and foremost protection resides in strengthening the judiciary's power, instead of weakening it.

## Notes

1. As numbered in the translation into English of the original Latin text. See this translation provided by the British Library and based on Holt (1992). http://www.bl.uk/collections/treasures/magnatranslation.html.

2. After five men (Sir Thomas Darnel and four others), known as the Five Knights, were imprisoned by King Charles I for refusing to contribute to forced loans.

3. Other, more specific procedural guarantees that are enshrined in some of the "substantive rights" (e.g., the right to privacy) are beyond of the scope of this chapter. Some of them are dealt with extensively in relevant sections of this book.

4. See the explanatory report of this protocol (CETS no. 177, adopted in 2000 and entering into force in 2005) for a better understanding of the limitation of Article 14 of ECHR with regard to equality and non-discrimination. Available on the Council of Europe Web site, http://conventions.coe.int/Treaty/en/Reports/Html/177.htm.

5. Called (e.g., in ACHR) "freedom from ex post facto laws."

6. To the extent that a group of members of the Council of Europe Parliamentary Assembly proposed, in May 2004, a resolution regarding the coherent translation into French of the expression "principle of the rule of law," stressing their concern related to possible misinterpretation, through inappropriate translations, of the substance of this principle. The motion is still pending since, according to the Council of Europe Parliamentary Assembly website, "this motion has not been discussed in the Assembly and commits only the members who have signed it." See http://assembly.coe.int/Documents/WorkingDocs/doc04/EDOC10180.htm.

7. For a general overview of this evolution, see Chevallier (2004). We use "rule of law" here as the English translation of the concept of "état de droit" rather than specifically as the concept of the British rule of law. A more comprehensive discussion is in Chevallier (2003).

8. "Une véritable rhétorique à laquelle ne peut plus échapper la souveraineté des états dans leurs rapports avec la communauté internationale" (Mockle 2000: 238).

9. Available at http://www.osce.org/item/4047.html. The CSCE became the OSCE (Organization for Security and Co-operation in Europe) in 1994.

10. Available at http://www.unhchr.ch/html/menu5/wchr.htm.

11. "L'état de droit est posé comme une valeur en soi, sur laquelle aucun compromis n'est possible: recouvrant des significations multiples et passablement contradictoires, il se présente comme une notion floue et à géométrie variable; enfin, son incorporation au discours politique le rend porteur d'effets de légitimation. L'état de droit apparaît ainsi comme un véritable mythe, dont la portée n'a d'égale que l'imprécision" (Chevallier 2003).

12. As discussed by Habermas (1997), who shows how these principles are the necessary conditions of a legitimate use of law, even without considering any normative content.

13. CETS no. 185. Adopted in Budapest on Nov. 23, 2001, and entered into force on July 1, 2004. Available at http://conventions.coe.int/Treaty/en/Treaties/Html/185.htm.

14. As of Apr. 30, 2005.

15. The treaty is supplemented by an additional protocol making dissemination of racist and xenophobic propaganda via computer networks a criminal offense.

16. Most of these criticisms may be found at http://www.treatywatch.org and at http://www.epic.org/privacy/intl/ccc.html.

17. See http://www.treatywatch.org/Draft_27_Comments.html.

18. EU Article 29 Data Protection Working Party Opinion 4/2001 on the Council of Europe's draft Convention on Cybercrime. March 22, 2001.

19. For details of the Patriot Act provisions and how they are breaching even minimal requirements of the rule of law, see ACLU main USA Patriot Act Web page, http://www.aclu.org/patriot.

20. "Il est vrai que le 31 décembre 2003, c'est loin, et que nous pouvons espérer revenir à la légalité républicaine, pour appeler les choses par leur nom, bien plus tôt." Michel Dreyfus-Schmitt, declaration at the French Senate session of Oct. 17, 2001. See http://www.senat.fr/seances/s200110/s20011017/s20011017_mono.html.

21. Available at http://europa.eu.int/smartapi/cgi/sga_doc?smartapi!celexapi!prod!CELEXnumdoc&lg=EN&numdoc=31997L0066&model=guichett.

22. See the letter sent by a large coalition of NGOs to the president of the European Parliament, available at http://www.gilc.org/cox_en.html, and other actions documented at http://www.epic.org/privacy/intl/data_retention.html.

23. In less than one week, more than 17,000 EU citizens signed a petition against the proposal.

24. *Golder v. United Kingdom*, A 18 (1975), para. 35.

25. Council of Europe, Multidisciplinary Ad Hoc Committee of Experts on the Information Society (CAHSI), "Draft Political Statement on the Principles and Guidelines for Ensuring Respect for Human Rights and the Rule of Law in the Information Society," approved by the CAHSI on Apr. 7, 2005. Available at http://www.coe.int/t/e/integrated_projects/democracy/02_Activities/00_Declaration_on_Information_Society

26. WSIS CS Human Rights Caucus press release, Dec. 7, 2003. Available at http://www.iris.sgdg.org/actions/smsi/hr-wsis/hris-pr-071203-en.html.

**References**

ACLU (American Civil Liberties Union). "Patriot Act Sunsets." New York: ACLU, Mar. 2005. Available at http://www.aclu.org/sunsets.

Chevallier, Jacques. *L'état de droit*. 4th ed. Paris: Monchrestien, 2003.

Chevallier, Jacques, ed. *L'état de droit*. "Problèmes politiques et sociaux" no. 898. Paris: La Documentation Française, 2004.

Electronic Privacy Information Center (EPIC) and Privacy International. "Privacy & Human Rights." Washington, DC: EPIC, 2001. Available at http://www.privacyinternational.org.

Electronic Privacy Information Center (EPIC) and Privacy International. "Privacy & Human Rights." Washington, DC: EPIC, 2004. Available at http://www.privacyinternational.org.

Frydman, Benoît, "Coregulation: A Possible Legal Model for Global Governance." In *About Globalisation: Views on the Trajectory of Mondialisation*. Ed. Bart de Schutter and Johan Pas. Brussels: VUB University Press, 2004.

Frydman, Benoît, and Isabelle Rorive. "Regulating Internet Content Through Intermediaries in Europe and the USA." *Zeischrift für Rechtssoziologie* (Max Planck Institute) 23, no. 1 (2002): 41–59.

Habermas, Jürgen. *Droit et démocratie: Entre faits et normes*. Paris: Gallimard, 1997.

Holt, James C. *Magna Carta*, 2nd ed., rev. Cambridge: Cambridge University Press, 1992.

ISHR (International Service for Human Rights). "Compilation of International and Regional Instruments for the Protection of Human Rights Defenders." Geneva: ISHR, 2002. Available at http://www.ishr.ch/about%20ISHR/HRDO/Publications/Human%20Rights%20Defenders%20Series/Compilation/CompilationContents.htm.

Jakubowicz, Karol. "Human Rights in the Information Society: A Preliminary Overview." Working paper prepared for the Council of Europe Preparatory Group on Human Rights, the Rule of Law in the Information Society. IP1(2004)47(web).

Strasbourg, Sept. 2004. Available at http://www.coe.int/t/e/integrated_projects/democracy/02_Activities/00_CAHSI/IP1%282004%2947_Jakub.asp.

Lessig, Lawrence. *Code and Other Laws of Cyberspace.* New York: Basic Books, 1999.

Lochak, Danièle. *Les Droits de l'homme.* Paris: La Découverte, 2002.

Marzouki, Meryem. "Petite histoire de la directive européenne sur la vie privée et les communications électroniques ou le revirement de l'Europe." *Terminal* no. 88, special issue: *Fichiers et libertés: Le cybercontrôle 25 ans après.* (Winter 2002–Spring 2003): 61–83.

Marzouki, Meryem. "Nouvelles Modalités de la censure: Le Cas d'Internet en France." *Le Temps des médias—Revue d'histoire* no. 1 (Autumn 2003): 148–161.

Marzouki, Meryem, "Informatique et Internet: De l'état de droit à l'arbitraire." In *L'État des droits de l'homme en France.* Ed. Ligue des Droits de l'Homme. Paris: La Découverte, 2005.

Marzouki, Meryem, and Rikke Frank Jørgensen. "A Human Rights Assessment of the World Summit on the Information Society." *Information Technologies and International Development* 1, no. 3–4, special issue: *The World Summit in Reflection: A Deliberative Dialogue on the WSIS.* (Summer 2004): 86–88.

Marzouki, Meryem, and Cécile Méadel. "Gouvernance technique et gouvernement politique d'Internet: Enjeux et questions de recherche." In *Proceedings of the 14th SFSIC National Congress on Information and Communication Sciences. Béziers, June 2004.* Paris: SFSIC, 2004.

Mockle, Daniel. "Mondialisation et état de droit." *Cahiers de droit* (Laval University) 41, no. 2 (Mar. 2000): 237–288.

Mueller, Milton. *Ruling the Root: Internet Governance and the Taming of Cyberspace.* Cambridge, MA: MIT Press, 2002.

Privacy International and GreenNet Educational Trust. "Silenced: An International Report on Censorship and Control of the Internet." London: GreenNet Educational Trust, 2003. Available at http://www.privacyinternational.org.

Schiavetta, Susan. "The Relationship Between e-ADR and Article 6 of the European Convention on Human Rights Pursuant to the Case Law of the European Court of Human Rights." *Journal of Information, Law and Technology* 2004, no. 1 (Apr. 2004). Available at http://www2.warwick.ac.uk/fac/soc/law/elj/jilt/2004_1/schiavetta.

Taylor, Graig. "The Council of Europe Cybercrime Convention. A Civil Liberties Perspective." Adelaide: Electronic Frontier Australia, 2001. Available at http://www.efa.org.au/Publish/coe_paper.html.

# III   Equal Treatment and Development

# 9   A Nondiscriminatory Information Society

Mandana Zarrehparvar

The World Summit on the Information Society's (WSIS) Declaration of Principles and Plan of Action have taken human rights principles as their point of departure and reiterate the essential principles of universality and indivisibility with references to the Charter of the United Nations, the Universal Declaration of Human Rights, and the Vienna Declaration. However, despite the proliferation of knowledge about discrimination and the value of information and communication technology (ICT) to the realization of human rights, the documents and debate on the visions for the Information Society fail to seriously address and refer to the fundamental principle of non-discrimination.

This chapter will address the challenges facing the information society and discuss in particular the need to translate the right to be protected against any form of discrimination or hate incitement. A prerequisite for this discussion is an understanding of the principle of non-discrimination. The chapter thus begins with an examination of how the principle is reflected through the instruments adopted by the international community since World War II. The chapter will further explore the ways in which discrimination manifests itself in relation to the information society. In particular, it will suggest that more attention be paid to two dilemmas of the information society: the backlash against any commitment to combat racism, gender discrimination, or any other form of intolerance through the Internet, and discrimination through lack of access to ICT.

## The Principle of Nondiscrimination

Basically, the purpose of the nondiscrimination principle is protection of all individuals from being discriminated against on grounds stipulated in the human rights instruments and obligating state parties to take action to ensure equal treatment.

Discrimination can roughly be defined as any distinction, exclusion, restriction, or preference that is based on certain prohibition criteria, and has the purpose or effect of nullifying or impairing the recognition, enjoyment, or exercise by certain persons, on an equal footing, of certain rights and freedoms.[1]

The common conceptions of discrimination are direct and indirect discrimination. Direct discrimination occurs when one person is treated less favorably than another is, has been, or would be treated in a comparable situation on prohibited grounds. For instance, when women do not get jobs because of their gender or when access to public services is denied to persons from certain minority groups.

Indirect (or concealed) discrimination, on the other hand, occurs when an apparently neutral provision, criterion, or practice would, without any objective justification, put certain categories of persons at a particular disadvantage compared with other persons. For example, a height requirement to enter a police academy can in effect restrict the number of women who can become part of the police force. The height requirement is not proportionate and objectively justifiable because one does not need to have a certain height in order to be a good and qualified policeman/woman.

Broadly, the principle of nondiscrimination refers to the requirement that the state parties treat similar cases alike, and different cases differently. In other words, the enjoyment of rights and freedoms on an equal footing does not necessarily mean identical treatment. Not all similar cases can be treated alike. For instance, the Convention on the Elimination of All Forms of Discrimination Against Women (CEDAW) requires that special protection be given to women against harmful work during pregnancy. The principle of nondiscrimination acknowledges that there is room for differential treatment, but only when it is objectively justified by a legitimate aim and the means of achieving that aim is proportionate and necessary.

The fundamental principle of nondiscrimination has since World War II become a central standard in the development of human rights. Recognized human rights ought to be applied to all human beings without discrimination and irrespective of a person's status and position. In a sense, nondiscrimination is what makes human rights universal, a red thread and an indispensable principle in the global endeavor to protect and promote human rights. The non-discrimination provisions in the various human rights instruments reflect this indispensability.

Chapter 1, Article 1, of the United Nations Charter (1945) states:

> ... To achieve international cooperation in solving international problems of an economic, social, cultural, or humanitarian character, and to promote and encourage respect for human rights and for fundamental freedoms for all without distinctions to race, sex, language, or religion ...

The Universal Declaration of Human Rights (1948) reaffirms and expands the principle of equal rights and nondiscrimination stipulated in the Charter. Article 2 states:

> Everyone is entitled to all the rights and freedoms set forth in the Declaration, without distinction of any kind such as race, colour, sex, language, religion, political or other opinion, national or social origin, property, birth or other status. Furthermore, no distinction shall be made on the basis of the political, jurisdictional or international status of the country or territory to which a person belongs, whether it be independent, trust, non-self governing or under any other limitation of sovereignty.

The principle of nondiscrimination also has a prominent position in the two covenants that transformed the Universal Declaration of Human Rights into binding treaty law. Article 2, Paragraph 1, of the International Covenant on Civil and Political Rights (ICCPR) and Article 2, Paragraph 2, of the International Covenant on Economic, Social and Cultural Rights (ICESCR) specify provisions by which the state parties guarantee that the human rights stipulated in each covenant are exercised without discrimination.

The indispensability of the principle of nondiscrimination is further underlined by the adoption of specialized human rights instruments aimed at the elimination of discrimination.

The Convention on the Rights of the Child prohibits, and thus protects the child against, discrimination in relation to the rights protected in the Convention and, moreover, adds ethnic origin and disability to the specifically mentioned categories against which discrimination is prohibited. Article 2 of the Convention further adds that the child is protected against all forms of discrimination based on the status, activities, expressed opinions, or beliefs of the child's family members.

The International Labour Organisation (ILO) and the U.N. Educational, Scientific, and Cultural Organisation (UNESCO) have adopted numerous conventions in which the principle of nondiscrimination is mentioned, in particular the ILO Convention on Discrimination in Respect of Employment and Occupation and the UNESCO Convention Against Discrimination in Education.

The ILO Convention, in Article 1, Paragraph 1(a), defines discrimination as

... any distinction, exclusion or preference made on the basis of race, colour, sex, religion, political opinion, national extraction or social origin, which has the effect of nullifying or impairing equality of opportunity or treatment in employment or occupation.

The definition of discrimination in the UNESCO Convention is formulated in Article 1, Paragraph 1, and is similar to the one in the ILO Convention, except that it mentions language, economic conditions, and birth as categories against which discrimination is prohibited. The UNESCO Convention does not merely aim at eliminating discrimination from legislative provisions and administrative practices. It also addresses the deliberate denial of the right to education to certain members of society, as well as indirect discrimination caused by a combination of social, geographical, economic, and historical circumstances.

The Convention on the Elimination of All Forms of Discrimination Against Women (CEDAW) and the Convention on the Elimination of All Forms of Racial Discrimination (CERD) not only provide protection against discrimination based on specific grounds but also obligate the state parties to take positive and constructive measures to ensure the elimination of discrimination. CEDAW and CERD confirm the standards stipulated in earlier conventions and add new dimensions and principles to them.

CEDAW guarantees the right of all women to be free from discrimination and formulates state obligations that are designed to ensure the legal and practical enjoyment of that right. It deals in greater detail with a variety of issues arising in the area of discrimination against women. The scope of the Convention is very broad, and there are provisions concerning all aspects of life. Article 1 of CEDAW defines discrimination against women as

... any distinction, exclusion or restriction made on the basis of sex which has the effect or purpose of impairing or nullifying the recognition, enjoyment or exercise by women, irrespective of their marital status, on the basis of equality of men and women, of human rights and fundamental freedoms in the political, economic, social, cultural, civil or any other field.

Article 1, Paragraph 1, of CERD defines racial discrimination as

any distinction, exclusion, restriction, or preference based on race, colour, descent, national or ethnic origin which has the purpose or effect of nullifying or impairing the recognition, enjoyment or exercise, on an equal footing, of human rights and fundamental freedoms in the political, social, cultural or any other field of public life.

CERD protects all persons exposed to acts of racial discrimination in all public aspects of life and, among other requirements, obligates state parties to declare punishable by law all dissemination of ideas based on racial superiority or hatred and incitement to racial discrimination, with due regard to the Universal Declaration of Human Rights, Article 19, on freedom of expression.

The development of the human rights instruments has had the overall aim of achieving international cooperation and fundamental respect for all human rights. Ever since the adoption of the United Nations Charter in 1945, the prohibition of discrimination based on personal characteristics has been an intrinsic part of the global protection and promotion of human rights. Therefore, provisions against all forms of discrimination have been developed and included in the human rights instruments. The development since the adoption of the Universal Declaration of Human Rights in 1948 also shows that it is essential to define discrimination more concretely by having specific instruments (ICERD and CEDAW) with provisions against discrimination to tackle different prohibition criteria or categories of persons who need protection.

## Nondiscrimination and ICT

As illustrated above, nondiscrimination is established as a bedrock principle of international human rights instruments. However, despite these instruments and the commitment on paper by state parties, combating discrimination and securing equal treatment is far from being globally realized.

Reasons for not realizing the principle by the state parties are many. It is not the objective of this chapter to dwell on what these are and to what degree the reasons are legitimate and plausible. However, it should be pointed out that the lack of a full implementation of the nondiscrimination principle has dire implications for the state of the world order. Social and political unrest, instability, a growing gap between the poor and the rich, environmental problems and catastrophes, epidemics such as HIV/AIDS, ethnic cleansing, and racism are just a few examples.

In regard to ICT and the development of the information society, the lack of implementation of the nondiscrimination principle also has its implications. I will go so far as to argue that without the principle of nondiscrimination, there can be no information society. In order to make my point, I will focus on how a lack of implementation of the nondiscrimination principle manifests itself (1) in relation to the Internet and (2) in relation to access to ICT by certain vulnerable groups.

### Hate Speech on the Internet

The Internet is a wonderful thing. It has made access to and exchange of information (for those of us who are so privileged) much quicker and easier. It is the medium in which many have the opportunity to exercise their right to freedom of expression and thereby express their opinions on any subject. It is relatively cheap and easy to maintain, and even individuals or small groups have the same circulation potential and availability capacity as the *New York Times* or television networks such as CNN. Last but not least, the Internet provides an easy and effective way of organizing, fund-raising, communicating, and merchandising. It can therefore be used effectively for the common good of mankind and be a strong instrument to promote human rights.

But the Internet is not being used only for the common good of mankind. It is also used very effectively to spread discriminatory and hate propaganda.

The structure of the Internet, its pervasiveness, and the possibility it affords for anonymity have made cyberspace a playground for those who wish to spread hateful propaganda and incite to hate and violence. A quick check on any search engine provides numerous home pages that target their propaganda against immigrants, Jews, Muslims, or homosexuals, inciting hate and encouraging violence against these groups. For instance, in The Netherlands, the Dutch Complaints Bureau has noted a steady increase in discrimination on the Dutch part of the Internet. During 2003 a total of 1,496 expressions were reported, of which 121 contained threats against individuals or ethnic or religious groups or called for violence against them.[2] According to the International Network Against Cyber Hate (INACH), in The Netherlands, Germany, the United Kingdom, and France there are more than 10,000 hate sites.[3]

Some free speech advocates believe that hate speech on the Internet cannot and should not be curbed.[4] They believe that any regulation of the Internet would be an infringement on the right to freedom of expression. There are also those who regard expressing hate to be a legitimate statement of political belief. What some tend to forget is that the right not to be discriminated against is just as much a human right as the right to freedom of expression. These rights are weighted equally in human rights and complement, protect, and enhance one another. Having the right to exercise freedom of expression will be senseless if that right is not protected by the right not to be discriminated against on grounds of, say, gender or ethnicity. On the other hand, it does not make any sense to use the right to freedom of expression to spread hate of various groups of people in the society and thereby infringe on their fundamental right not to be discriminated against.

There is a need to protect freedom of expression *and* to combat discriminatory and hateful speech, even though in attempting to do so, we risk "impairing core aspects of one or the other"[5] right. An example of how such a balance can be struck is the European Court of Human Rights' decision in the case of *Jersild v. Denmark*.[6]

*Jersild v. Denmark* is a case involving a journalist (Jens Olaf Jersild) who broadcast an interview with three youngsters belonging to a group who called themselves the Green Jackets. During the interview the Green Jackets expressed extreme racist attitudes and support for eugenics and apartheid,[7] which led to a subsequent conviction in the City Court of Copenhagen of the three youngsters and Jersild, in accordance with Section 266b[8] of the Danish Penal Code. Jersild appealed the court's decisions to the High Court of Eastern Denmark, where it was dismissed, and then to the Supreme Court, where it also was dismissed. Once the national remedies were exhausted, Jersild submitted an application to the European Court on Human Rights, on the ground that his conviction was in violation of Article 10 of the European Convention on Human Rights—his right to freedom of expression.[9]

The European Court of Human Rights, in its final decision on September 23, 1994, acquitted Jersild. In its decision the Court made it clear that "incitement to racial hatred does not deserve protection under the right to freedom of expression, whilst at the same time protecting the right of the media to report on issues of public interest, however controversial or offensive, without national or international courts 'substituting their own views for those of the press as to what technique of reporting should be adopted by journalists.'"[10]

Another aspect that some may not realize is that online propaganda is used to commission hate crimes, and the persons behind the hate sites are not just unsophisticated thugs. The reality is that these groups and individuals are the generation that has grown up in a digitized world and sees greater potential for cyberspace than their predecessors. They communicate in cyberspace ever more frequently and effectively. And they use the Internet for planning actions (such as the organization of demonstrations), for fund-raising, and for the recruitment of new group members.[11]

Despite the worries expressed by free speech advocates, combating hate sites does not necessarily imply curbing freedom of expression. On the contrary, in order to protect the right to freedom of expression, it is necessary to combat discrimination. It must not be forgotten that these types of home pages have, apart from disseminating hate and violence, another serious effect: they undermine democracy and the fundaments of a democratic society, which in turn are the underlying premises for people to exercise their right to freedom of expression. Situations in which hate speech can be harmful should be illegal, for the simple fact that whereas freedom of expression is a condition for a successful democracy, tolerance is essential for the survival of a democracy.[12]

Combating discrimination on the Internet is very complex. Yet, however complex it may be, state parties and the international community cannot leave the responsibility for regulation to Internet service providers.

A report prepared by the Swiss Institute of Comparative Law for the European Commission Against Racism and Intolerance[13] concludes that the Internet, like any other means of communication, does not fall outside the scope of the law. The problem, though, is that

... the legal instruments at the source of international judicial cooperation have not adapted to the era of digitalised, world-wide electronic communications. Their lengthy and cumbersome procedures, which are linked with national sovereignty, scarcely favour the cooperation and coordination indispensable to effective action against transient communications which know no frontiers.[14]

On a regional level, the Council of Europe (CoE) has adopted the Convention on Cybercrime and an additional protocol to the Convention concerning the criminalization of racist and xenophobic acts committed through computer systems. The Convention and its additional protocol provide a source of international judicial cooperation, at least at the European level, but since only ten out of forty-six member states have ratified the Convention, the prospects seem quite bleak.

Despite bleak prospects, the existing human rights instruments do provide some possibilities. Application of the principle of non-discrimination as stipulated in the various human rights instruments does indeed provide not only a definition of what is discriminatory but also guidelines for nondiscriminatory practices on the Internet. Article 7 of the Universal Declaration of Human Rights declares that all human beings are entitled to the equal protection of the law against any incitement to discrimination. Article 20 of the ICCPR declares that any advocacy of national, racial, or religious hatred that constitutes incitement to discrimination, hostility, or violence shall be prohibited by law. Article 4 of the ICERD obliges all state parties to enact laws prohibiting and punishing the dissemination of racist material.

Even though the Universal Declaration on Human Rights, ICCPR, and ICERD were drafted and adopted at a time when the Internet was not a widely used communication medium, they provide the possibility to put into effect positive measures to prevent discriminatory home pages. State parties that have adequate legal instruments to combat discrimination usually make no reference to a technical means of communication, and therefore the existing legal provisions intended to combat hateful statements in the physical world are perfectly capable of barring hateful statements on the Internet. It is a question of political will and commitment to secure nondiscriminatory, democratic societies.

### Discrimination in Access to ITC

Addressing the issue of discrimination in access to ICT concerns the right not to be discriminated against when wanting to access ICT at the national or state level rather than the right to have access as such. With regard to the latter, it is, however, necessary to acknowledge the link between the global and the local levels.

Looking at statistics and surveys by various international research institutions, it becomes clear that the majority of ICT users and owners of PCs live in the United States, Canada, and western Europe. A survey published on February 23, 2003,[15] shows that the United States alone accounted for 29 percent of the global Internet access and Latin America accounted for only 2 percent. The same survey showed that Europe accounted for 23 percent, and Asia–Pacific for 13 percent. Africa was not even mentioned. The survey does not say why Africa is not mentioned, but perhaps the answer can be found by looking at data collected by the International Telecommunication Union. In 2003, out of 10,000 Africans only 149 persons used the Internet, and out of 100 persons only 1.38 had a PC. In comparison, in the United States, out of 10,000 persons, more than 5,000 were Internet users, and out of 100 persons, 66 had PCs.[16]

The general lack of access to ICT globally and the "digital divide" between south and north implicate discrimination due to poverty and lack of social, economic, and political development. In fact, it could be argued that the lack of access to ICT in the developing regions adds to human rights violations such as discrimination against vulnerable groups. ICT is a gateway to accessing knowledge and information. Having access will, for example, enable the creation and distribution of information to develop business opportunities, and ensure that rural areas have access to education and to information on, for instance, family planning, medical treatment, one's right not to be discriminated against, and, more generally, means to create and partake in different types of networks.

It is no secret that access to information empowers individuals and groups to combat poverty and support their participation in the development of democratic societies. However, it is also no secret that vulnerable groups, due to discrimination, do not have equal access to the information provided through ICT.

Generally speaking, information and communication technologies are a commodity available to the general public, and as such are within the scope of the provision of goods and services. The term "goods and services" potentially extends across a wide range of private and public activities, including the provision of education, housing, transport, service delivery, and the supply of goods.[17] When a product, commodity, service or good is intended for the general public, the provider must guarantee the right to access to it for everyone, without distinction as to race, ethnicity, color, religion, gender, disability, age, or civil or political status. This applies to both private and public telecommunication and ICT providers.

Nevertheless, discrimination in the provision of goods and services can involve the manifestation of some of the most virulent and overt forms of prejudice against certain groups in a society.[18] As mentioned before, the general lack of global access to ICT and the existence of the digital divide imply the existence of discrimination. But there are few or no disaggregated data as to which *groups of persons* have or don't have access to ICT. Collecting such data is very difficult. The difficulty lies in the fact that the violations are often committed indirectly or as an accepted traditional and social behavior. Discrimination is often institutionalized as neutral practices embedded in the traditions and institutions of a society.

Women, for instance, due to existing gender stereotyping and their traditional status and position in society, are denied access to a large range of goods and services, and access to ICT is no exception. For example, in societies where women are not allowed to be visible in public, they are denied entrance to Internet cafés. They also are indirectly discriminated against because most women live in rural areas and are not very mobile. Generally speaking, ICT providers do not prioritize rural areas or the state does not ensure an infrastructure that enables ICT to be accessed in those areas. Seemingly a neutral practice/policy, but in effect a practice/policy that excludes a particular group of people: women.

Dr. Heike Jensen, an expert in the field of gender, argues further in her chapter in this book:

Many global and pervasive structural human rights violations against women and girls have intersected with the digital divides based on north–south, urban–rural, rich–poor, and racially or ethnically motivated divisions, and have constituted formidable barriers to many women's and girls' access to ICTs. Among these are the discrimination against girls and women in education and access to technology (CEDAW, Articles 5 and 10; BPfA, Critical Areas of Concern 2 and 12); job opportunities, career development, and level of income (CEDAW, Articles 11, 13(b), and 16(g); BPfA, Critical Area of Concern 6); business autonomy and money at their free disposal (CEDAW, Articles 15(2) and 16(h); BPfA, Critical Areas of Concern 1 and 7); leisure time and cultural participation (CEDAW, Article 5); political participation (CEDAW, Articles 7 and 8); and decision-making in all spheres of society (BPfA, Critical Area of Concern 7).

In other words, discrimination against women in access to ICT is closely linked to the fact that they are being discriminated against in other areas that would have, had they not been discriminated against, enabled them to gain access.

Similar patterns of discrimination in goods and services, and thereby access to ICT, occur with regard to race, color, and ethnicity.

Looking back in history for the reasons why, in the European context, legal steps were taken to combat racial and ethnic discrimination, one finds that, apart from discrimination in employment, discrimination in goods and services bears considerable responsibility. According to Colm O'Cinneide, a human rights lawyer at University College London:

Many of the most overt and aggressive forms of racial and ethnic discrimination that gave rise to the US civil rights movements in the early 1960's involved unequal treatment in the provision of goods and services, often involving the vicious segregation of Afro-Americans in education, public transport, restaurants and housing. Equivalent patterns of discrimination occurred in the UK in the same period with the influx of Afro-Caribbean and South Asian migrants, epitomised by the "no blacks, no Irish, no dogs" signs that often appeared on signs for rented accommodation in London.[19]

Blatant and outright prejudice such as the signs "no blacks, no Irish, no dogs" are no longer found in Europe. But racial and ethnic discrimination still exists, often involving more hidden and insidious forms of prejudice, continuation of the same-procedure-as-last-year mantra, and policies regarding integration of ethnic minorities into society. When the state provides information for its citizens—nationals as well as non-nationals—on the Internet, the information is most likely to be found only in the majority language, which in effect excludes those who do not speak the majority language or have difficulty understanding it. Dissemination of information often begins in the majority and the homogeneous society, and thereby excludes the minorities (for instance, due to language barriers).

The impact and implications of discrimination can vary from one vulnerable group to another. But despite differences, all groups subject to discrimination experience exclusion and vulnerability.

A prerequisite for nondiscriminatory access to ICT is mainstreaming of nondiscrimination and prohibition of discrimination, as stipulated in the various human rights conventions. Mainstreaming nondiscrimination can be defined as incorporation of equal treatment into all actions, programs, and policies from the start. For instance, development of an action program for ICT should accommodate the impact of the actions on gender, race, and so on.

States have a duty not only to prohibit discrimination through laws and regulations, but to also take positive measures to guarantee all persons equal and effective protection against discrimination. Article 2 of ICESCR expresses this duty quite clearly:

Each State Party to the present Covenant undertakes to take steps, individually and through international assistance and co-operation, especially economic and technical, to the maximum of its available resources.

This duty includes guaranteeing all persons the right and equal access to ICT without being discriminated against.

## Conclusion

No other human rights can be claimed if the nondiscrimination principle is not applied. Nondiscrimination is the principle that makes the other rights operational and, in a sense, makes human rights universal, not only in judicial discourse but also, to a great degree, in political and moral discourse.

The WSIS Declaration of Principles and the Action Plan for the development of a global information society, although only political documents that state parties have committed themselves to, serve as platforms from which the development of the global information society should occur. The documents signal the importance of the information society, and such a society cannot exist as a democratic one if the principle of nondiscrimination is not applied. The documents ought to remind the states of their obligations to combat discrimination and to recommend implementation and mainstreaming of the non-discrimination principle in national legislation and policies to protect individuals from violations of human rights and secure their rights to access ICT. The information society can become a reality only when all human beings can claim their rights without prejudice and discrimination.

### Notes

1. Morten Kjærum, "The Principle of Non-discrimination in the Field of Human Rights," in *Discrimination and Prevention of Torture. Collected Papers from the First*

*Roundtable Under the EU–Iran Human Rights Dialogue, Tehran, 16–17 December 2002* (Copenhagen: Danish Institute for Human Rights, 2003).

2. MDI (Dutch Complaints Bureau for Discrimination on the Internet), *Annual Report 2003* (Amsterdam: MDI, 2003).

3. www.inach.net.

4. Especially in the United State there is a tradition of more absolute freedom of expression, whereas Europe puts more emphasis on balancing freedom of expression with the protection of other rights.

5. Lene Johannessen, *New Limits: A Legal Comment on a Case About Freedom of Expression and Hate Speech* (Copenhagen: Danish Centre for Human Rights, 1996), 3.

6. Ibid.

7. Ibid., 4.

8. Section 266b of the Danish Penal Code prohibits racist propaganda and incitement to racial hatred.

9. Johannessen, *New Limits*, 10.

10. Ibid., 3.

11. From a unpublished speech by Michael Whine, "Online Propaganda and the Commission of Hate," presented at the Organization for Security and Co-operation in Europe meeting on the relationship between racist, xenophobic, and anti–Semitic propaganda on the Internet and hate crimes (Paris, June 16–17, 2004).

12. David Matas, *Bloody Words, Hate and Free Speech* (Winnipeg, Canada: Bain & Cox, 2000), 38.

13. Swiss Institute of Comparative Law, *Legal Instruments to Combat Racism on the Internet* (Strasbourg, France: European Commission Against Racism and Intolerance, 2000).

14. Ibid., 89.

15. www.nua.ie/surveys/index.

16. www.itu.int.

17. Colm O'Cinneide, "Goods and Services: Setting the Scene," paper delivered at the seminar "Discrimination in the Fields of Goods and Services," Danish Institute for Human Rights, Mar. 17, 2004.

18. Ibid.

19. Ibid.

# 10   Women's Human Rights in the Information Society

Heike Jensen

Human rights can be understood as abstract norms and values enshrined in laws, constitutions, and international conventions. At the same time, human rights are cultural concepts that are slowly evolving in response to social change or contestation. In this chapter I explore how human rights have become applicable to the realities of women's lives, and how we can build on the international conventions and agreements that have accomplished this task to understand the dimensions of women's human rights in the information society. I wish to show that women's human rights instruments provide fundamental insights into the causes, manifestations, and consequences of human rights violations experienced by women and girls. They hence can serve as an important lens for examining how old and new information and communication technologies (ICTs) can either redress existing human rights violations or augment them and even add new ones.

The fundamental challenges to women's human rights that present themselves with the move toward the information society are not new at all. They have been identified for quite some time, but they have not been fought in a systematic, thorough, and committed manner. Human rights violations multiply where different forms of arbitrary social stratification intersect, so that girls and women are most severely affected by them if they are also disadvantaged in terms of race, class, and other determinants. The uneven spread of ICTs compounds these violations if it is not expressly directed to counter them. Hence, what needs to be understood is the evolving relationship between existing human rights provisions and human rights violations regarding women and girls, on the one hand, and media and ICTs, on the other. This deliberation is needed to establish frameworks in which ICTs can serve as tools that help promote, protect, and fulfill human rights, including women's human rights.

## Articulating Women's Human Rights Provisions at the UN Level

The principle of equality between women and men and the prohibition of discrimination on the basis of sex are laid down in the United Nations Charter (1945)[1] as well as in the three central documents that together constitute the International Bill of Human Rights: the Universal Declaration of Human Rights (1948),[2] the International Covenant on Civil and Political Rights,[3] and the International Covenant on Economic, Social and Cultural Rights.[4] However, the overall framework of interpretation for these human rights documents has been a traditional liberal one, in which human rights violations are tacitly understood as actions by state agents against politically active men in the public sphere. Violations of women's human rights have in this framework largely remained hidden from view, and have often appeared either as private matters or as cultural or religious traditions. Starting from the lived realities of girls and women and tracing how and by whom they are hindered from enjoying their fundamental rights and freedoms has enabled decisive reconceptualizations of human rights violations. Since the general human rights instruments have often proved to be insufficient, in terms of both thematic scope and application, to address these violations, distinct human rights instruments for women have been developed alongside them.

The first legal instrument of the United Nations focusing solely on women's rights was the Convention on the Political Rights of Women, which entered into force in 1954.[5] As stressed by Hazou, it constitutes "the first worldwide treaty in which a charter principle of equal rights for men and women has been applied to a concrete problem."[6] Other such instruments followed, which were adopted by either the U.N. General Assembly or its specialized agencies.[7] In 1981, the Convention on the Elimination of all Forms of Discrimination Against Women (CEDAW) entered into force.[8] It constitutes the most comprehensive convention concerning women to date, and more than 90 percent of the states of the world are now parties to it.[9] CEDAW addresses a broad range of issues that are of particular relevance to women's and girls' human rights, and it insists on seeing human rights as indivisible, interdependent, and integral parts of any space and all spheres of society, from the most private to the most public.

CEDAW defines human rights violations as any form of intentional or unintentional discrimination that prevents women's equality with men—understood as an abstract standard. Governments that are parties to CEDAW are held responsible not only for committing human rights violations themselves but also for systematically failing to protect women's and girls' human rights against violations perpetrated by any other actor, for failing to address or punish violations in a systematic manner, and for failing to promote and bring about equality between women and men. Beyond CEDAW, it was primarily the series of U.N. world conferences during the 1990s that further promoted and fleshed out women's human rights. Summit declarations, in contrast to conventions such as CEDAW, do not have the force of law. Nevertheless, they constitute a strong global normative consensus and may have a direct impact on how existing conventions are interpreted and refocused in the light of new developments. Experience also shows that summit declarations may exert a considerable influence on future conventions.

A very important contribution to the articulation of women's rights was made at the World Conference on Human Rights in Vienna in 1993, where violence against women was denounced as a human rights violation, and the rallying cry "Women's rights are human rights" went around the world.[10] The Beijing Declaration and Platform for Action,[11] formulated at the Fourth World Conference on Women in 1995, builds on this and constitutes a comprehensive touchstone for women's human rights. It is also a vital point of reference as far as media and communications issues are concerned. But with regard to these issues, it is instructive to go a little farther back in history and consider the World Conference on Women in Nairobi (1985) as well.

The Forward-looking Strategies for the Advancement of Women,[12] adopted at Nairobi, contain a wealth of paragraphs concerned with all kinds of media, from traditional cultural media, to mass media, to communication and information networks. The Nairobi document thoroughly addresses the need to combat stereotypes[13] and pornography, and to work for positive portrayals of women and peace. Further media content issues that are stressed are the need to inform the public about women's rights and to provide useful information for women, particularly in developing and rural regions. Other media issues that receive attention are the development of communication and information networks, and the need to bring women into decision-making positions and to train them in the mass communication sector. The Beijing Declaration and Platform for Action of 1995 takes up several of these issues, stating as one of its twelve Critical Areas of Concern the "Stereotyping of women and inequality of women's access to and participation in all communication systems, especially in the media." Section J, "Women and the Media," provides an elaboration of these points.

It is generally agreed that the Beijing document was decisive in putting ICTs firmly on the global women's agenda.[14] But it also needs to be stressed that the document attests to another vital change when compared with older documents such as the Nairobi one: almost all calls for a revision of media content and new guidelines for content are qualified in the Beijing document by the clause "to the extent consistent with freedom of expression." Freedom of expression is here acknowledged as a right of commercial media institutions to safeguard against content or programming obligations imposed by states. While this right can be used by media businesses to refuse to transmit state propaganda, it can also be invoked by them to avoid public service obligations or women's right to nonstereotyped depictions.[15] These issues go to the heart of a fundamental tension at the root of the mass media: even though most media are commercial enterprises, they simultaneously are understood and called upon as public resources, which raises the questions of how to finance and govern them.

With the dawn of the Internet, with new paradigms of communication via the World Wide Web and e-mail, and with the increasing deregulation of the telecommunications sector, the media landscape has changed profoundly. Simultaneously, the tension between media as commercial enterprises and media as potential public resources or public service providers has intensified, so that new models of regulation are needed to balance the two. At this stage, advocates for gender equality have turned to ICT policy as a new field for political intervention to try to ensure that all women will benefit from the new technologies.[16] From a human rights perspective, the overarching challenge has been to create frameworks in which the new ICT tools can be harnessed on the basis of a global human rights consensus to redress human rights violations instead of augmenting them.[17] At present, it appears that in the wake of the stipulation of the Millennium Development Goals (MDGs),[18] a dangerous shift and backsliding may be under way from a human rights paradigm to an "aid to victims" approach.[19] Such a protectionist approach is reminiscent of old and faded development policy schemes. These schemes often disempowered women in particular, limiting their individual agency and freedoms and favoring universal technical approaches within questionable economic frameworks.[20]

The gender divide has been recognized as "one of the most significant inequalities to be amplified by the digital revolution."[21] It has been brought about by the far-reaching impact on all spheres of society of the new digital and networked ICTs, of which computers and the Internet, as well as mobile phones and their networks, are the most prominent examples. Many of the human rights violations against women that are being augmented—but could also be ameliorated—by ICTs have been noted for a long time. In what follows, I will use key women's human rights documents such as CEDAW and the Beijing Platform for Action (BPfA), and the insights they provide into the causes, manifestations, and consequences of discrimination, as a lens to focus on prime women's human rights issues in the information society. I will discuss the status quo and its human rights implications for women, as well as some current political issues and their possible implications for women's human rights in three overlapping, central spheres: ICTs as tools, ICTs as careers, and ICT ideology. The sample of relevant women's human rights provisions from CEDAW onward that I will cite in the text is by no means meant to be exhaustive, but is to illustrate the long-standing identification of these issues.

## ICTs as Tools: Whose Tools and Tools for What?

ICTs have been the driving force of an increasingly globalized economy, orchestrating the division of labor, the movement of goods, the operation of the financial markets, and knowledge exchange. Despite this profound worldwide impact of ICTs, the vast majority of people so far have not come into direct contact with them. In 2002, 600 million people were online (9.6 percent), which means that more than 5.5 billion (90.4 percent) of the people of the world were offline. Of the onliners, 66 percent were in the developed countries, in which 19 percent of the world's population lives.[22]

ICTs and Internet connections have so far been a predominantly urban and northern phenomenon, and the commercial logic that has guided their spread makes it likely that this development may intensify.[23] The global impact of ICTs on many aspects of life, coupled with their highly uneven spread and accessibility, has given rise to the notion of "digital divides," gaps separating those who can access, use effectively, and shape the new ICTs and the spheres they alter, and those who cannot. Research has shown that digital divides open up along the lines of established economic and social inequalities, and that they become deepest where multiple forms of arbitrary social stratification intersect. This severely disadvantages women and girls, who also suffer from additional forms of discrimination.

The profound north–south and urban–rural digital divides and their ties to the global economy have arguably had a detrimental effect on the fundamental right to development of the global south.[24] And they have without a doubt had particularly strong implications for women's human rights, because the majority of women in the developing world, especially in Africa, live in rural areas.[25] The human rights of rural women constitute a specific focus of CEDAW, which calls for wide-ranging human rights actions on their behalf in Article 14. Closely connected to the north–south and the urban–rural divides is the issue of poverty, which constitutes another digital divide. This issue is also of particular relevance for women because more than 70 percent of the world's poor are women. The majority of poor women live in developing regions, but poverty in general, and women's poverty in particular, is increasing everywhere. This "feminization of poverty" has been observed for quite some time, and it constituted the first Critical Area of Concern addressed in the Beijing Platform for Action of 1995.

Racial and ethnic discrimination is another determinant of digital divides, both between and within countries. The differential impact of racial and ethnic discrimination on men and women was duly noted in the report of the World Conference Against Racism, Racial Discrimination, Xenophobia and Related Intolerance, held in Durban, South Africa, in 2001.[26] The digital divide based on racial and ethnic discrimination in turn has strong connections to poverty, and is particularly salient for women in situations of migration, displacement, and armed conflict. Many global and pervasive structural human rights violations against women and girls have intersected with the digital divides based on north–south, urban–rural, rich–poor, and racially or ethnically motivated divisions, and have constituted formidable barriers to many women's and girls' access to ICTs. Among these are the discrimination against girls and women in education and access to technology (CEDAW, Articles 5 and 10; BPfA, Critical Areas of Concern 2 and 12); job opportunities, career development, and level of income (CEDAW, Articles 11, 13(b), and 16(g); BPfA Critical Area of Concern 6); business autonomy and money at their free disposal (CEDAW, Articles 15(2) and 16(h); BPfA, Critical Areas of Concern 1 and 7); leisure time and cultural participation (CEDAW, Article 5); political participation (CEDAW, Articles 7 and 8); and decision-making in all spheres of society (BPfA, Critical Area of Concern 7).

Given the multidimensional barriers that have hindered many girls' and women's access to ICTs, the potential benefits that ICTs provide have largely not helped them but, rather, men and women in the north and south who are already well-off and advantaged. The gap between the groups has widened with the growth of the social, economic, political, and other advantages and opportunities derived from information and expertise gained through ICTs. Two central compensatory strategies have been identified that would counter these trends systematically, one involving traditional media and the other involving ICTs. First, knowledge gaps and expertise differentials between users and non-users of ICTs need to be bridged by other, readily accessible media, such as the radio, which must be meaningfully related to and socially integrated with the new ICTs. Also, older technologies must be expanded, particularly in forms that allow women ready access not just as users and consumers, but also as producers of content and media structures. An example would be community radio stations run by women and geared to their needs. Concurrently, women need to be empowered to shape the technologies and their social, economic, and political meanings.

Second, strong and consistent ICT policy measures are required to turn ICTs into tools for inclusion and social balancing, community development, and the promotion of women's human rights. There is a wide consensus in the gender-sensitive literature on ICT policy that all decisions, be they concerned with infrastructure, networks, technology, tariffs, regulation, licensing, or any other matter, need specifically to take into account the situation of women, particularly of women in the south, and rural and poor women, and to promote their right of inclusion, hence furthering their right to development.[27] This will involve the availability of phone lines, relay stations for mobile phones, and earth stations for satellites, as well as the accessibility of the technology. Accessibility, on the one hand, refers to physical locations within reach of the girls and women (i.e., shared public access facilities such as multimedia centers, cybercafés, telekiosks, or other places were ICTs might be used). On the other hand, it refers to opening hours that fit girls' and women's time management duties, equipment that is most suitable, and personnel who are approachable and helpful. Finally, the services need to be affordable.[28]

In terms of content, ICTs could provide services that ameliorate specific human rights violations against girls and women. With respect to education and training, they could, for instance, provide distance education and e-learning, with a view to increasing girls' opportunities to receive the same amount and quality of education as boys. This goal was fixed in the pre–ICT era by CEDAW's Article 10, elaborated in the BPfA Strategic Objectives B and L.4., stipulated in Millennium Development Goal (MDG) 2 and indicators 9 and 10 for MDG 3, and reaffirmed with respect to ICTs in Paragraph 29 of the World Summit on the Information Society (WSIS) Declaration of Principles (DoP) and Paragraphs C4.11, C7.19.d, and C8.23 of the WSIS Action Plan (AP). Despite all of these provisions, and in fact prompting them, no steady progress can be stated with respect to girls' education on a world scale, which may also suggest that the literacy ratio between the genders will not improve significantly. At present, of the 1 billion illiterate adults, two thirds are women.[29] This also means that special interface concepts are required for ICTs that circumvent the illiteracy obstacle, foreign language barriers, or low levels of computer skills and information literacy that may be particularly salient for women without much formal education.

In a manner comparable with education, ICTs could provide health information in general and health information for women and girls in particular, including information on family planning. They would thus strengthen women's human rights in this area, as laid down in CEDAW and stressed as vital by the high number of provisions to this effect (Articles 12 and 14(b) with a particular view to rural areas; and 10(h) and 16(e)). Women's health was also reaffirmed as a central issue for women in the BPfA Strategic Objective C and in a very truncated form in MDG 5 and Indicator 18 of MDG 7. Compliance with women's human rights with respect to health would simultaneously benefit society at large, because women provide the bulk of unpaid health-care services around the world.

This line of reasoning, however, should not be understood as an argument to cement women's multiple burdens of gainful employment and unpaid domestic and care work.[30] These multiple burdens in fact violate the human rights principle of equality between the genders. They leave women and girls less time for personal development, education (CEDAW, Article 10) and career development (CEDAW, Article 11), as well as for participation in cultural life (CEDAW, Article 13(c)) and the political development of their communities (CEDAW, Articles 7 and 8). Currently, we are in fact witnessing an increase in women's multiple burdens, and hence an intensification of these human rights violations. This is the case because governments worldwide follow the neoliberal doctrine and cut social spending; and girls and women take up the largest share of the resulting increase in unpaid work. UNICEF has acknowledged this dynamic as "invisible adjustment."[31]

In terms of creating increased business opportunities for those most in need of them, ICTs and their content would have to be particularly geared to meeting the information needs of poor women and women in developing and rural regions (constituencies addressed in CEDAW, Article 14, and BPfA, Strategic Objective A.1). With respect to political content, ICTs could be used to inform women about their human rights and how to apply them for empowerment and decision-making in all areas of individual and community life (BPfA, Strategic Objectives I and G). Beyond content dissemination, ICTs should allow women to form networks, be these self-help groups, economic cooperatives, or political pressure groups. While this is important for women worldwide, it carries a particular significance for women living in comparative isolation (e.g., rural women, older women, or handicapped women, and women who face other types of structural discrimination and human rights violations, such as extreme poverty or displacement). There is increasing evidence that political networks dedicated to furthering women's human rights have been proliferating and expanding with the help of ICTs. This development needs to be strengthened, as expressly mandated by the BPfA Strategic Objective J, Paragraph 239(f).

Strengthening women's rights and women's development would also appear to be the prime way of combating trafficking in women and forced prostitution and its facilitation through ICTs. Trafficking and forced prostitution are human rights violations denounced in CEDAW, Article 6, and the BPfA Strategic Objective D.3., and it is safe to assume that in many cases they build on previously existing, multiple human rights violations suffered disproportionately or distinctively by women, such as extreme poverty, unemployment, stereotyping, and racism.[32] These violations have the underlying consequence of cementing women's subordinate role in the societies affected, as explained in CEDAW, General Recommendation 19,[33] and the flaunting of these crimes over the World Wide Web further consolidates the impression of girls' and women's subordination and easy victimization. Other real-life threats to women and girls in virtual reality are their intimidation by cyberstalking and flaming (verbal haiassment) on the World Wide Web. Mainstream pornography and spam advertising sex aids for men are other reminders of an outside world catering to northern male fantasies and buying power. Many women consider these uses of ICTs undesirable at best and deeply threatening at worst, and it has been convincingly argued that these practices, insofar as they testify to northern male power and intimidate or weary women, have the effect of curtailing women's right to freedom of expression.[34]

These issues raise complex questions of Internet governance and security that cannot easily be answered with calls for censorship or surveillance. Surveillance is a particularly crucial issue with respect to the new ICTs, because these technologies may record all manner of activities and allow the production, aggregation, cross-matching, and storage of unprecedented amounts and kinds of personal data. Infringements on the human rights to privacy and confidential correspondence, stated in the Universal Declaration of Human Rights (UDHR, Article 12), and to freedom of association (UDHR, Article 20) might help police agencies locate the criminals exploiting women. But these infringements could just as easily be turned against women's interests at the whim of governments, business entities, or other interested parties.[35]

To understand in which contexts women using ICTs might be particularly vulnerable to surveillance or censorship, we have to understand the specific uses women make of the World Wide Web. In this context, it is also important to know that in several First World countries, women make up from almost 50 percent to the majority of the Internet users.[36] In terms of use strategies, it appears that women differ most markedly from men in that they are more goal-oriented and have less leisure time to spare. Men read online newspapers, play games, download software, tinker with the technology, and consume pornography. Women, in contrast, network and correspond, look up health-care information, and engage in online shopping.[37] Various parties might have a stake in monitoring these activities as closely as possible.

Quite generally, in some cultures women are particularly vulnerable to surveillance in the outside world, and it needs to be ascertained that the invasions of privacy that they potentially suffer offline are not carried over into monitoring their online activities. With respect to glaring human rights violations targeted at women, such as violence in the family and honor killings, there is evidence that the World Wide Web offers women and the organizations supporting them new possibilities to circumvent physical surveillance, to network, and to tell their stories without compromising their need for anonymity. However, there is an entirely new trail of digital data that these women and their organizations leave behind, and this information needs to be shielded from surveillance, from infringements of the right to privacy, and from serving to facilitate physical human rights violations. The same care is needed to ascertain that women's political groups and networks will be able to work confidentially without surveillance and infringements on the women's rights to expression, association, and democratic participation. These infringements could take the form of surveillance as well as censorship (e.g., in the form of content filters).

With respect to the health-care system, it needs to be made certain that any data produced neither infringe on women's right to privacy nor form the basis for discrimination against women in health-care systems. The role of women as online shoppers also needs to be considered, keeping in mind that initiatives in northern countries for bringing more women online are in large part advanced by companies that wish to turn these women into buyers of the technology, into online shoppers, and into online audiences for advertisements.

With the rise of the new ICTs, the psychologizing approach to audience profiling that was inaugurated in the late 1920s and early 1930s can be augmented by information which severely violates the right to privacy and the dignity of potential customers.[38] This information could encompass the amount of time a woman lets her cursor hover over a specific part of a Web page in virtual space, and even her state of arousal and her eye movements when entering a shop in the outside world, as transmitted by sensors installed in a shop, and subsequently processed and stored as data, without her knowledge and beyond her reach.[39] Such a scenario suggests that invasion of privacy, which is a human rights violation that was initially conceptualized as states' penetrations into their citizens' privacy, must be reconceptualized to include potentially far-reaching violations by businesses vis-à-vis potential customers.[40] These, in the present circumstances, put women at particular risk.

### ICTs as Careers: Whose Careers?

ICTs have changed the ways in which business has traditionally been set up and conducted, and ICTs themselves constitute new industries. As such, their introduction has created new kinds of jobs and skills. Just as with other realms of global restructuring of employment, these changes have benefited women only to a limited degree, if at all. Most obviously, women have hardly made any inroads into the established centers of economic and political power. As Primo states:

> Whether at the global or national level, women are under-represented in all ICT decision-making structures, including policy and regulatory institutions, ministries responsible for ICTs, and boards and senior management of private ICT companies. ... In 2001 women held only 9% of senior management jobs and 9% of positions in the supervisory bodies of the telecommunications industry across 18 countries in Europe. In the United States in 2001, women held 13% of top executive positions, and made up just 9% of board members of major telecommunications and e-companies.[41]

Thus, with respect to decision-making positions in business and politics, the familiar picture of human rights violations against women continues: women are denied the same employment opportunities (CEDAW, Article 11(b)), the right to free choice of profession and employment (CEDAW, Article 11(c)), and the right to equal remuneration or to equal treatment with respect to work of equal value[42] (CEDAW, Article 11(d); see also BPfA Strategic Objective F, "Women and the Economy," and Strategic Objective G, "Women in Power and Decision-Making").[43] On the governmental level, women's rights to hold public office (CEDAW, Article 7(b)) and to represent their governments at the international level (CEDAW, Article 8) on equal terms with men are still severely curtailed. It is particularly striking to see how swiftly new industries and new kinds of jobs have been stereotyped in terms of gender. Considered from a human rights perspective, the gender-role stereotyping connected with ICT-related jobs and businesses constitutes a seamless continuation of previous human rights violations in the sphere of work that women have faced: it violates CEDAW Article 5(a) and its call to abolish stereotyped roles and gender hierarchies.

Within the dynamics of globalization, stereotyping has become a decisive process shaping the worldwide division of labor, the latter being enabled by minute coordination via the new ICTs. This process has led to an outsourcing of manufacturing and service jobs from the global north to the global south, most notably to the free trade zones of developing countries, such as Jamaica and Barbados.[44] While women's occupations in the ICT field constitute new opportunities for gainful employment, they have generally been characterized by low pay, low recognition, repetitiveness of duties, and limited career opportunities. Hence, women have been employed in the production of electronics and computer hardware, but generally restricted to assembly line and low-level technical occupations. In addition, women dominate the global service sector of computer-aided data processing and telecommunications, centered in the Caribbean and in Asia.[45]

In the Philippines, India, and Malaysia, ICT industries expand primarily in the form of call centers staffed by female teleworkers. In Europe, telework in call centers or at home also constitutes a feminized work option, in general characterized by single-task, repetitive duties, while male telework from home is usually more varied, considered more prestigious, and better paid.[46] Depending on the employment circumstances, women's right to social security may be violated (CEDAW, Article 11(e)), as may be the core labor standards stipulated by the International Labour Organisation (ILO), such as workers' right to organize. These human rights violations may occur in all world regions, but they have become glaringly apparent in free trade zones, where other human rights violations, such as sexual harassment, may be added to them. While women gain new job opportunities, other feminized job sectors are diminishing due to an increased application of ICTs, so that, for instance, women lose their employment as bank tellers and telephone operators.[47]

The new economy of the global north as the center of the ICT industry has generated its own share of gender stereotypes, which have had detrimental effects on women's job and career opportunities. The new economy is symbolized as a masculine sphere, crowned by the mythical male figure of the self-taught software developer–genius, who either builds an evil empire or is a hero of free and open source software.[48] It has spurred a corporate culture of long work hours and total commitment that is next to incompatible with family and child-rearing responsibilities. These characteristics limit many women's inclinations and possibilities to work in the new economy. For one thing, it is harder for women to succeed as employees, given the multiple burdens many of them have to shoulder (CEDAW, Articles 5 and 11). For another, it is also harder for them to obtain credit or venture capital to build up their own enterprises, a violation of their right to equality addressed in CEDAW, Article 13 (b), and in the BPfA, A.3.[49]

Only in a few countries (e.g., Brazil, India, and Malaysia) have women been promoted as skilled workers such as software programmers or computer analysts.[50] Concerted political action is called for everywhere to combat the gender stereotypes and other human rights violations that keep girls and women away from sophisticated interaction with technology, so that they can establish careers shaping ICTs and the societies in which these are embedded. This promise is gestured toward in WSIS, DoP, Paragraph12, and WSIS, AP, Paragraphs C4.11, C6.13, and C7.19.[51]

## ICT Ideology: Whose Ideology?

A huge conceptual blurring lies at the heart of the term "information," and consequently carries over into the concept of the information society. This blurring is infused with power relations, which makes it an ideological issue as well as a human rights issue. In order to get to its core, a distinction between the terms "data" and "information" needs to be introduced. With this distinction, it can be stated that the new ICTs produce and make available huge amounts of data. These data are turned into information only if the person receiving them and trying to interpret them finds them to be a resource (i.e., comprehends the language and the content, and has use for it). It is fair to assume that as far as the World Wide Web is concerned, most of the content constitutes data to most people, and not information, because very little of it is of value to any single individual. Such an assessment exposes the technological positivism that is at the heart of the claim that the new ICTs automatically create the information society.[52]

Turning to the gender dimension of information, it is particularly vital to address supposedly fact-producing endeavors such as the news, government statistics, and academic and scientific research. Given the ongoing predominance of men as decision-makers in all of these endeavors and the institutions running and financing them, at least two kinds of ideological distortions need to be stressed. One is the distortion produced by a focus on male-dominated fields, experiences, viewpoints, and perspectives, which leads to a marginalization or exclusion of insights, opinions, experiences, or knowledge arrived at by women as a result of their specific, gender-defined, and gender-circumscribed places in society. The other distortion is produced by the predominant ideology of universality. For one thing, this ideology elevates the dominant male perspective to the status of universal truth and validity.[53] For another, this ideology of universality masks situations of inequality by omitting reference to them. For instance, statistics describing a population may not differentiate between men and women, let alone between men and women of different racial, ethnic, or migratory backgrounds. This, of course, throws the information value of the data into question, particularly if large gaps of social, economic, or political significance between the groups are concealed in this way.

In sum, what is now canonized as information or knowledge is heavily indebted to the positions of dominance and control under which it is produced. As such, it is characterized by an infringement on women's right to participate in the political and cultural life of the community (CEDAW, Articles 7 and 13(c)) and the academic world (CEDAW, Article 10) on the same footing as men. And further, it interferes with women's basic democratic human right to inform themselves about their own situations and to arrive at informed political and other decisions on this basis. This is an issue everywhere around the globe, irrespective of the wealth or level of education of the people. It takes various forms, from a lack of disaggregated statistics (which would differentiate between men and women and further subgroups), to the male definition of news value and its attendant stereotypes in news reporting, to an undervaluation of women's knowledge, areas of expertise, and learning styles.[54]

With respect to the well-meaning call for an increasing public domain of knowledge to be created with the help of the new ICTs, it needs to be stressed that such a domain is compatible with women's human right to "seek, receive and impart information and ideas" (Universal Declaration of

Human Rights, Article 19) only if its definition of knowledge departs decisively from the present ideology. It would consequently have to encompass women's knowledge—which would not only add to the pool of knowledge but also, in effect, disqualify much of what is considered knowledge under the present ideological regime. Hence, in this context, from a women's human rights perspective it is not only intellectual property rights and the costs of ICTs that jeopardize any public domain of knowledge, even though these are crucial issues. In addition, women have to battle much more insidious, hegemonic arrangements that structurally disqualify many of their intellectual contributions.[55]

A related problem arises with respect to the concept of a "right to communicate" that has been advanced as a new take on the right to freedom of expression. This new right is to supersede the appropriation of freedom of expression by media businesses, as explained above, with a more democratic notion that all people should be able to express themselves and get in contact with each other, which includes the democratization of access to information and communication facilities and technological resources. From the perspective of women's human rights, it is questionable if such a new right would really benefit women in a global social climate in which their views, knowledge, and issues are marginalized and suppressed. It is true that the new ICTs do have the potential to be used in a way that ameliorates this situation. For instance, it is often pointed out that ICTs constitute a medium of communication that is unique with respect to the ease with which individuals can express their concerns to a mass audience.

While the "one-to-many" type of communication associated with the traditional mass media is indeed augmented by the "many-to-many" possibilities offered by the new ICTs, this state of affairs says nothing about the reception side of the communication process. Thus an important human rights issue that has not received much attention is how to safeguard not only the ease of utterance but also its potential reception. This is an issue that also concerns the workings of search engines and catalogs on the World Wide Web and their crucial role in directing potential audiences to the kind of data they might be looking for. Given the proliferation of content and the users' reliance on instruments to navigate it, there is a strong need to conceive (of) search engines and catalogs as tools for e-democracy which point to data that are of social, political, and developmental concern rather than see them as tools facilitating business.[56] This issue echoes the tension between media as businesses and media as public resources described above. The question remains to what extent marginalized views and voices will reach the mainstream, generate a deeper interest, and be able to move the mainstream toward non-discrimination and social balancing.

The area of e-democracy also links more broadly to the ideological issues discussed here; and the general public discussion so far has been dominated by gender-blind considerations. In such a framework, e-democracy would in effect only extend the present hegemonic arrangements to the sphere of ICTs, thus violating women's human right to receive and transmit data that will add up to socially useful information, and consequently infringing on their right to equal participation in a democratic political system, on their right to have equal access to public services, and on their possibilities to hold their governments accountable. Other issues that connect to questions surrounding e-democracy are those of the educational level, language, and literacy requirements, as well as information literacy, needed to participate. Given that women's human right to the same level of education enjoyed by men continues to be violated, e-democracy runs the risk of exacerbating this human rights violation by adding a violation of the human right to equal opportunities for political participation in the digital world.[57]

The question of online elections also raises a particular privacy issue for women. In the outside world, strong pressure may be applied by male heads of households to influence women's votes or take them out of their hands entirely. Online elections might facilitate this violation of women's right to self-determination and participation in the political sphere, because such violation might take place in the private sphere with no outside social scrutiny. At the same time, the hope is held out that e-democracy will reshape democratic processes in a manner that allows citizens more direct participation in and oversight of government activities, which could be a key element in women's empowerment and in the quest for gender equality.[58]

## Conclusion

The protection, promotion, and fulfillment of women's and girls' human rights is the prerequisite for shaping societies in a more just and sustainable manner within and among world regions.[59] The existence of digital divides, and in particular of the gender dimensions of these digital divides, has thrown into stark relief the fact that ICTs on the whole, under the present circumstances, compound human rights violations experienced by many women and girls rather than ameliorate them. Specifically, ICTs have exacerbated the forms of discrimination faced by those women and girls who are already disadvantaged by multiple forms of arbitrary social stratification. They thus block and hinder the constituencies that are most in need of tools and routes for positive change.

The existence of this chapter on women's human rights in the information society testifies to the fact that an awareness of violations of women's human rights has so far not informed the general debate. Yet international conventions and summit declarations aimed at furthering women's and girls' human rights have long identified the manifestations, consequences, and causes of discrimination, and have embodied a global normative consensus to counter all forms of discrimination against women. To move from lip service to the realization of women's and girls' human rights in the information society, women's human rights instruments can serve as a grid for working through the challenges posed by the possibilities ICTs might offer with regard to women's and girls' human rights. In this chapter, I have explained how this might be done with respect to ICTs as tools, ICTs as careers, and ICT ideology.

At bottom, ICTs could be of crucial service for the move toward gender equality and non-discrimination, but only if these principles guide their spread and application. Such a process would require special interventions on behalf of girls and women in all spheres, from the ideological to the material. Also needed would be new blueprints for the roles of boys and men in societies in order to enable nondiscriminatory, nonhierarchical, and truly cooperative relationships between the genders and sustainable development in all world regions. Much more serious work and commitment are required to accomplish these goals.[60]

## Notes

I would like to thank Angela M. Kuga Thas, Susanne Kempf, and Dace Kavasa for their valuable comments on draft versions of this chapter.

1. UNX.122(73) C613, Preamble and Art. 1.3.

2. A/RES/217 A (III), Preamble and Art. 2.

3. A/RES/2200 A (XXI), Arts. 2(1) and 3, adopted in 1966 and entered into force in 1976.

4. A/RES/2200A (XXI), Arts. 2(2) and 3, adopted in 1966 and entered into force in 1976.

5. A/RES/640 (VII), adopted by the General Assembly in 1952.

6. See Hazou, *The Social and Legal Status of Women*, 133.

7. Three additional types of conventions are important in this context. The first type is conventions that focus on the rights of specific groups of women, such as the Convention on the Nationality of Married Women (A/RES/1040 (XI)), adopted by the General Assembly in 1957 and entered into force in 1958. The second type is conventions that address issues of equality between the genders, such as the Convention Concerning Equal Remuneration for Men and Women Workers for Work of Equal Value (C100), adopted by the ILO in 1951 and entered into force in 1953. The third type is other problem-oriented conventions that contain specific references to women's or girls' status, such as the Convention Against Discrimination in Education, adopted by UNESCO in 1960 and entered into force in 1962.

8. A/RES/2263 (XXII), adopted by the General Assembly in 1979. In 2000, CEDAW was strengthened by an optional protocol (A/RES/A/54/4, adopted by the General Assembly in 1999).

9. See www.un.org/womenwatch/daw/cedaw/states.htm. Among the less than 10 percent of countries of the world that are not parties to CEDAW, the United States is the only OECD country.

10. See International Women's Tribune Centre, *Rights of Women*, 20. According to Jutta Joachim, it was Charlotte Bunch who laid the conceptual groundwork for this kind of women's rights frame in her article "Women's Rights as Human Rights." For the broader political context, see Joachim, "Shaping the Human Rights Agenda."

11. A/CONF.177/20/Rev.1 (96.IV.13).

12. A/CONF.116/28/Rev.1 (85.IV.10).

13. The connection between sex-role stereotyping and media was very much an issue during the U.N. International Decade for Women (1975–1985). See the historical overview in United Nations, Office of the Secretary-General, "Elimination of Stereotyping in the Mass Media," Report of the Secretary-General to the 40th session of the Commission on the Status of Women, esp. Introduction, Para. 4.

14. See Burch and Leon, "Directions for Women's Advocacy on ICT," 36.

15. On a supranational level, this understanding of freedom of expression also raises the issues of whether northern media monopolies may "colonize" other world regions with their content and silence local articulations. These issues were

heatedly debated at UNESCO from 1975 to 1985 under the heading "New World Information and Communication Order."

16. According to Nancy Hafkin, gender advocacy in ICT policy was inaugurated on the international level in the context of the World Telecommunications Development Conference organized by the International Telecommunication Union (ITU) in Valletta, Malta, in 1998. In its wake, ITU established its Gender Task Force. See Hafkin, "Gender Issues in ICT in Developing Countries," 3.

17. See Hurley, *Pole Star*. Much hope was invested in the U.N. World Summit on the Information Society (WSIS) in this respect. However, the Declaration of Principles (WSIS-03/GENEVA/DOC/0004) and Plan of Action (WSIS-03/GENEVA/DOC/0005) of the first summit in Geneva (Dec. 2003) fell short of many human rights activists' expectations.

18. Available at www.developmentgoals.org.

19. The relationship between human rights and the Millennium Development Goals (MDGs) is hotly debated within feminist and women's rights communities. There are many attempts to make the MDGs meaningful within a women's human rights framework. See, for instance, Painter, "Gender, the Millennium Development Goals, and Human Rights. . . ." See also Women's International Coalition for Economic Justice, *Seeking Accountability on Women's Human Rights*.

20. According to Arundhati Roy's 2004 Sydney Peace Prize lecture, "Peace and the New Corporate Liberation Theology," the violation of human rights is in fact an integral aspect of the neoliberal political and economic reordering of the world that has been taking place. The whole human rights discourse, in her understanding, serves as a deceptive side show that obscures this connection and provides a bandage for the losers.

21. Khan, "Preface," 5.

22. See ITU, *World Telecommunication Development Report 2003*. The ITU Report counts western Europe, Australia, Canada, Japan, New Zealand, and the United States as developed countries and all others as developing ones. According to the figures of the U.N. Development Programme (UNDP) *Human_Development Report 2004*, 155, the population ratio would be closer to 15 to 85 percent, even including Korea with the developed countries.

23. As Hurley states, "There are more telephone lines in metropolitan Tokyo than in all of sub-Saharan Africa, including South Africa. Moreover, there are plans to lay even more telephone lines in metropolitan Tokyo than in all of sub-Saharan Africa." See her *Pole Star*, 21.

24. This is the case insofar as the spread of ICTs has been directed by the overall neoliberal policy framework inaugurated by the Washington Consensus of the

1980s, which is widely held to have exacerbated poverty, social inequality, and debt. Main features of that framework are the opening of markets, a diminishing role of the state in the economy, privatization, and export-oriented growth. See, for instance, the discussions of this framework in Women's International Coalition for Economic Justice, *Seeking Accountability in Women's Human Rights*.

25. Primo, *Gender Issues in the Information Society*, 39.

26. A/CONF.189/12, esp. Paras. 69–72.

27. For an excellent overview of the different kinds of ICT policy issues and their gender aspects, see Hafkin, "Gender Issues in ICT Policy." As the basis for her overview, see Jorge, *Gender Perspectives in Telecommunications Policy*.

28. Hafkin, "Gender Issues in ICT Policy," 5.

29. Estimates vary tremendously. Compare, for instance, the figures provided by UNDP, *Human Development Report 2004* (table 26), UN, *The World's Women 2000*, UNIFEM, *Progress of the World's Women 2000*, UNESCO, *World Education Report 2000*, and www.developmentgoals.org/Gender_Equality.htm.

30. In this context, the phrase in the WSIS AP "recognizing women's roles as health providers in their families and communities," in the context of e-health (Para. C7.18.), appears dubious because it omits any reference to monetary compensation and hence seems to naturalize this role.

31. See UNICEF, *The Invisible Adjustment*.

32. Abeyesekera, "Development and Women's Human Rights," quotes the U.N. Special Rapporteur on Violence Against Women as stating that "economically disadvantaged women are more vulnerable to sexual harassment, trafficking and sexual slavery" (7). Trafficking and forced prostitution compound the situation because they deprive the victims of dignity, liberty, and self-determination and impact their health negatively. Reproductive health, including self-determination with respect to pregnancy, on the one hand, and sexuality, on the other, was emphasized as a fundamental human right for women at the World Summit on Population in Cairo in 1994 and the Fourth World Conference on Women in Beijing in 1995, respectively. The concept of health in general encompasses the physical, mental, emotional, and social dimensions. The crucial connection for women between health and the absence of violence has been reiterated for a long time and has recently come back into stark focus in connection with the rising numbers of women infected with HIV/AIDS.

33. Available at www.un.org/womenwatch/daw/cedaw/recommendations/recomm. htm#recom19.

34. See Brail, "The Price of Admission."

35. Online pornography and trafficking have been instrumentalized by governments to argue for increased opportunities for cyberspace surveillance and censorship in general.

36. See ITU, *World Telecommunication Development Report 2003*, 78. It needs to be stressed that in these countries, the gender digital divide is qualified by other variables of social stratification, including urban–rural divides; age, racial, and ethnic background; education; income level; and number of children. Those who are most connected are urban, well-educated, and well-off women in early adulthood and middle age. While in this subgroup no gender digital divide exists in terms of access to the new ICTs, research has shown that gender still constitutes a decisive variable in terms of how ICTs are used.

37. Primo, *Gender Issues in the Information Society*, 31.

38. For a "classical" account of the rise of the advertising industry in the United States, see Ewen, *Captains of Consciousness*; for a seminal investigation into the targeting of female audiences, see Coward, *Female Desires*.

39. As Hurley emphasizes, a crucial human rights issue is not only the amount and quality of the data gathered and whether this is in proportion to the aim underlying its gathering, but also who controls and owns the information. The latter question is inflected by further concerns about who can access the information and correct potential errors.

40. Violations of the right to privacy encompass the mining of personally identifiable information, including information gathered through forms of bodily intrusion, e.g., in cases in which medical implants emit data. Another form of intrusion comes in the form of unsolicited advertisements and other spam messages, which have, for instance, occupied the political system in the United States for years. Examples from 2003 are the Telemarketing Intrusive Practices Act introduced in the Senate (S 1661 IS), the Restrict and Eliminate the Delivery of Unsolicited Commercial Electronic Mail or Spam Act introduced in the Senate (S 1327 IS), and the Wireless Telephone Spam Protection Act introduced in the House of Representatives (HR 122 IH).

41. Primo, *Gender Issues in the Information Society*, 55. She cites FrauenComputerZentrumBerlin, *European Database on Women in Decision-making 2001*, and Jamieson, "Progress or No Room at the Top?," as her sources. For an update, see Falk and Grizard, "The Glass Ceiling Persists."

42. Women are still paid considerably less than men for comparable work. The mean difference is 20 percent, but this number is almost insignificant, given the high variability among countries and employment sectors. See UNIFEM, *Progress of the world's women 2000*.

43. As Huyer observes, women are diverted from becoming decision-makers in their fields at every stage of their career, from education and training through work experiences. See her *The Leaky Pipeline*.

44. Primo, *Gender Issues in the Information Society*, 50.

45. See Freeman, *High Tech and High Heels*; Pearson, "Gender and New Technology in the Caribbean"; or Ng and *Keying into the Future*.

46. See Prügl, *The Global Construction of Gender*.

47. Primo, *Gender Issues in the Information Society*, 24.

48. See Coyle, "How Hard Can It Be?"

49. It is worthwhile to stress that these obstacles for women have sprung up in a field in which a central impediment that often disqualifies women for careers does not matter: the lack of formal education. IT specialists are often self-taught, but the gender stereotypes relating to technology have created a virtual male homosocial sphere rather than equal opportunities for men and women for pursuing this field of expertise.

50. Primo, *Gender Issues in the Information Society*, 49.

51. But political decisions on Internet governance, intellectual property rights, and free and open source software will also influence the form of ICT careers, in that they affect the economic chances that small innovators and businesses will have in relation to multinational corporations. From a gender perspective, it would appear that—all other things being equal, which they are in fact not—small businesses hold greater promise for women than multinationals to exercise human rights as self-determined business owners or employees.

52. For a good elaboration, see Burkett, "Beyond the 'Information Rich and Poor.'"

53. Such an effect has also existed with respect to the traditional liberal framework for the articulation of human rights, whose detrimental effect on women and on an understanding of their rights I addressed at the beginning of this article.

54. The content on the World Wide Web, however, is even more narrowly defined by the prevalence of a worldview of the global north and of only a few languages, most notably English.

55. The sole area that is broadly acknowledged as one in which hegemonic gender arrangements have a direct bearing on knowledge production and even on IPR issues is women's expertise in the field of agriculture and biodiversity, as made visible in the Political Declaration of the World Summit on Sustainable Development (A/CONF.199/20* (03.II.A.1)) in Johannesburg in 2002.

56. The operation of search engines may be guided by economic imperatives that the users are unaware of, just as users in general often have only limited knowledge about how profit-generating mechanisms may enter into the online picture.

57. For an excellent investigation of this matter, see Martínez and Reilly, "Looking Behind the Internet."

58. See, for instance, Ramilo, "National ICT Policies and Gender Equality Regional Perspective."

59. See Jensen, "Enabling Cooperative and Gender-Equitable Information Societies."

60. While rights-based articulations are well suited to work through human rights violations against girls and women, they seem less suited to theorize the relationship between social gender constructions and the constructions' readjustment for the promotion of just and sustainable development. This is the case because the current framework for understanding human rights ultimately relies on concepts of the individual and individual entitlements, and not on concepts of community building and cooperation. Further articulations in this direction are needed.

## References

Abeyesekera, Sunila. "Development and Women's Human Rights." In *Seeking Accountability on Women's Human Rights*, 6–7. Ed. Women's International Coalition for Economic Justice. Navi Mumbai: Women's International Coalition for Economic Justice, 2004.

Brail, Stephanie. "The Price of Admission: Harassment and Free Speech in the Wild, Wild West." In *Wired Women: Gender and New Realities in Cyberspace*, 141–157. Ed. Lynn Cherny and Elizabeth Reba Weise. Seattle, WA: Seal Press, 1996.

Bunch, Charlotte. "Women's Rights as Human Rights." *Human Rights Quarterly* 12 (1990): 486–500.

Burch, Sally, and Irene Leon. "Directions for Women's Advocacy on ICT: Putting New Technologies on the Gender Agenda." In *Networking for Change: The APCWNSP's First 8 Years*, 31–47. Philippines: APCWNSP, 2000.

Burkett, Ingrid. "Beyond the 'Information Rich and Poor': Futures Understandings of Inequality in Globalising Information Economies." *Futures* 32 (2000): 679–694.

Coward, Rosalind. *Female Desires: How They Are Sought, Bought and Packaged.* New York: Grove, 1985.

Coyle, Karen. "How Hard Can It Be?" In *Wired Women: Gender and New Realities in Cyberspace*, 42–55. Ed. Lynn Cherny and Elizabeth Reba Weise. Seattle, WA: Seal Press, 1996.

Ewen, Stuart. *Captains of Consciousness: Advertising and the Social Roots of the Consumer Culture.* New York: McGraw-Hill, 1976.

Falk, Erika, and Erin Grizard. "The Glass Ceiling Persists: The 3rd Annual APPC Report on Women Leaders in Communication Companies." Philadelphia: Annenberg Public Policy Center, University of Pennsylvania, 2003. Available at www.annenbergpublicpolicycenter.org/04_info_society/women_leadership/2003_04_the-glass-ceiling-persists_rpt.pdf.

FrauenComputerZentrumBerlin. "Women in the Telecommunications Industry." In *European Database on Women in Decision-making 2001, 2007.* Available at www.db-decision.de/IuK_E.htm.

Freeman, Carla. *High Tech and High Heels in the Global Economy: Women, Work, and Pink-Collar Identities in the Caribbean.* Durham, NC: Duke University Press, 2000.

Hafkin, Nancy. "Gender Issues in ICT Policy in Developing Countries: An Overview." Presented at UN DAW Expert Group Meeting "Information and Communication Technologies and Their Impact on and Use as an Instrument for the Advancement and Empowerment of Women." Seoul, Republic of Korea, Nov. 11–14, 2002. EGM/ICT/2002/EP.1 (dated Oct. 25, 2002).

Hazou, Winnie. *The Social and Legal Status of Women: A Global Perspective.* Westport, CT: Praeger, 1990.

Hurley, Deborah. *Pole Star: Human Rights in the Information Society.* Montreal: International Centre for Human Rights and Democratic Development, 2003.

Huyer, Sophia. *The Leaky Pipeline: Gender Barriers in Science, Engineering and Technology.* Washington, DC: World Bank, 2002. Presentation video. Available at http://info.worldbank.org/etools/bspan/PresentationView.asp?PID=693&EID=356#RM

International Women's Tribune Centre. *Rights of Women: A Guide to the Most Important United Nations Treaties on Women's Human Rights,* 2nd ed. New York: International Women's Tribune Centre, 1998.

International Telecommunication Union. *World Telecommunication Development Report 2003: Access Indicators for the Information Society.* Available at www.itu.int/ITU-D/ict/publications/wtdr_03/.

Jamieson, Kathleen Hall. "Progress or No Room at the Top? The Role of Women in Telecommunications, Broadcast, Cable and E-Companies." Philadelphia: Annenberg Public Policy Center, University of Pennsylvania, 2001. Available at www.annenbergpublicpolicycenter.org/04_info_society/women_leadership/telecom/2001_progress-report.pdf.

Jensen, Heike. "Enabling Cooperative and Gender-Equitable Information Societies." In *Creating an Enabling Environment: Toward the Millennium Development Goals. Proceedings of the Berlin Global Forum of the United Nations ICT Task Force,* 51–60. Ed. Denis Gilhooly. New York: U.N. ICT Task Force, 2005.

Joachim, Jutta. "Shaping the Human Rights Agenda: The Case of Violence Against Women." In *Gender Politics in Global Governance*, 142–160. Ed. Mary K. Meyer and Elisabeth Prügl. Lanham, MD: Rowman & Littlefield, 1999.

Jorge, Sonia Nunes. *Gender Perspectives in Telecommunications Policy: A Curriculum Proposal*. Geneva: ITU, 2000. Available at www.itu.int/ITU-D/gender/projects/GenderCurriculum.pdf.

Khan, Abdul Waheed. "Preface." In Natasha Primo, *Gender Issues in the Information Society*, 5–6. Paris: UNESCO, 2003.

Martínez, Juliana, and Katherine Reilly. "Looking Behind the Internet: Empowering Women for Public Policy Advocacy in Central America." Presented at UN/INSTRAW *Virtual Seminar Series* on Gender and ICTs, Seminar Four: "ICTs as Tools for Bridging the Gender Digital Divide and Women's Empowerment," Sept. 2–14, 2002. Available at www.un-instraw.org/en/docs/gender_and_ict/Martinez.pdf.

Ng, Cecilia, and Anne Munro-Kua, eds. *Keying into the Future: The Impact of Computerization on Office Workers*. Kuala Lumpur: WDC Sdn. Bhd. 1994.

Painter, Genevieve Renard. "Gender, the Millennium Development Goals, and Human Rights in the Context of the 2005 Review Process." Report for the Gender and Development Network, Oct. 2004. Available at www.choike.org/documentos/mdg_women2004.pdf.

Pearson, Ruth. "Gender and New Technology in the Caribbean: New Work for Women?" In *Women and Change in the Carribean*, 287–296. Ed. Janet Momsen. Bloomington: Indiana University Press, 1993.

Primo, Natasha. *Gender Issues in the Information Society*. Paris: UNESCO, 2003.

Prügl, Elizabeth. *The Global Construction of Gender: Home-Based Work in the Political Economy of the 20th Century*. New York: Columbia University Press, 1999.

Ramilo, Chat. "National ICT Policies and Gender Equality Regional Pespective: Asia." Presented at UNDAW Expert Group Meeting "Information and Communication Technologies and Their Impact on and Use as an Instrument for the Advancement and Empowerment of Women." Seoul, Republic of Korea, Nov. 11–14, 2002. EGM/ICT/2002/EP.2 (dated Oct. 29, 2002).

Roy, Arundhati. "Peace and the New Corporate Liberation Theology." Lecture delivered at the Seymour Theatre, University of Sydney, in acceptance of the Sydney Peace Prize, Nov. 3, 2004. Available at www.arts.usyd.edu.au/centres/cpacs/publications.htm.

United Nations. *The World's Women 2000: Trends and Statistics*. New York: United Nation, 2000.

United Nations Children's Fund. *The Invisible Adjustment*. Santiago, Chile: UNICEF, 1987.

United Nations Development Fund for Women. *Progress of the World's Women 2000*. New York: UNIFEM, 2000.

United Nations Development Programme. *Human Development Report 2004*. Available at http://hdr.undp.org.

United Nations Division for the Advancement of Women. *Assessing the Status of Women: A Guide to Reporting Under CEDAW*. New York: UNDAW: 2000.

United Nations Educational, Scientific and Cultural Organization. *World Communication and Information Report, 1999–2000*. Paris: UNESCO, 1999. Available at www.unesco.org/webworld/wcir/en/pdf_report/chap17.pdf.

United Nations Educational, Scientific and Cultural Organization. *World Education Report 2000*. Paris: UNESCO, 2000.

United Nations Office of the Secretary-General. "Elimination of Stereotyping in the Mass Media." Report of the Secretary-General to the 40th Session of the Commission on the Status of Women. E/CN.6/1996/4 (dated Jan. 23, 1996).

Women's International Coalition for Economic Justice. *Seeking Accountability on Women's Human Rights: Women Debate the UN Millennium Development Goals*. Navi Mumbai: Women's International Coalition for Economic Justice, 2004.

## 11 Ensuring Minority Rights in a Pluralistic and "Liquid" Information Society

Birgitte Kofod Olsen

Economic, technological, and cultural globalization has led to a world characterized by flexibility and liquidity. The term *liquid*[1] is used to illustrate the form of modernity that we are experiencing today and that is taking us down an avenue of transnationality; increased mobility of money, services, and persons; and restructuring of sovereignty, power, and freedom.[2] This development leaves us in a flux of uncertainty rather than stability in all aspects of life, including marriage, family life, local community, work, and communication. But at the same time, it provides us with the possibility to easily change our residence or location, to engage in work-related migration, to visit places outside our home countries, and to retrieve and disseminate information of all kinds. Distance does not matter any longer. Mobility and accessibility make us capable of staying in touch with family, friends, colleagues, and others with whom we share a common interest.

The information society and the Internet represent a perfect setting for such behavior and needs. They are instrumental for free communication and dialogue across borders, and thus represent efficient tools for maintaining and developing cultural, religious, and social traditions and norms, as well as for preserving language and other elements of identity of persons. At the same time, the Internet serves as a platform for accessible pluralistic information, and for dialogue and interchange of such information irrespective of language.

For members of minority groups, this tool is of paramount importance. It enables minority groups to communicate and compare the situations in different countries and—if the groups are spread over a cross-border area—among the jurisdictions they are covered by. Thus a new way of maintaining and developing the common culture within the minority group is possible.

Also, it enhances the possibilities for monitoring the protection and promotion of minority rights by states that have signed legally binding international and regional conventions. International organizations and NGOs may review the situation via access to information made available on the Web by the states and, just as important, by minority groups.

Immediate response to risks of or actual violation of minority rights is made possible via easily accessible digital communication channels, including the Internet, satellite TV, and mobile phones. State organs, citizens, and organizations may have instant knowledge about minorities at risk and an opportunity to initiate efficient measures to stop or prevent violations.

Full and effective protection of minority rights presupposes a general acceptance of pluralism in society and of inclusion and equality as basic values and principles. It also requires a willingness to make policy and to adopt legislation, program, and plans of action to implement these standards.

If all this is accomplished, we may, from an optimistic perspective, benefit from the new ways of "liquid" living and the communicative platform given by the Internet, and create a society that exhibits pluralism, tolerance, broad-mindedness, and a common set of values; embraces diversity; and—within this ambit—protects the right to identity of members of minorities and ensures the principle of substantive equality between members of minorities and members of majority populations.

This chapter will briefly map the traditional minority protection and explain the interrelation of the concepts of minority rights and a pluralistic society. It seeks to exemplify how the information society may contribute to strengthening of that linkage and to enhancing of traditional minority protection. Since the societal transformation from a traditional to a digitized setting carries with it a number of challenges, the chapter highlights the challenges related to enjoyment of their rights by members of minority groups. Finally, it lists issues of fundamental importance for the realization of a society in which minorities are fully included and at the same time are provided with the possibility to preserve and develop their identity and enjoy equality with the rest of the population.

## Traditional Minority Protection

Minority protection today reflects a traditional approach to the activities, interaction, and communication within and among minority groups, their participation in society, and their relation to the majority population, which may be seen as linked to an analogue perception of our daily living. Before turning to the impact of digitizing minority rights, it is necessary to get acquainted with existing regulation of minority issues.

International initiatives and provisions for the protection of religious, ethnic, and linguistic minorities date back to the religious peace treaties of Augsburg (1555) and Westphalia (1648). In the twentieth century this protection was further institutionalized in the League of Nations and, after World War II, within the system of the United Nations.[3]

Within the U.N. system, minority protection has been dealt with in various ways, encompassing human rights initiatives and documents that include the setting up of the Subcommission on Prevention of Discrimination and Protection of Minorities,[4] the appointment in 2001 of a special rapporteur of the U.N. Human Rights Commission on the situation of human rights and fundamental freedoms of indigenous peoples, and the adoption in 1992 by the U.N. General Assembly of a declaration on minority rights.[5] It is, however, noteworthy in this connection that the basic international human rights document, the U.N. Universal Declaration on Human Rights (1948), is silent about minority protection.

If one approaches human rights from the perspective of citizens, and thus seeing them as a vehicle to ensure efficient protection of the individual vis-à-vis the state, it is remarkable that only one provision in a legally binding instrument lays a general obligation on the signatories to protect minorities. The only legally binding international provision on minority rights is found in the U.N. Covenant on Civil and Political Rights (1966, Art. 27).[6] According to this provision, persons belonging to ethnic, religious, or linguistic minorities "shall not be denied the right, in community with the other members of their group, to enjoy their own culture, to profess and practise their own religion, or to use their own language."

Apart from the general protection of peoples enshrined in the African Charter on Human and People's Rights (1981), a stronger and more specific protection—legally speaking—of minorities is found Europe. An explicit prohibition against discrimination on grounds of membership in a national minority is found in the European Convention on Human Rights and Freedoms (1956, Art. 14). Thus, even though the Convention does not provide for specific minority rights, the prohibition ensures that persons belonging to national minorities have the right to enjoy their civil and political rights without being discriminated against because of their specific status.

The Council of Europe has taken the protection a step further; inspired by the so-called CSCE (now OSCE) Copenhagen Document,[7] the Council of Europe adopted the Framework Convention for the Protection of National Minorities (1995), covering a number of specific rights and principles.[8] Prior to that, the European Charter for Regional or Minority Languages had been adopted in 1992.[9]

Within the European Union, an obligation to protect national, ethnic, and religious minorities flows from the basic principles of the EU,[10] but is not explicitly identified as a core value or principle in the Treaty of the European Union. This will change if, eventually, the treaty establishing a European Constitution is agreed upon by the EU member states, because this document specifically identifies respect for the rights of persons belonging to minorities as one of the founding values of the EU. Also, the EU European Charter of Fundamental Rights (2000)[11] contains a prohibition against discrimination[12] similar to that of the European Convention on Human Rights, and an obligation to respect cultural, religious, and linguistic diversity.[13]

### The Term "Minority": Now and in a Future Perspective

Despite the consensus on both the global and the regional level on the need for protection of minorities, and the efforts of political and monitoring bodies, legal scholars, and others, a clear definition of the term "minority" is not available. A number of criteria have been suggested to distinguish minority populations from the majority, encompassing both objective and subjective criteria. The list includes numerical inferiority; nationality of state of residence; a nondominant position in society; characteristics differing from those of the rest of the population; a sense of solidarity within the group concerning the preservation of their common culture, religion, or language; and stability in the form of long presence in the state.[14]

Diverging from this set of mainly objective criteria, a pragmatic approach rather than a legal definition has been discussed at the U.N. level,[15] and explicitly adopted in the explanatory report to the Council of Europe Framework Convention for the Protection of National Minorities.[16] In other bodies, such as the U.N. Human Rights Committee and the OSCE High Commissioner for National Minorities, the lack of a definition leaves room for both a continuation of the pattern presented by the list of objective criteria, and for a move toward a margin of appreciation to determine whether the members of a group of people should be perceived and treated as having minority status.

Embedded in this uncertainty as to the level of protection that may be claimed by persons belonging to a minority is an important question with far-reaching impact in practice. Thus, the requirement of nationality of the state of residence gives rise to a core human rights problem: Who enjoys protection of minority rights in a country? Old minorities who have been in the country for centuries? New minorities stemming from the influx of migrant workers and/or refugees? Asylum seekers? Exchange students? Tourists or other visitors?

From a state perspective, an inclusion of the whole spectrum of those groups as minorities would have a somewhat unpredictable socioeconomic, financial, and political impact if applied fully. Especially the inclusion of visitors has been deemed unrealistic and difficult to defend by some.[17] From the perspective of the person concerned, however, the fulfillment of a general requirement for efficient protection of human rights and of a specific need for special protection due to the vulnerable position of members of a minority may be seen as covered by the state obligation to protect and promote human rights.

Supporting an argument of application of human rights in general to noncitizens is a recent General Comment from the U.N. Committee on the Elimination of Racial Discrimination. The committee recalls in its interpretive comment on discrimination against noncitizens that "although some fundamental rights such as the right to participate in elections, to vote and to stand for election, may be confined to citizens, human rights are, in principle, to be enjoyed by all persons."[18]

As to inclusion of all minorities under the protection found in ICCPR (Art. 27), a General Comment by the U.N. Human Rights Committee suggests this line of thinking by putting forward an interpretation of the provision that rejects the requirement of nationality and states that the length of residence is an irrelevant criterion. On this basis, the committee opens the way for an understanding according to which immigrants and even visitors could qualify as minorities in the sense of Article 27.[19]

It is exactly such inclusive and pragmatic approaches to human rights and minority rights protection that is needed in the information society when it is seen as both pluralistic and "liquid." Transnationality, migration, and cross-border interaction are not easily combined with traditional measures to protect and promote minority rights. On an abstract level, achieving efficient protection of minorities in an information society presupposes an openness in the perception of minority groups and a willingness among states to take responsibility to respect and promote the rights of members of minority groups residing permanently or temporarily within the jurisdiction.

Such transformation from a one-dimensional perception of the state into a new setting is indeed difficult, but a way has been, if not paved, then at least identified by the U.N. treaty bodies.

## Basic Principles for Minority Protection

Moving to a more concrete level, existing and applied basic principles are not only necessary but also suitable for application in the information society. As in a traditional setting, protecting minority rights in a pluralistic and liquid setting demands both a prohibition against discrimination and special measures to enable the members of minorities to preserve and develop their own, separate characteristics.[20]

It is clear from the preparatory work of the ICCPR and the legal literature[21] that the obligation which may be derived from Article 27 goes beyond a prohibition of discrimination and contains elements of a right to de facto equality—for instance, by means of positive measures to combat discrimination. The requirement for the states to do more than not interfere has been stressed by the U.N. Human Rights Committee with regard to the horizontal effect of Article 27 (i.e., the application of Article 27 to private interference with protected rights). Hence, the committee has stated that "positive measures of protection are . . . required not only against the acts of the State party itself, . . . but also against the acts of other persons within the State party."[22]

In Europe, the double approach is directly reflected in Articles 4 and 5 of the European Framework Convention for the Protection of National Minorities. Article 4 contains both a prohibition against discrimination based on belonging to a national minority and an obligation for the state to guarantee the right of equality before the law and to equal protection under the law. Moreover, a positive obligation to promote full and effective equality between persons belonging to national minorities and those belonging to the majority in the state is stipulated in Article 5. According to this provision, the states shall undertake promotional activities to maintain and develop the cultures of persons belonging to national minorities, and to preserve essential elements of their identity, including their religion, language, traditions, and cultural heritage.

Article 6 calls for a commitment by the state parties to encourage a spirit of tolerance and intercultural dialogue. This provision should be read in light of the preamble, which states that "the creation of a climate of tolerance and dialogue is necessary to enable cultural diversity to be a source and a factor, not of division, but of enrichment for each society."

Conceptually linked to the need for cultural diversity is the connection drawn by the European Court of Human Rights between democracy and pluralism. On several occasions, the Court has stated that pluralism is an inherent part of the concept of democracy applied in a European human rights context. This is illustrated below in connection with specific rights relevant to minorities in an information society.

## Specific Minority Rights

It seems evident that a minority right of paramount importance in an information society is the freedom of expression and the rights, derived from this freedom, to receive and impart information. Both as a general human right[23] and as a specific minority right,[24] the freedom of expression enables minorities to express themselves and to impart information and ideas in the minority language.

Not only does the freedom of expression give room for expressions of minorities that diverge from those of the majority, but it also plays a vital role for both minorities and the majority in ensuring and facilitating access and dissemination of pluralistic information, and access to receive such information via media[25] and means of information technology, such as satellite television.[26]

In addition, the European Court of Human Rights has frequently stressed the freedom of expression as an imperative in a democratic state and has demonstrated the intimate link between democracy and pluralism. Thus, the Court has stated that freedom of expression applies "not only to 'information' or 'ideas' that are favorably received or regarded as inoffensive or as a matter of indifference, but also to those that offend, shock or disturb; such are the demands of that pluralism, tolerance and broad-mindedness without which there is no 'democratic society.' "[27]

Case law of the Court also reveals that the principle of pluralism should form the basis of all regulation of the freedom of expression.[28] Such a principle may be derived from the *Informationsverein Lentia case*[29] concerning broadcasting of programs via audiovisual media of information and ideas of general interest, in which the Court stated, "Such an undertaking cannot be successfully accomplished unless it is grounded in the principle of pluralism, of which the State is the ultimate guarantor."

The interrelation between the requirement for pluralism and minority protection is not as clear. In two cases against Turkey,[30] the Court stated that "democracy thrives on freedom of expression. From that point of view, there can be no justification for hindering a political group solely because it seeks to debate in public the situation of part of the state's population and to take part in the nation's political life in order to find, according to democratic rules, solutions capable of satisfying everyone concerned." This statement may lead to the assumption that a line can be drawn from the overarching principle of pluralism as an integral part of the European democratic society to actual or potential protection of members of minorities.[31]

In the *Informationsverein Lentia case*, the Court did not, however, take the opportunity to discuss the question of minority protection even though it was invoked by the complainant, a member of the Slovene minority in Austria. This may suggest a reluctance to contribute to defining and furthering a system of efficient protection of minorities.[32]

In another case against Turkey,[33] the Court dealt with the right to freedom of expression of a member of the Kurdish minority in Turkey who claimed that measures taken by the authorities against small-scale illegal trading had a direct effect on Kurdish persons. However, the Court did not enter into a discussion of minority rights, but addressed the issue within the usual interpretive framework as an assessment of the necessity of interference in a democratic society and its proportionality. The case has been perceived as confirming a tendency toward a stronger awareness and acknowledgment by the Court of the importance of effective protection of the political freedom of members of minorities.[34] These and other cases do, however, leave us with the impression that protection and promotion of minority rights and the importance and impact of those rights in a pluralistic society are not actively integrated as core factors in the interpretation of the European Convention on Human Rights.

Other specific minority rights that are relevant in the information society cover the right to assembly, the right to establish and maintain free and peaceful contacts across borders, and the right to participate in cultural, social, and economic life. These substantial rights are found in the European Framework Convention for the Protection of National Minorities, but have no equivalents in binding international documents. A right to enjoy cultural life is derived from Article 27 of the U.N. Covenant on Civil and Political Rights.

The impact of these rights in a digitized setting has not yet been tested by human rights monitoring bodies, but does represent a challenge in a society with an increase in the number and diversity of ethnic, religious, and linguistic minorities. Consequently, this will be addressed below.

### Challenges of Digitizing Minority Rights

Efficient protection of the right to peaceful assembly and freedom of association for minorities is a prerequisite for the gathering of minorities and their possibility to share common interests and to maintain and develop their specific culture.[35] Also, it contributes to the realization of a pluralist society and thus is instrumental for the development of an information society capable of addressing the needs and interests of a diverse population.

In a future perspective, the right represents a substantial challenge if invoked in cases of protection of virtual associations—and a number of issues will be added to the list of implications if combined with cross-border activities and communication.

The right to enjoy the cultural life of the minority and to participate in the cultural, social, and economic life of society may be effectively facilitated by the Internet and other ICTs. ICT-based reforms of public-sector and government services, including education and health, and of programs aimed at effective public administration within agriculture and taxation, have been carried through in a number of countries worldwide.[36] An inherent risk in initiatives like these is, however, that their full potential is exploited only if a set of demands is met. It must be ensured that everybody with a need to receive services or other forms of government support via ICT systems has access to the Internet. The fulfillment of this demand may require that the state accept a positive obligation to provide public access to call centers, telecenters, or similar operators of telephone, fax, and Internet services, and to complement such services with regulatory and policy initiatives ensuring equal access for members of minorities as well as of the majority.

In some countries, including Estonia, India, and South Africa, so-called community-based multipurpose community telecenters (MCTs) have been established in rural and remote areas that incorporate Internet access, e-mail, and other computer applications into existing community access telephone centers, and also offer educational and cultural services.[37] Similar models are worth considering in the context of maintaining and developing minority cultures, because they seem suitable for ensuring the enjoyment of both specific minority rights and the basic right to equality, and for facilitating intercultural dialogue within communities.

In a broader perspective, ICT may contribute to understanding of and knowledge about diverse cultural traditions among the majority population and, thus, enhance the promotion of a diverse and pluralist society.

A specific right that needs attention in the information society when applying ICT is the human right to (information) privacy in conjunction with nondiscrimination. For many members and groups of minorities it is essential to their daily life, integrity, and participation in society to be able to communicate with private and public actors without the risk of being registered as belonging to an ethnic, religious, or linguistic minority.

On the other hand, states with pluralistic societies are required to combat discrimination, and to achieve this, in many countries registration of ethnicity is seen not only as a legitimate aim but also as a sufficient means to combat discrimination, raise awareness of discrimination as a societal phenomenon, and disseminate knowledge of discriminatory structures and practices.

## Monitoring Minority Rights in a Digitized Setting

A central element in safeguarding the adequate fulfillment of the state's obligations to protect and promote minority rights is the monitoring bodies established within the United Nations and regional human rights systems.

Active inclusion of ICT as a means to enhance the enjoyment of minority rights, and to move the pluralistic society toward diversity, tolerance, and mutual respect, has a positive side effect on monitoring mechanisms. The gathering of information from state organs regarding compliance with international and regional standards is easier, since documents, assessments, judicial reviews, and case law in their original form typically are available on the Web sites of state organs. Also, it is possible to have national human rights institutions, NGOs, labor market organizations, minority groups themselves, and other relevant actors submit material in far more easily than today. The huge amount of available material may— on the other hand—give rise to longer and/or more intense preparatory work within the monitoring bodies. It should, however, be seen as a qualitative improvement rather than an obstacle to efficient monitoring.

## Multicultural Jurisdictions

A major challenge envisaged by all societies today is represented by the question of how to deal with the consequences of globalization, including cross-border activities and flows of information, within a traditional perception of the nation-state as autonomous both in territorial terms and in legislative, executive, and administrative powers.[38]

Vis-à-vis minority groups this challenge goes to the root of a core issue of minority protection, the possibility—and in reality often barriers—for minorities to achieve acknowledgment of their status as a group and to enjoy their common culture within this group.[39] It is a crucial aspect of the right of minorities to know that the right not only is an individual right but also is closely linked to the existence of the minority as a group. Self-determination and autonomy of the minority group may, as a consequence of this line of thinking, be seen as a sine qua non for efficient and substantive protection and promotion of individual minority rights.[40]

When focusing on the special features of the information society, the Internet and other information and communication devices may play an important role in de facto strengthening and furthering the enjoyment of minority rights. The setting up of Web sites, chat rooms, and virtual conferences enables members of minority groups spread throughout a country or a region, or across borders, to stay in contact and thereby actively maintain and develop their specific identity and culture. Moreover, it creates a basis for a new perspective on structuring a pluralistic society that acknowledges the right of minorities to live in accordance with their own norms and traditions within their ethnic or religious group or community.

A structure that has been suggested as accommodating differences and at the same time respecting human rights is that of jurisdictional authority shared between the state and the minority groups.[41] In such a structure, the minority is allowed, upon delegation of powers from the state, to regulate life within the minority group. ICT would be an excellent instrument to technically support the implementation of shared jurisdiction. Moreover, it could be used to put in place a system that facilitates and contributes to ensuring that basic principles of the rule of law were governing within the minority group.

From a pure minority approach, a society building on diversification of rights and obligations in this way represents a major step forward in the acknowledgment and promotion of minority rights. It does, however, carry a number of serious human rights problems concerning the protection of the rights of the individual. Would it, for instance, be acceptable for the minority group to interfere with the members' individual rights? And, in the affirmative, what would be the limits for such interference? How would we, for instance, handle restrictions on women's rights to participation and nondiscrimination set up as a consequence of jurisdictional authority within the minority group?

Other questions are linked to the delegation itself, and cover principles guiding the delegation, limitations on the ability/power to delegate, subsequent performance of delegated powers, and monitoring of those powers by the delegating state.[42]

Considering the development of populations and societies worldwide, the possibilities offered by the Internet and other ICT devices, and the—however vague—tendency within the international and regional systems to acknowledge the importance of protection and promotion of minority rights, the time may be ripe to introduce and discuss in depth new perspectives on and systems for efficient minority protection in the information society.

## Public or Private Governance of the Internet

Yet another challenge that should be mentioned in the context of minority rights in the information society stems from the governance of the Internet. Thus, it cannot be foreclosed that the choice of private or public governance may have an impact on the efficient protection of minority rights. When addressing this issue, the point of departure may be the assumption that the principle of pluralism applies, in the sense that it must form the basis of the regulation of ways and means of expression, communication, and interchange of thoughts and ideas.

If it is made applicable to the basic minority rights to enjoy cultural life, use minority language, and practice the culture's religion, the principle of pluralism would lead to a requirement for the governing actor of the Internet to ensure that communication and interchange of information in minority languages on minority and other issues are not restricted or interfered with in other ways.

Moreover, it may be argued that a positive obligation exists to adopt measures ensuring and enhancing equality between Internet users from minorities and the majority, as well as to promote conditions for participation and for maintenance and development of minority cultures. This is true at least for a public governing actor, but may also follow from the acknowledged horizontal effect of human rights obligations.

## Concluding Remarks

The challenges posed by the development in society toward increased communication and interaction, mobility and migration, as well as cultural, ethnic, and linguistic diversity, make it necessary to address minority rights, issues, and conditions from a new perspective. The perils of a new perspective may be set by available ICTs, especially the Internet, which has the potential to serve as an efficient structure for accessible pluralistic information, and for dialogue and interchange of information, irrespective of language, among members of minorities and between minorities and majorities.

Improvement of minority rights also has to take into consideration new ways of structuring an information society that is pluralistic in its composition but founded on basic principles and values that should be shared by everybody. This does indeed present a major challenge, and a focal point here will be to strike a balance between self-determination within a minority group and adequate safeguard mechanisms for external protection against restrictions on the rights of members of minorities set up by internal regulation within the minority group.

In this context the principle of pluralism should be applied in order to ensure that cultural life, religious practice, communication, and interchange of information in minority languages concerning minority and other issues, are not restricted or in other ways interfered with in a way incompatible with international human rights norms and standards. Application of the same principle to governance of the Internet would ensure a similar protection and create a framework for improving the enjoyment of minority rights.

Information technologies are indeed instrumental for the protection and promotion of minority rights and do possess a potential for facilitating the transformation of society into an information society capable of embracing diversity and creating mutual respect for and understanding of differences in traditions, norms, and ways of living. "Liquid" living is a suitable background for addressing traditional concepts of nationality and affiliation of members of minorities from a new perspective. But it requires human beings, resources and reflections to vitalize the vision of efficient minority protection in a pluralistic information society.

**Notes**

1. Bauman, *Liquid Modernity*.

2. Bauman, *Globalization*, 57ff.

3. See Nowak, *CCPR Commentary*, 635, with references.

4. The Subcommission was renamed the Subcommission on the Promotion and Protection of Human Rights in 1999.

5. U.N. Declaration on the Rights of Persons Belonging to National Ethnic, Religious and Linguistic Minorities, GA Res. 47/135, Dec. 18, 1992.

6. Specific protection of indigenous peoples' human rights is found in ILO Indigenous and Tribal Peoples Convention, No. 169, June 27, 1989.

7. The Concluding Document of the Second Meeting on the Human Dimension of the Conference on Security and Co-operation in Europe (1991), which lists the rights of persons belonging to national minorities in sec. IV. In 1992, the CSCE appointed a high commissioner on national minorities.

8. Entered into force Feb. 1, 1998.

9. Entered into force Mar. 1, 1998.

10. See Treaty on European Union, Art. 6, and Network of Independent Experts on Fundamental Rights, Thematic Comment no. 3, "The Protection of Minorities in the European Union, Apr. 25, 2005, p. 6.

11. The Charter is not yet legally binding, but serves as an important political instruments insofar as it is accepted as guiding all EU actions and policies.

12. Art. 21 (Art. II-81 of the Constitution Treaty).

13. Art. 22 (Art. II-82 of the Constitution Treaty).

14. The list builds on the Capotorti–Deschênes standard. For further details and references, see Nowak, *Commentary to ICCPR*, 642ff.; and Henrard, *Devising an Adequate System of Minority Protection*, 16ff.

15. See U.N. Working Group on Minorities of the U.N. Subcommission, Report of the Third Session, U.N. Doc. E/CN.4/Sub.2/1997/18, July 10, 1997, p. 22.

16. See items 12 and 26 of the explanatory report.

17. See, for example Michalska, "Migrant Workers as a 'New' Minority," 135, 143. A similar rationale has been put forward in discussion on the assumption of direct, positive obligations to guarantee linguistic rights in, for instance, multiethnic states. See Tomuschat, "Equality and Non-Discrimination Under the International Covenant on Civil and Political Rights," 965.

18. U.N. Committee on the Elimination of Racial Discrimination, General Comment no. 30, para. 5.

19. U.N. Human Rights Committee, General Comment no. 23, para. 27.

20. U.N. Subcommission on the Prevention of Discrimination and the Protection of Minorities, Cf. the Report of the First Session, UN Doc.E/CN.4/52, sec. V.

21. See, e.g., Nowak, *Commentary to ICCPR*, 657ff.

22. General Comment no. 23, para. 6.1.

23. See ICCPR, Art. 19; ECHR, Art. 10; ACHPR, Art. 9.

24. See European Framework Convention, Art. 9.

25. A specific provision on granting the possibility to access to create and use own media is contained in the European Framework Convention for the Protection of National Minorities, Art. 9 (3).

26. In Denmark, the High Court has addressed the issue of compatibility of denial of the right to set up satellite antennas on the balconies of apartments in order to receive programs in Turkish with the right to receive information. In both cases (U99.656V, U97.190V), no violation was found.

27. The principle was introduced in *Handyside v UK*, Eur. Ct. H.R., 7 Dec. 1976, ser. A, no. 24; Eur. Ct. H.R., §49 and reiterated in a number of cases, such as *Incal v Turkey*, Eur. Ct. H.R., 9 June 1998, para. 46.

28. See Cohen-Jonathan, "Article 10"; and Harris et al., *Law of the European Convention on Human Rights*, 384–386.

29. *Inforamtionsverein Lentia and Others v Austria*, Eur. Ct. H.R., 24 Nov. 1993, para. 38.

30. *United Communist Party of Turkey and Others v Turkey*, Eur. Ct. H.R., 30 Jan. 1998, para. 57; *Socialist Party and Others v Turkey*, Eur. Ct. H.R., 25 May 1998, para. 45.

31. See Henrard, *Devising an Adequate System of Minority Protection*, 91.

32. See also ibid., 94. Examples of similar reluctance are found in *Otto Prenninger v Austria*, Eur. Ct. H.R., 20 Sept. 1994; and *Wingrove v UK*, Eur. Ct. H.R., 25 Nov. 1996.

33. *Incal v Turkey*.

34. See Henrard, 99f.

35. Minority protection is stressed in connection with ECHR, Art. 11, in *Sidiropoulos and Others v Greece*, Eur. Ct. H.R., 10 July 1998, paras. 41, 44.

36. See Grace et al., "Information and Communication Technologies and Broad-Based Development," 32f.

37. Ibid., 37, 38. A plan of action to develop best-practice models of MCT was adopted at the World Telecommunication Development Conference in Buenos Aires in 1994.

38. The concept of autonomy is analyzed in skurbaty, *Beyond a One-Dimensional State*. The division into forms and types of autonomy is suggested by Max van der Stoel in the book's prolegomenon, xix f.

39. The complexity of combining individual rights with collective rights.

40. Similar viewpoints are found in Henrard, Devising an Adequate System, 2.; and Tomuschat, *Equality and Non-Discrimination*, 966.

41. See Shachar, *Multicultural Jurisdictions*.

42. A discussion is in Martin Scheinin, *How to Resolve Conflicts Between Individual and Collective Rights?*, 219 ff. See also, on autonomy, Skurbaty, *Beyond a One-Dimensional State*, 565 ff.

## Bibliography

Bauman, Zygmunt. *Globalisation: The Human Consequneces*. Cambridge: Polity Press, 1998.

Bauman, Zygmunt. *Liquid Modernity*. Cambridge: Polity Press, 2000.

Cohen-Jonathan, G. "Article 10." In *La Convention Européenne des Droits de l'Homme. Commentaire article par article*. Ed. L. E. Pettiti et al. Paris: Economica, 1995.

Grace, Jeremy, Charles Kenny, and Christine Zhen-Wei, Qiang. "Information and Communication Technologies and Broad-Based Development. A Partial Review of the Evidence," World Bank working paper no. 12. Washington, DC: World Bank, 2004.

Harris, D. J., M. O'Boyle, and C. Warbrick. *Law of the European Convention on Human Rights*. London: Butterworth, 1995.

Henrard, Kristin. *Devising an Adequate System of Minority Protection: Individual Human Rights, Minority Rights and the Right to Self-Determination*. The Hague: Martinus Nijhoff, 2000.

Michalska, A. "Migrant Workers as a 'New' Minority. Sociological and Legal Definitions of Minority." In *The Role of the Nation-State in the 21ˢᵗ Century: Human Rights, International Organisations, and Foreign Policy*. Ed. M. Custermans et al. The Hague: Kluwer Law International, 1998.

Nowak, Manfred. *U.N. Covenant on Civil and Political Rights: CCPR Commentary*, 2nd rev. ed. Arlington, VA: N. P. Engel, 2005.

Shachar, Ayelet. *Multicultural Jurisdictions: Cultural Differences and Women's Rights*. Cambridge: Cambridge University Press, 2001.

Scheinin, Martin. "How to Resolce Conflicts Between Individual and Collective Rights?" In *Rethinking Non-Discrimination and Minority Rights*. Ed. Martin Scheinin and Reetta Toivanen. Turku: Institute for Human Rights, Åbo Akademi University; Berlin: German Institute for Human Rights, 2004.

Skurbaty, Zelim A., ed. *Beyond a One-Dimensional State: An Emerging Right to Autonomy?* Leiden: Martinus Nijhoff, 2005.

Tomuschat, Christian. "Equality and Non-Discrimination Under the International Covenant on Civil and Political Rights." *Staatsrecht, Völkerrecht, Europarecht: Festschrift für Hans-Jürgen Schlochauer zum 75. Geburtstag am 28. März 1981.* Ed. Ingo von Münch. Berlin: Walter de Gruyter, 1981.

## 12 The Right to Development in the Information Society

Ran Greenstein and Anriette Esterhuysen

Since its adoption by the U.N. General Assembly in 1986, the "right to development" has been controversial. This chapter will examine the right to development, its relationship to inequality within and between countries, and collective versus individual rights. It will discuss the notion of the right to development in the context of information and communications for development, and reflect on how this notion needs to be integrated into the broader discussion of human rights in the information society.

In its Declaration of Principles, the World Summit on the Information Society (WSIS), which convened for its first phase at Geneva in December 2003, asserted a commitment "to build a people-centred, inclusive and development-oriented Information Society, where everyone can create, access, utilize and share information and knowledge."[1] The goal of this commitment is to enable "individuals, communities and peoples to achieve their full potential in promoting their sustainable development and improving their quality of life."[2] The Declaration also states, as a result of successful lobbying by human rights advocates, that all of this is to be achieved in accordance with the principles of the Charter of the United Nations and the Universal Declaration of Human Rights.

The links in the WSIS Declaration between information, development, and human rights are indeed crucial for our understanding of the contemporary challenges of development. But, as we argue in this chapter, there are many ways in which these notions can be interpreted, and the links between them conceptualized. After discussing some of these ways later on in the chapter, we will outline how a rights-based perspective can be applied to the analysis of the socioeconomic and political aspects of development.

There is a notion, frequently found in official WSIS documents, that closing the "digital divide" is the key to development. However, the "digital divide" itself is a consequence of deep-rooted local and global structural inequalities. The spread of the "knowledge economy" is unlikely to result in a more egalitarian distribution of wealth and power. In fact, it can reinforce and deepen existing inequalities, introduce new forms of exclusion, and increase the gap between rich and poor. It is not merely access to information that will empower people to achieve their full potential; it is also more equitable access to the world's resources and the ability to participate effectively in decisions that impact their lives.[3] Moreover, the term "knowledge economy" implies the commodification of knowledge, a process that transforms experience and information into marketable products and services. Access to these products and services is then supposed to be regulated by the law of demand and supply. This trend might result in more widespread distribution of knowledge and information, but it is also likely to result in restricted access for those without the resources needed to buy their way into this economy.

A major question that is not addressed by WSIS is the extent to which issues of power and inequality are major obstacles to development. In fact, while the document talks about problems of poverty and disempowerment, it avoids identifying any individuals, institutions, processes, or social relations responsible for such conditions.

In contrast, and with a clear focus precisely on such issues, the Civil Society Declaration of the WSIS in Geneva in December 2003 argues that a commitment to people-centered development means "consciously redressing the effects of the intersection of unequal power relations in the social, economic and political spheres, which manifests in differential access, choice, opportunity, participation, status and control over resources between women and men as well as communities in terms of class, ethnicity, age, religion, race, geographical location and development status."[4]

To combat these conditions, the Civil Society Declaration states, there needs to be a focus on social justice, an endeavor that must take into account "geo-political and historical injustices along economic, social, political and cultural lines" resulting from "the inter-linkages of global economic liberalisation, cultural globalisation, increased militarism, rising fundamentalisms, racism and the suspension and violation of basic human rights."[5]

From this perspective, then, development is not simply an outcome of developing countries, regions, and communities catching up with their more developed counterparts; it means also (and primarily) addressing the unequal and unjust conditions that gave rise to such underdevelopment in the first place. Digital exclusion, or the "digital divide"—referring to unequal distribution of and access to information and communication technologies—cannot be seen in isolation, since it is in fact "a mapping of new asymmetries onto the existing grid of social divides."[6] In other words, the issue here is not a mere technological "divide" or gap that can be bridged, but the underlying social relations that sustain it. Tackling them involves dealing with questions of power and resources.

Perhaps the most important challenge facing us today, then, is to identify correctly the main obstacles to development (whether social, political, or technological) and outline a way of overcoming them in the specific context of the information society. In doing that, an understanding of notions of human rights and their role in development is essential.

It is to this issue that we now turn, with an emphasis on the right to development. After discussing the right to development and related rights, we will return to ICTs and their role in development. We will examine their relevance to development with a focus on the socioeconomic and political aspects of development and the information society.

## The Right to Development

The right to development, adopted by a U.N. General Assembly resolution in 1986, is best examined against a background of other U.N. declarations on human rights. Prominent among these are the Universal Declaration of Human Rights of 1948 and the International Covenant on Economic, Social and Cultural Rights, which was adopted in 1966 and entered into effect in 1976. When assessing the meanings and implications of the notion of the "right to development," we must look at the definition of the right, its relations to other rights, the extent to which it fits within the general discourse on development, and the practices and institutions associated with it.

The 1986 Declaration on the Right to Development, drawing on previous international agreements and documents, identifies development as "a comprehensive economic, social, cultural and political process, which aims at the constant improvement of the well-being of the entire population and of all individuals." It emphasizes the need for "meaningful participation in development" and the "fair distribution of benefits" resulting from it.[7] The Declaration is rife with the notions of development, well-being, participation, human rights, self-determination, sovereignty, and so on, but makes little attempt to give these concrete content, if only to illustrate what they might mean in practice. This is essential, however, for the right to be realized. The ritual invocation of these standard notions provides no guidance on application.

It is in the nature of such general declarations that they are strong on buzzwords and vague on specifics. One of the inevitable side effects of seeking to use all the right words, and to be as inclusive as possible, is that potential contradictions creep into the text, affecting the ways in which it may be interpreted and applied. Within this context, one area to consider is the identification of the "agents" and "beneficiaries" of development.

Article 1 of the Declaration mentions development as a right of "every human person" and of "all peoples."[8] Article 2 identifies "all human beings," "the community," and the "entire population" and "all individuals" of states, as the potential beneficiaries of and participants in development. Article 3 goes a step further by referring to the role of states in facilitating the realization of the right to development, as well as their own right to "sovereign equality" in the context of a new international economic order.

The international context is highlighted in Article 4, which calls on states to take steps to formulate "international development policies." It further calls for "sustained action" in order to "promote more rapid development of developing countries," and for international cooperation to provide those countries with "appropriate means and facilities to foster their comprehensive development" (thus implying that countries—rather than their citizens—may be regarded as bearing the right). These calls are combined in Article 5 with assertions of the need to eliminate the legacy of colonialism, foreign domination and occupation, foreign interference and threats against national sovereignty, national unity and territorial integrity, and the need to "recognize the fundamental right of peoples to self-determination."

Having listed agents and beneficiaries, the Declaration concludes that "all human rights and fundamental freedoms are indivisible and interdependent," and they must receive "equal attention and urgent consideration" (Article 6). In the process of facilitating the full realization of human rights, states should encourage "popular participation" in all spheres (Article 8). On an important note, the Declaration asserts that all aspects of the right to development are "indivisible and interdependent and each of them should be considered in the context of the whole" (Article 9).

The idea of indivisibility of rights presents interesting challenges to our understanding of the right to development. Extending the notion of human rights, usually understood as rights of individuals or of "all human beings," to collectives such as communities, populations, and states entails two problematic moves. The first is treating abstract categories, which do not always have clear identities and boundaries, as if they were individuals. The second is regarding these categories as if they were unified actors, ignoring their internal divisions and the extent to which they are prone to conflict among different components. Let us consider each of these moves in turn.

Treating abstract categories as if they were individuals blurs the distinction between human beings, who can be identified with precision, and collectives with fuzzy boundaries, whose nature and composition shift with time and according to who defines them. This is not a mere technical distinction, but a distinction between tangible and intangible bearers of rights. The former are concrete; the latter, open to interpretation. This has implications for the way in which rights may be realized, as will be explored later in the chapter.

Perhaps of greater concern here is the move to regard collectives as unified actors. This approach usually results in giving some elements within a group the power to speak on behalf of the entire membership. Since groups are invariably diverse, and include people and factions with different and competing interests and concerns, this move elevates some to a position of priority while marginalizing others. It is particularly problematic in that both victims and perpetrators of human rights abuses frequently hail from the same group. In many respects the source of obstacles to development is internal rather than external. Identifying groups as bearers of rights is thus problematic.

When we regard "developing countries" and states as bearers of the right to development, our attention is directed *toward* relations *between* countries and *away* from relations *within* them. This can serve the interest of local elites in obscuring relations of domination and exploitation from which they benefit, while highlighting global relations in which they occupy a subordinate position. This trend was in evidence during the WSIS. Many of the countries that were most vocal in insisting on their right to receive support to "bridge the digital divide" had made little progress in improving their human rights practice at the national level. In other words, when the Declaration on the Right to Development calls for developing countries to become beneficiaries of sustained international action, it ignores the fact that many poor people in the world are deprived of development by their own governments and social elites. Giving those governments more power and greater access to resources will probably harm the cause of development more than it will help it.

That this may be the outcome of the U.N. declaration is not surprising since, like all U.N. resolutions, it is a product of negotiations between government representatives, with little direct participation of local people, communities, and civil society organizations. And even when civil society does participate, as in the case of the WSIS, these inputs do not carry the same weight as those of governments.

This does not mean that the right to development is meaningless. Rather, it means that on its own, as a concept adopted and interpreted by representatives of states, it may fall victim to social and political relations that work for the benefit of some people and groups in developing countries, at the expense of others. To overcome this state of affairs, and embark on a transformative course of action, we need to discuss the relations between development and human rights.

Having discussed the concept of the right to development critically, it is important to recognize that it did not remain in a frozen state. In the late 1990s the U.N. Office of the High Commissioner on Human Rights appointed an independent expert on the right to development, and convened an open-ended working group on the matter. Both of these have produced a number of reports addressing different aspects of the right and its relations to issues of trade, economic growth, and poverty alleviation, all seen in the context of globalization. These reports are important contributions to the elaboration of the concrete meanings of the right to development.

## Rights in the International Context

The relationship between notions of human rights and development has been a controversial topic for some time. Historically, human rights revolved around issues of civil liberties and political expression (first-generation rights), whereas development has been seen primarily as an economic issue. Socioeconomic rights (second-generation rights) gained legitimacy within the human rights discourse as a national issue, but third-generation rights (dealing with development, peace, and so on) lag behind. The international dimension of the latter set of rights made them a useful rhetorical tool in debates but very difficult to implement in practice.

The crucial questions to consider here are "Development of what, of whom, and at whose expense?"[9] We argued above that the Declaration on the Right to Development is oriented toward state rights, though Rajagopal sees a potential for social movements, local communities, and individuals to claim rights as well. By doing that, they would be challenging the practices of the states within which they are located. However, by the same token, states could use this notion of rights to assert their own claims vis-à-vis communities and other states. The ability of actors to use the notion for different and sometimes contradictory ends opens up a contested terrain in which public and private forces may debate and fight over the interpretation of the right to development. A meaningful use of the right would see it applied as a critical tool against restrictive and oppressive practices by local, national, and international agencies, and as a vehicle for empowerment of individuals and communities rather than of states. To facilitate this, a look at other rights and processes would be helpful.

The collectivist approach of the Declaration on the Right to Development can be contrasted with the more individualist approach of previous international declarations. The Universal Declaration of Human Rights of 1948 addresses itself to the rights of "all members of the human family," men and women.[10] It clearly regards the individual ("the human person") as the elementary unit of concern. Of particular interest here is that the only reference to "development" (Article 22) is made specifically in the context of education, which should be directed "to the full development of the human personality" (article 26).

Although not using the term "development" in the same sense as the 1986 Declaration, the Universal Declaration mentions a range of social rights that embody social development. Among them are the rights to social security, to work, to an adequate standard of living to ensure the health and well-being of individuals and their families (providing them with food, clothing, housing, and medical care), and to education. Most of these are to be realized by governments and states, which are seen as providers of, rather than beneficiaries from, these rights.

The only significant move from individual to collective rights is made in Article 28, which asserts that "everyone is entitled to a social and international order in which the rights and freedoms set forth in this Declaration can be fully realized." This is supplemented by Article 29, with its notion of "duties to the community," which provides everyone with the necessary context "in which the free and full development of his personality is possible." These statements are too vague, however, to entail specific obligations and policies, and can serve to highlight further the focus of the rest of the Declaration on the rights of individuals.

Two decades after the Universal Declaration, the General Assembly adopted another rights document, the International Covenant on Economic, Social and Cultural Rights. It begins with the notion of the right of self-determination of "all peoples," who may "freely dispose of their natural wealth and resources" (Article 1).[11] The reference to "peoples" rather than to "people" introduces a collectivist element that endows states (as the embodiment of populations) with rights in relation to each other, but potentially also in relation to elements within their populations. Having said that, the bulk of the document does impose obligations on states vis-à-vis their citizens.

These obligations include recognition of the right to work, which entails "policies and techniques to achieve steady economic, social and cultural development" (Article 6, para. 2); the right to social security, protecting the family as "the natural and fundamental group unit of society" (Article 10); the right of everyone to "an adequate standard of living for himself and his family, including adequate food, clothing and housing, and to the continuous improvement of living conditions" (Article 11); the right of everyone to "the enjoyment of the highest attainable standard of physical and mental health" (Article 12); the right to education (Article 13); and the right of everyone to take part in cultural life and enjoy the benefits of scientific progress and its applications (Article 15).

The long list of rights is similar to that included in the Universal Declaration. Without using the term "development" explicitly, the 1966 Covenant gives concrete content to the notion of social rights and covers extensive ground in this area. It does not introduce new notions of rights beyond those used in 1948, however. Whether there is indeed a need for such a move in the early twenty-first century is a question explored below.

On the eve of the third millennium, a flurry of activity around social development issues took place on the international stage. Of particular interest in this context are the Copenhagen Declaration on Social Development of 1995 and the U.N. Millennium Declaration of 2000.

The Copenhagen Declaration, adopted by the World Summit on Social Development, identifies social development as "central to the needs and aspirations of people throughout the world and to the responsibilities of Governments and all sectors of civil society."[12] It defines development as a state that allows all people, especially those living in poverty, to "exercise the rights, utilize the resources and share the responsibilities that enable them to lead satisfying lives and to contribute to the well-being of their families, their communities and humankind."[13]

This approach is relevant for the discussion of the right to development in the information society and is implied in the discourse around "the right to communicate." In the charter of the Communication Rights in the Information Society campaign, the "vision of the 'Information Society' is grounded in the Right to Communicate, as a means to enhance human rights and to strengthen the social, economic and cultural lives of people and communities."[14]

Indicators of development that are identified in the Copenhagen Declaration are economic (volume of trade, the global wealth of nations), social (life expectancy, literacy, access to primary education and basic health care), and political (democratic institutions and civil liberties). In line with that, the indicators of developmental gaps include poverty, unemployment, inequalities between and within countries, unsustainable patterns of consumption and production, social exclusion, and violence.

The Copenhagen Summit participants pledged to give attention to the conditions that hamper development, and outlined a program of action that focuses on the need to place people at the center of development and to direct economies to meet human needs, recognizing that social development is a national responsibility but cannot be successfully achieved without the commitment and efforts of the international community and the integration of economic, cultural, and social policies so that they become mutually supportive. With a focus on rights, the program includes a commitment to "promote universal respect for, and observance and protection of, all human rights and fundamental freedoms for all, including the right to development."[15]

These commitments were reasserted in the United Nations Millennium Declaration of 2000, which includes a chapter on development and poverty alleviation. With a focus on poverty, debt, and trade relations, it is clear that the Declaration regards development primarily as an economic issue. However, it also mentions issues of hunger, access to water, primary schooling, infectious diseases, housing, gender equality, job creation, and so on. In dealing with the challenges of development, it calls specifically for "strong partnerships with the private sector and with civil society organizations in pursuit of development and poverty eradication,"[16] and for the benefits of "new technologies, especially information and communication technologies,"[17] to be made available to all. In line with trends current at the time, it places great faith on the capacity of the market to facilitate meeting the Millennium Development Goals and other development goals, and less on notions of "empowerment" and human rights.

A more sustained focus on human rights can be found in a strategy document, released by the Office of the High Commissioner on Human Rights in 2002, that deals with rights and poverty reduction strategies.[18] The document asserts that "policies and institutions for poverty reduction should be based explicitly on the norms and values set out in the international law of human rights."[19] This normative framework should govern the formulation of national and international policies, including poverty reduction strategies, and facilitate empowerment of the poor by recognizing their "entitlements that give rise to legal obligations on the part of others."[20]

Of course, in typical U.N. fashion, in most of these documents the list of problems, solutions, challenges, and goals is very long, but the list of social and political actors responsible for problems such as hunger, poverty, inequalities, and environmental destruction is very short. There is virtually no mention of who or what might be responsible for such problems, or what kind of local and international interests might be served by the current state of affairs. The implication is that the signatories to such declarations—nation-states and their leaders—are expected to fix the problems they themselves created. It seems to be a case in which the cat is expected to watch over the cream, and also to make amends for previous times when she neglected her duties. . . .

## Development, Rights, and ICTs

The point in the Millennium Declaration regarding information and communication technologies has been taken up by the U.N. ICT Task Force, which was established in the wake of the 2000 declaration of the U.N. Economic and Social Council (ECOSOC) on development and international cooperation in the twenty-first century.[21]

Focusing on the role of information technology in economic and social development, the ECOSOC raised a concern that the potential of ICT for development has not been realized in full. As a result, a "digital divide" was created, and it must be bridged by fostering "digital opportunity" to enhance "development for all." To do that, there is a need to address issues such as lack of infrastructure, education, capacity-building, investment, and connectivity.

What, precisely, is meant by the potential of ICT for development? The ECOSOC document refers to a wide range of development applications, from electronic commerce to access to financial markets; from generating employment to providing opportunities for investment to entrepreneurs, in particular small and medium-sized enterprises; from improved agricultural and manufacturing productivity to the empowerment of all sections of society; from long-distance education to telemedicine; from environmental management and monitoring to prevention and management of disasters. The assumption is that ICTs' potential to foster sustainable development is enormous, but unless access to and use of ICTs is broadened, the majority of people, particularly in the developing countries, will not enjoy the benefits of the new knowledge-based economy.

To ensure improved access and capacity to use new technologies, the ECOSOC document emphasizes the need for coordinated action at the national, regional, and international levels, and for collaborative efforts involving governments, multilateral development institutions, bilateral donors, the private sector, civil society, and other relevant stakeholders.

Most people would agree that addressing an issue at multiple levels, and promoting partnerships between multiple stakeholders, are good ideas that can open up opportunities for enhancing development from a rights-oriented perspective. At the same time, this approach also gives rise to challenges and possible contradictions, in particular over the issue of how to deal with inevitable tensions between different levels, partners, and rights.

Why are such tensions inevitable? Because having multiple stakeholders means having to resolve clashes between different interests, priorities, concerns, and perspectives. This involves pursuing a course of action that would necessitate making choices between competing agendas. Attempting to disguise disagreements and conflicts of interest through the use of vague language that would appeal to all—as is frequently is done in U.N. meetings and other international summits—offers only temporary reconciliation. It cannot address underlying issues, and thus cannot form a basis for a sustained, long-term development agenda. Such an agenda must be built, rather, on a foundation of two fundamental principles: *promoting human rights* and *meeting human needs*. The two are of course related, and it may be argued that the only way to meet basic needs is by promoting socioeconomic and human rights. This calls for a clear identification of both problems and potential solutions.

### Promoting Human Rights

The fundamental importance of human rights as a foundation is asserted in a joint statement, "The Millennium Development Goals and Economic, Social and Cultural Rights," issued in 2002 by the U.N. Committee on Economic, Social and Cultural Rights and the U.N. Commission on Human Rights' special rapporteurs on economic, social, and cultural rights: "We believe that chances for attaining Millennium Development Goals will improve if all U.N. agencies and governments adopt a comprehensive human rights approach to realizing the MDGs, including in the formulation of the corresponding indicators."[22]

A recent contribution by the Civil Society Human Rights Caucus to the WSIS declaration argues that a human rights approach would imply using the improvement of human rights standards, "such as human and social development, democracy and participation," as focus points for setting goals and measures for progress.[23] From this perspective, the right to development can be regarded not as an additional new right that stands on its own but as a way of referring to a cluster of existing social, cultural, and political rights. This notion of rights would involve shifting focus away from infrastructure and the growth of markets (without necessarily abandoning them) and toward issues such as

• Human development (using indicators such as health, education, and livelihood)
• Social and cultural development (using indicators such as economic opportunities and employment, and cultural and linguistic diversity)
• Democracy (or political development, using indicators such as freedom of expression, access to information, privacy protection, media pluralism, transparency, participation in decision-making, and local capacity-building)

Linking notions of rights and development, the Human Rights Caucus maintains that the realization of human rights, such as freedom of expression and access to information and knowledge, is "essential to education, citizen empowerment, democratic participation, equal opportunities, cultural and linguistic diversity, economic development and innovation, leading to overall social wealth." In other words, rights with specific information content are a precondition for other rights with a broad developmental content.

At the same time, factors interfering with the exercise of these developmental rights include poverty and inequality, which lead to massive disparities in access to information and to the means of communication. These are "at the same time a cause and a consequence of the unequal distribution of wealth in the world and within countries. It severely diminishes the capabilities of people to enjoy their human rights, especially the right to an adequate standard of living, and prevent economic and social development."

The current international relations of power and allocation of resources—what the Caucus terms "Internet topography," which include international communication routes and traffic rate agreements—result in "unfair distribution of resources and massive inequalities" regarding costs. People-centered, inclusive development requires addressing this situation.

## Meeting Human Needs

Using the approach of the Human Rights Caucus, with slight modifications, we argue that the right to development in the information society requires looking at the following clusters of rights, and breaking them down into specific components:

- Human development
- Social and economic development
- Cultural development
- Political development
- Cross-cutting issues.

**Human Development**   From the perspective of information and communications for development, the realization of rights to human development requires governments to mainstream and integrate the use of information and communications, and related technologies, in the areas of health, education, training, and other relevant sectors.

Among specific areas within this context is access to health information, including information about illnesses and epidemics, their causes, risk factors, and steps that can be taken to contain their spread and facilitate prevention and cure. This would require not only efforts to extend access to such information to individuals and communities that do not have regular contact with the formal health system, but also mechanisms to allow input by those directly affected to medical professionals, in a two-way flow of information between experts and laypeople.

Particular attention must be paid to the language in which health information is conveyed. It should be plain and, as far as possible, free of technical jargon that creates distance between the conveyers and receivers of information. It should also take into account the multilingual reality of most developing countries, in which many languages with different status are spoken and used for various aspects of life. An example of a successful initiative that made use of ICTs is the Tanzania Essential Health Interventions Project (TEHIP).[24] This partnership between the International Development Research Centre and the Tanzania Ministry of Health piloted innovations in gathering and processing data for health planning and resource allocation. The project adopted an integrated approach, with the use of ICTs being one part of a process that included research, capacity-building, infrastructure development, and community participation. The impact of the planning interventions that resulted from TEHIP in the two districts in Tanzania where it was piloted can now be observed:

Child mortality in the two districts fell by over 40% in the 5 years following the introduction of evidence-based planning; and death rates for men and women between 15 and 60 years old declined by 18%. During the same period, the health indicators for other districts in Tanzania, and in fact across Africa, have become stagnant. This suggests that the project provided the Tanzanian health reform with the appropriate tools needed for development of an evidence-based health system and policies.[25]

With regard to education, the Civil Society Declaration argues that "Knowledge creation and acquisition should be nurtured as a participatory and collective process and not considered a one-way flow."[26] The use of ICTs in education started in the early 1990s, and the lessons can inform future practice. One of the best-documented examples of national initiatives is from Chile. Red Enlaces, the initiative started ca. 1994 and has been able to build on experience, integrate learning, and show positive results. One of its critical success factors is consistent support from the Ministry of Education.[27]

**Social and Economic Development**   This area covers most of the rights that are usually referred to as socioeconomic rights, including the right to water, food, jobs, housing, social security, and other basic services. Though it is related to human development, the focus on socioeconomic rights directs our attention to services crucial for physical survival as well as services that aim to develop the human person as a whole (such as education and health). In addition, labor rights, such as the rights to organize unions and to strike, and the rights to decent working conditions and a living wage, also belong in this category, as essential for ensuring people's ability to organize and to demand and realize their social and economic rights.

Information and communications technologies can contribute greatly to the economic development of institutions and individuals—for example, access to information about investment opportunities, microcredit, and online banking. A recent publication by the Swiss Agency for Development and Cooperation and the Global Knowledge Partnership, "ICT4D—Connecting People for a Better World: Lessons, Innovations and Perspectives of Information and Communication Technologies in Development," explores the risks and opportunities involved in using ICTs as a development tool. The text is available on the Web and includes a detailed list of resources.[28]

Addressing these rights in the context of the information society would mean a focus on the dissemination of information about the content of rights and the circumstances under which they can be realized, the national and international obligations of governments in these respects, and the extent to which governments have committed themselves to minimum standards of provision by signing international conventions.

Learning about international best practices that serve as benchmarks for other countries, and about legal and political achievements by social movements in some countries that can be replicated elsewhere, may also be facilitated by an environment of increased networking and access to sources of information. Such an environment is also more conducive to effective solidarity campaigns with social and political struggles that involve the use of tactics such as boycotts and sanctions, and for organization across and beyond borders.

**Cultural Development**    The Civil Society Declaration notes that "cultural and linguistic diversity is an essential dimension of people-centred information and communication societies" and that "ICTs including traditional communications media have a particularly important role to play in sustaining and developing the world's cultures and languages."[29]

While the information society may facilitate access to the means needed to protect endangered cultures and languages, raise awareness of threats, and encourage networking and joint action between groups that find themselves in similar situations, it also presents its own dangers to the cause of indigenous and minority cultures.

Economic globalization, the growing spread of the Internet, and the rise of new types of media and means of communications have resulted in increasing dominance of European languages and, in particular, English. In most instances of networking that bring together indigenous activists and movements representing other cultural and minority groups, English is the lingua franca (in some regional cases it is French or Spanish). The implications of this paradoxical situation need to be explored further.

An example of effective and low-cost use of ICTs to enable content creation in minority languages is Atavik.net. It is a project of an APC (Association for Progressive Communications) member in Canada, Web Networks, and it facilitates easy online content publishing in the Inuit language, Inuktitut.[30]

A particular aspect of cultural development includes indigenous peoples' knowledge, which is threatened by existing intellectual property regimes. There is need for measures to maintain knowledge diversity and to protect the cultural, intellectual, and natural resources of indigenous peoples, especially botanical and agricultural knowledge, from commercial exploitation and appropriation.[31] At the same time it is necessary to be proactive and accept that cultural mixing and remixing is not just a reality of contemporary culture; it is also a means for cultural producers to assert their rights—rights that in many cases are being appropriated and abused by publishers (e.g., in the music industry). The alternative licensing movement is finding new ways, such as Creative Commons, for authors and creators to reclaim their rights.[32]

**Political Development**   A major concern in the area of political development is freedom of expression. Article 19 of the Universal Declaration on Human Rights establishes the right of everyone to freedom of opinion and expression, and the right to seek, receive, and impart information and ideas, through any medium. Obviously this right is central to the exercise of all other rights in the information society (though its application and importance are of course not new).

As the Civil Society Declaration argues, this implies free circulation of ideas, pluralism of the sources of information and the media, press freedom, ability to access information and share knowledge, and protection of the right to privacy. The last "faces new challenges in information and communication societies, and must be protected in public spaces, online, offline, at home, and in the workplace. Every person must have the right to decide freely whether and in what manner he or she wants to receive information and communicate with others."[33] This is a particular problem in recent times because of the increasing risk of abuse of personal data by governments, private sector companies, and individuals.

Other issues related to political freedoms revolve around public access to information produced and kept by governments. This applies to legislation, policies, plans, tenders, and other acts of governments and other public bodies that potentially impact the lives of people. Mandatory consultation with stakeholders, public hearings before new legislation is formulated and enacted, and mechanisms that allow people to challenge policies publicly and through the courts are all essential procedures to guarantee political development; access to relevant information and the use of communication technologies to facilitate these processes are important tools in the context of the information society.

Perhaps of most importance for political development is the ability of citizens and civil society organizations to participate in governance, voice their concerns, hold government accountable, and ensure that resources are used to benefit the population rather than politicians and bureaucrats (in other words, to prevent corruption). Innovative ways in which ICTs can be used to facilitate the realization of these goals need to be formulated and implemented further. An example of this is the innovative work done by Colnodo, an APC member in Colombia, to use an open source application to promote transparency and public participation at the level of local government.[34]

**Cross-Cutting Issues**   Some issues cannot be clustered under a separate label because they cut across different rights and aspects of development. These include gender justice, youth issues, and the rights of people with disabilities. Specific attention to gender sensitivity training and use of ICTs, the need to train and empower young people, and the need to consider the specific access needs of people with disabilities are challenges facing all development practitioners in the information society.

Different components will assume priority based on concrete circumstances, and to make them meaningful, and facilitate implementation, indicators that reflect national realities—in accordance with international standards—need to be developed. Moreover, accountability and responsibility need to be identified to guide implementation and monitoring of progress. An example of indicators and how they may be used to measure progress can be found in the work of Social Watch, an international citizens' network on poverty eradication and gender equality.[35]

Another cross-cutting issue is financing. During the first phase of the WSIS, the matter of "financing the information society" was contentious and remained unresolved. There was a standoff between developed and developing countries on the issue of who should finance the information society. In the context of the "right to development," the issue is a critical one: Who takes responsibility for ensuring that the basic conditions in which the rights that relate to development can be realized?

Two opposing perspectives on the matter emerged in the WSIS, with developing countries insisting that a "digital solidarity fund" be established, while developed countries called for a more effective use of the existing financial mechanisms. A task force was convened by the UNDP to explore the issue and submit a report to the second preparatory committee meeting of the second phase of the WSIS (February 2005).[36]

Debate over the implications of the task force's report emerged at the WSIS 2 PrepCom meeting in Geneva (February 2005). One of the key issues was the relative weight placed on private and public sector finance for ICTs for development. It seems, though, that there is growing recognition that private sector finance is not adequate on its own to address the infrastructure needs of developing countries, and it needs to be supplemented by public and community-driven initiatives. It remains to be seen, though, how this recognition will translate into concrete policies and allocation of resources. It is encouraging that the digital solidarity fund has been welcomed as a voluntary fund open to interested stakeholders and functioning as a complementary financial mechanism. It should be accompanied by new policy and financial models based on notions of public good, public finance, and open access as crucial for national and international development strategies.[37]

## Conclusion

In conclusion, we would argue that the right to development is a composite concept. To be meaningful, it has to be broken down into components that are framed by fundamental human rights and address specific needs.

In order to ensure the realization of these rights, indicators that are measurable and relevant to the intended beneficiaries need to be developed in an inclusive and transparent manner. The information society angle requires the systematic integration of information, communications, and supportive technologies into all aspects of development policy and practice. Without giving priority at the national and global levels to the need to integrate information and communication considerations in development, we run the risk of missing out on the important contribution these can make to the development process.

This integrated approach to development and information and communications relies not only on breaking the right to development into components, and exploring the role of information and communications in realizing this right. It also requires the recognition that the right to information, communications, services, and technologies is fundamental. This in turn requires a contemporary reinterpretation of rights enshrined in the Universal Declaration of Human Rights in the context of the information society, as argued by the Association for Progressive Communication in the publication "Involving Civil Society in the Information Society."

Specific agents need to be identified and made responsible for implementing needed change, thus avoiding the vague notion of "partnership" that is rife in information society discourse. In particular, the role, responsibility, and accountability of national governments at three primary levels must be emphasized:

- To create enabling environments for communities and individuals to drive development themselves
- To provide the basic public services and infrastructure without which development cannot be sustained
- To avoid policies that hamper the ability of other states to meet their needs at the national level, and to follow those which facilitate international cooperation for development and social justice.

### Notes

1. WSIS, "Declaration of Principles, Building the Information Society: A Global Challenge in the New Millennium," sec. A, para. 1, http://www.itu.int/wsis/docs/geneva/official/dop.html.

2. Ibid.

3. APC and CRIS, "Involving Civil Society in the Information Society: The World Summit on the Information Society," Sept. 2003, http://www.apc.org/books/policy_wsis_EN.pdf.

4. WSIS, Civil Society Declaration, "Shaping Information Societies for Human Needs," Dec. 8, 2003, sec. 2, http://www.smsitunis2005.org/plateforme/pdf/civil-society-declaration-en.pdf.

5. Ibid., sec. 2.1.

6. Ibid.

7. Declaration on the Right to Development, adopted by General Assembly, resolution 41/128, Dec. 4, 1986, http://www.unhchr.ch/html/menu3/b/74.htm.

8. Ibid., art. 1. All subsequent references to the Declaration on the Right to Development refer to specific articles within the document mentioned in note 7.

9. Balakrishnan Rajagopal, *International Law from Below* (Cambridge: Cambridge University Press, 2003), 220.

10. The Universal Declaration on Human Rights, adopted and proclaimed by General Assembly resolution 217 A (III), Dec. 10, 1948, http://www.unhchr.ch/udhr/lang/eng.htm.

11. International Covenant on Economic, Social and Cultural Rights, adopted and opened for signature, ratification, and accession by General Assembly resolution 2200A (XXI) of Dec. 16, 1966, http://www.ohchr.org/english/law/cescr.htm.

12. Copenhagen Declaration on Social Development, adopted by the World Summit for Social Development, Mar. 6–12, 1995, Introduction, art. 7, http://www.un.org/esa/socdev/wssd/agreements/decparti.htm.

13. Ibid., Introduction, art. 9.

14. CRIS Charter, http://www.crisinfo.org/content/view/full/98/.

15. Programme of Action for the World Summit for Social Development, Mar. 6–12, 1995, chap. 4, art. 71, http://www.un.org/esa/socdev/wssd/agreements/poach4.htm.

16. United Nations Millennium Declaration, adopted by the General Assembly, 55/2, Sept. 6–8, 2000, art. 20, http://www.un.org/millennium/declaration/ares552e.htm.

17. Ibid.

18. OHCHR, "Draft Guidelines: A Human Rights Approach to Poverty Reduction Strategies," 10 Sept. 2002, http://www.unhchr.ch/development/povertyfinal.html.

19. Ibid., art. 3.

20. Ibid., art. 5.

21. U.N. Economic and Social Council, Development and International Cooperation in the 21st Century: The Role of Information Technology in the Context of a Knowledge-based Global Economy, July 25–Aug. 1, 2000, http://www.un.org/documents/ecosoc/docs/2000/e2000-52.pdf.

22. Joint statement of the U.N. Committee on Economic, Social and Cultural Rights and the U.N. Commission on Human Rights' Special Rapporteurs on Economic, Social and Cultural Rights, "The Millennium Development Goals and Economic, Social and Cultural Rights," Nov. 29, 2002, para. 3. Full text of the declaration is available at http://193.194.138.190/housing/MDG.doc.

23. "Comments on the Political Chapeau and the Operational Part," Human Rights Caucus contribution to the work of the Group of the Friends of the Chair, Mar. 4, 2005. Available at: http://www.iris.sgdg.org/actions/smsi/hr-wsis/hris-gfc-040305-en.html.

24. http://www.idrc.ca/tehip/.

25. Overseas Development Institute, "Research-Policy Case Study: Tanzania Essential Health Interventions Project (TEHIP)—a 'Good News' Research-policy Case Study, Feb. 2005, http://www.odi.org.uk/Rapid/Lessons/Case_studies/TEHIP.html.

26. Civil Society Declaration. Declaration of Principles (WSIS-03/GENEVA/DOC/4-E), para. 2.1.7. Available at: http://www.itu.int/wsis/docs/geneva/official/dop.html.

27. More information on this initiative is available in Spanish from http://www.educarchile.cl/home/ and http://www.enlaces.cl/.

28. http://www.globalknowledge.org/ict4d/.

29. Civil Society Declaration. Declaration of Principles (WSIS-03/GENEVA/DOC/4-E), para. 2.3.1. Available at: http://www.itu.int/wsis/docs/geneva/official/dop.html.

30. http://www.apc.org/english/news/index.shtml?x=27592; http://www.attavik.net, http://www.web.net; http://news.bbc.co.uk/1/hi/technology/3975645.stm.

31. Civil Society Declaration. Declaration of Principles (WSIS-03/GENEVA/DOC/4-E), para. 2.3.3.1. Available at: http://www.itu.int/wsis/docs/geneva/official/dop.html.

32. http://www.creativecommons.org.

33. Civil Society Declaration. Declaration of Principles (WSIS-03/GENEVA/DOC/4-E), para. 2.2.2. Available at: http://www.itu.int/wsis/docs/geneva/official/dop.html.

34. http://www.apc.org/english/news/index.shtml?x=17998;          http://www.municipios.colnodo.apc.org/.

35. Social Watch is a project of the Third World Institute, http://www.socialwatch.org/en/portada.htm.

36. Report of the Task Force on Financial Mechanisms, Feb. 2005, http://www.itu.int/wsis/tffm/index.html.

37. See APC, "Finance of Information and Communication Technologies for Development (ICTD)," presented at Prepcom 2, Apr. 2005, http://www.apc.org/english/news/index.shtml?x=31483.

# About the Authors

**David Banisar**   is director of the Freedom of Information Project of Privacy International in London and a visiting research fellow at the Faculty of Law, University of Leeds, United Kingdom. Previously he was a research fellow at the Kennedy School of Government at Harvard University and cofounder and policy director of the Electronic Privacy Information Center in Washington, D.C. He has served as an adviser and consultant to numerous organizations including the Organization for Security and Cooperation in Europe, the Organization for Economic Cooperation and Development, Justice Canada, the Open Society Institute, Article XIX, and Consumers International. He has worked in the field of information policy for over fourteen years and is the author of numerous books, studies, and articles on freedom of information, freedom of expression, and privacy. His most recent study of FOI laws is available at http://www.freedominfo.org/survey.htm.

**William J. Drake**   is the Director of the Project on the Information Revolution and Global Governance at the Graduate Institute of International Studies in Geneva, Switzerland, and the President (2004–2006) of Computer Professionals for Social Responsibility. In addition, he is co-editor of the MIT Press book series "The Information Revolution and Global Politics." He has been a Visiting Senior Fellow at the Center for International Development and Conflict Management, University of Maryland, College Park; a Senior Associate and the founding Director of the Project on the Information Revolution and World Politics at the Carnegie Endowment for International Peace, Washington, D.C.; the founding Associate Director of the Communication, Culture and Technology Program, Georgetown University; and an Assistant Professor of Communication at the University of California, San Diego. He also served on the United Nations Working

Group on Internet Governance. His primary research interests are the global governance of information and communication technology, and the impact of the information revolution on world politics. Among his publications are: *Governing Global Electronic Networks: International Perspectives on Policy and Power* (co-editor, forthcoming); *Reforming Internet Governance: Perspective from the UN Working Group on Internet Governance* (editor); *From the Global Digital Divide to the Global Digital Opportunity: Proposals Submitted to the G-8 Kyushu-Okinawa Summit 2000—Report of the World Economic Forum Task Force; Toward Sustainable Competition in Global Telecommunications: From Principle to Practice; Telecommunications in the Information Age* (editor); and *The New Information Infrastructure: Strategies for US Policy* (editor). He received his Ph.D. in political science from Columbia University.

**Anriette Esterhuysen**  is the executive director of the Association for Progressive Communications, an international NGO that focuses on the use of information and communication technologies by civil society for social justice and development. She was executive director of SANGONeT, an electronic information and communications service provider for the development sector in South Africa, from 1993 to 2000. She is also a founder of Women's Net in South Africa and served on the African Technical Advisory Committee of the Economic Commission for the African Information Society Initiative. Currently she is a member of the Social Science Research Council's Information Technology and International Cooperation Steering Committee and of the U.N. ICT Task Force.

**Ran Greenstein**  is an associate professor of sociology at the University of the Witwatersrand in Johannesburg, South Africa. His areas of research and teaching include political theory, research methodology, and social development. He received a Ph.D. from the University of Wisconsin-Madison, and has published *Genealogies of Conflict: Class, Identity and State in Palestine/Israel and South Africa* (Wesleyan University Press, 1995) and *Comparative Perspectives on South Africa* (Macmillan, 1998). He has worked on a large number of applied research projects, including studies of infrastructure delivery, civil society and the state, and human and socioeconomic rights, for national and international agencies as well as NGOs.

**Robin D. Gross**  is founder and executive directive of IP Justice, an international civil liberties organization that promotes balanced intellectual property law and protects freedom of expression. An attorney, she advises policy makers throughout the world on the impact of intellectual property rules.

Gross is a member of the High Technology Legal Advisory Board for the Santa Clara University School of Law, where she teaches international copyright law. She represents the Non-Commercial Users Constituency on the Generic Names Supporting Organization Policy Council at the Internet Corporation for Assigned Names and Numbers. She is a member of the board of directors of the Union for the Public Domain, a nonprofit organization in Washington, D.C., that is dedicated to protecting the public domain. She also is a member of the Advisory Board for Computer Professionals for Social Responsibility–Peru, and of FreeMuse, an independent international organization based in Copenhagen that advocates freedom of expression for musicians and composers worldwide.

**Gus Hosein** is a visiting fellow at the London School of Economics (LSE) in the Department of Information Systems, where he lectures on topics relating to the politics of technology, privacy and data protection, regulation, and civil liberties. At the LSE he researches technology policy and regulation, international agreements and standards, and civil liberties and surveillance. He is a senior fellow with Privacy International (PI), a London-based NGO. At PI he directs the Project on Terrorism and the Open Society, and coordinates a project on policy laundering. He is also an adviser to a number of NGOs. He holds a B.Math. from the University of Waterloo and a Ph.D. from the University of London.

**Heike Jensen** teaches in the Department of Gender Studies at Humboldt University in Berlin. Her teaching and research foci are media theories, media politics and media strategies, women's movements and women's organizations, and globalization and global governance. She received her education at the Free University of Berlin, the University of Minnesota-Minneapolis, Brown University, the International Women's University 2000 (Hamburg, Germany), and Humboldt University, where she obtained her doctorate in gender studies. Dr. Jensen's volunteer work is dedicated to promoting women. She is a member of Terre des Femmes, the NRO-Frauenforum, and the Association for Women's Rights in Development. In the WSIS process, she has worked with the German Civil Society Coordinating Committee, the Gender Strategies Working Group (an NGO), and the WSIS Gender Caucus, where she is a member of the Steering Committee. She was a civil society representative in the German governmental delegation to the Geneva Summit.

**Rikke Frank Jørgensen**   is Senior Adviser at the Danish Institute for Human Rights, Copenhagen; is adviser to the Danish governmental delegation to the World Summit on the Information Society (WSIS); and is co-chair of the WSIS Civil Society Human Rights Caucus. She previously was a special adviser in the Danish Ministry of Research and Information Technology, dealing with the social impacts of information technology. She cofounded the Danish NGO Digital Rights, and is on the board of European Digital Rights. She has been a member of several governmental committees, and has authored a number of presentations and articles on the interface between human rights and technology. She holds a master's degree in information science and a European master's degree in human rights and democratization.

**Hans Klein**   is associate professor in the School of Public Policy at the Georgia Institute of Technology. His research interests are in global Internet governance, sociotechnical systems, and alternative media. Klein is the former chair of Computer Professionals for Social Responsibility. He holds a B.S.E. in computer science from Princeton University, an M.S. in technology policy from MIT, and a Ph.D. in political science from MIT.

**Charley Lewis**   is a lecturer, researcher, and consultant at the LINK Centre of the School of Public and Development Management at the University of the Witwatersrand, South Africa, where his areas of focus include labor, work, and ICT; telecommunications regulation; and ICT policy development. Before joining LINK, Lewis headed the Information Technology Unit of the Congress of South African Trade Unions. During this time, he represented organized labor in a range of information society processes and activities, including the National Science and Technology Foresight Project and its ICT Working Group, the South African Acacia Advisory Committee, the South African Information Technology Industrial Strategy Project, South Africa's national e-commerce policy process, and the National Information Technology Forum. He has written numerous speeches and articles on information society regulation and development. He holds a Master of Commerce degree in management of information systems from the University of the Witwatersrand, and an honors degree in English from the University of Cape Town.

**Meryem Marzouki**   a senior researcher with the French National Public Research Center, is currently with the Computer Science Laboratory of

Paris 6 (LIP6). Dealing with relationships between ICTs, public policies, and the public space, using a multidisciplinary approach, her current research interests include Internet governance and the transformation of the rule of law, privacy and personal data protection issues, and communication usages on a mobile campus. She is the author of several publications and talks on Internet governance, human rights, and democracy, as part of both her scientific and her NGO activities. Marzouki holds a Ph.D. in computer science and a *habilitation à diriger des recherches*, both from the National Polytechnic Institute of Grenoble, France. Prior to entering to her current research field in 2002, she conducted extensive research in computer science and microelectronics, dealing with test and diagnosis of heterogeneous systems. She is president of the French NGO IRIS (Imaginons un Réseau Internet Solidaire) and co-chair of the WSIS Civil Society Human Rights Caucus.

**Birgitte Kofod Olsen** is director of the National Department at the Danish Institute for Human Rights, Copenhagen, where she is responsible for the Institute's activities on protection and promotion of human rights and equal treatment in Denmark. She is also a senior lecturer in law and philosophy at the University of Copenhagen. Her fields of expertise encompass minority rights, civil and political rights, identification technology and privacy, antidiscrimination and equal treatment, and the functioning of national human rights institutions. She is currently involved in a number of projects related to the development of methodologies applicable in a human rights and discrimination context. She holds a L.L.M. and a Ph.D. from the University of Copenhagen. Her Ph.D. thesis is on identification technology (biometrics) and data protection.

**Kay Raseroka** is the director of library services of the University of Botswana Library. She was elected president of the International Federation of Library Associations and Institutions, the global voice of library and information professionals and users of libraries, for the period 2003–2005. Raseroka's interests are in exploring ways of integrating indigenous knowledge systems, orality, and information technology to facilitate an inclusive access to the benefits of the emerging knowledge society. She is committed to the principles of freedom of access to information, ideas, and works of imagination, and to freedom of expression as a basis for unhindered access to information.

**Adama Samassékou** was Mali's minister of education for seven years (1993–2000), and a spokesperson for the government of Mali (1997–2000), and is currently president, with ministerial rank, of the African Academy of Languages. He was president of the WSIS preparatory process leading to the Geneva Summit. Playing an active role in community life, Samassékou was the founding president, for Mali and Africa as a whole, of the People's Movement for Human Rights Education, in partnership with PDHRE (People's Decade for Human Rights Education). In the political sphere, he was the founding chairman of ADEMA-France. He holds a Master of Arts in philology and linguistics from Lomonossov State University in Moscow, a DEA postgraduate diploma in African linguistics from the Sorbonne, and a DESS specialist postgraduate diploma in organizational science from the Université de Paris-IX (Dauphine). Subsequently he was head of the Linguistics Department of the Institute of Social Sciences of Mali, director of the National Library of Mali, and adviser to the minister of culture.

**Mandana Zarrehparvar** heads the Team on Anti-discrimination and Equal Treatment at the Danish Institute for Human Rights, Copenhagen. She has worked in the field of ethnic equality since 1993, and was executive director of the Danish Board on Ethnic Equality from 1998 to 2002. Zarrehparvar is a member of several governmental committees, an active public debater and speaker, and author of articles for numerous books and journals. She trained as a social worker, holds a B.A. in political science, and is currently studying for a master's degree in globalization and integration.

# Afterword: The Tunis Commitment

The Tunis Summit resulted in two political documents, the Tunis Commitment and the Tunis Agenda, plus a civil society Statement: "Much more could have been achieved." The three main issues of the second WSIS phase, Internet Governance—financing for development, and WSIS follow-up and implementation—resulted in: (1) No change to ICANN's role in the short term, but a political commitment to work toward greater internationalization of public policy issues related to internet governance, and a decision to create a new global policy mechanism: the so-called Internet Governance Forum (IGF). (2) An affirmation of the Digital Solidarity Fund established on a voluntary basis in March 2005, but with no concrete commitment to provide funding for development. (3) Establishment of a UN group on the Information Society within the UN's Chief Executives Board for coordination, and a mechanism for stocktaking and implementation under ECOSOC's Commission on Science and Technology for Development.

Human rights came into play both in the form of human rights violations at the Summit itself, and as a baseline for future GIS policies.

In the days leading up to the Summit, the Citizens Summit on the Information Society (CSIS), which was organized as a side event to the official summit, was prevented from happening by the Tunisian authorities. In response, a large number of international journalists, diplomats, and prominent human rights speakers, including Nobel prize winner 2003 Shirin Ebadi and the UN special rapporteur on freedom of expression, assembled in the office of the Tunisian Human Rights League and expressed their support of human rights, not least freedom of expression and freedom of assembly in Tunisia.

The Tunis Commitment and Tunis Agenda reaffirm the Geneva commitment to human rights as the foundation for the global information society. Paragraph 3 of the Tunis Commitment underscores "the universality, indivisibility, interdependence and interrelation of all human rights and fundamental freedoms, including the right to development." Hereby it establishes human rights as a broad baseline for assessing GIS policies, including both civil and political rights, social, economic, and cultural rights, and the right to development.

The role of human rights is also explicitly linked to Internet governance in paragraph 42 of the Tunis Agenda: "We reaffirm our commitment to the freedom to seek, receive, impart and use information, in particular, for the creation, accumulation and dissemination of knowledge. We affirm that measures undertaken to ensure Internet stability and security, to fight cybercrime and to counter spam, must protect and respect the provisions for privacy and freedom of expression as contained in the relevant parts of the Universal Declaration of Human Rights and the Geneva Declaration of Principles." This explicit linkage between human rights and internet governance can provide a basis for addressing human rights compliance when assessing proposals for future IG mechanisms and arrangements.

In sum, both the Geneva and Tunis Summit affirmed that GIS and IG policies must have human rights as their point of departure. However, analysis on how the agenda should carry forward and how human rights principles translate into concrete policy recommendations is still at a very early stage. So far it is merely a formal commitment to standards agreed upon more than 50 years ago. It is our hope that this book will contribute to bridging the gap between human right standards and information society policies and thus start a process whereby we move from formal human rights affirmation to concrete policy implementation.

# Index